>>>>>>>>>>>>>>>>>>>>>>>> *MAN O' WAR*

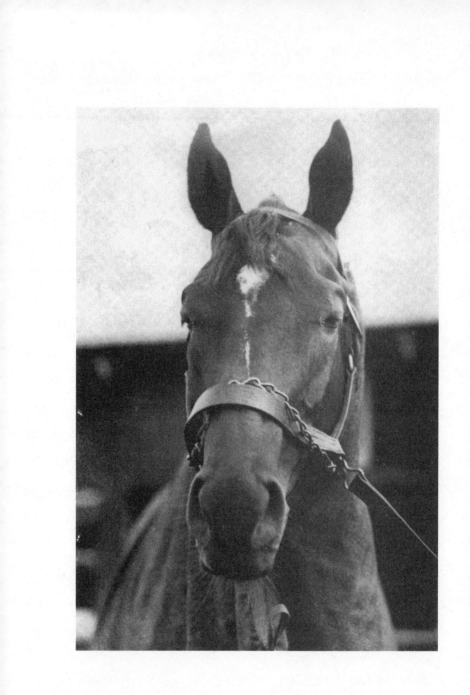

MAN O' WAR

by

PAGE COOPER

and

ROGER L. TREAT

WESTHOLME
Yardley

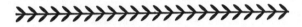

Originally published by Julian Messener, Inc. in 1950
Additional material © 2004 Westholme Publishing
First paperback edition, August 2004

Westholme Publishing, LLC
Eight Harvey Avenue
Yardley, Pennsylvania 19067

www.westholmepublishing.com

Printed in Canada on acid-free paper

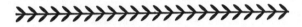

ISBN 1-59416-005-8

First Printing
10 9 8 7 6 5 4 3 2 1

Historical charts and statistical information compiled
by the authors from *The Daily Racing Form* and *The
Blood Horse*.

CONTENTS

≫≫≫≫≫≫≫≫≫≫≫≫≫≫≫≫≫≫≫≫≫≫≫≫

INTRODUCTION

≫≫≫≫≫≫≫≫≫≫≫≫≫≫≫≫≫≫≫≫≫≫≫≫

THE READERS of MAN O' WAR are going to meet a strange, exciting personality—an individual—a legend come alive. There never was another horse like Big Red and there never will be, for he was all thoroughbred—and something else, too. He was always a horse you referred to as "who" instead of "which." I know I always did, accustomed though I was to the careful, stilted requirements of what some horsemen call "bloodlines language."

If you can understand that, then this book is most certainly for you. If you can't, then it is twice as surely a book you will read, and read again. For in the pages that follow, the fabulous Big Red comes alive again. So do his records and all the thrills and climaxes of his life, and the stories they told about him.

With care and accuracy and color, the authors have here set down a fascinating story. We see Man o' War as a colt at play, as the most promising young star of the then-unknown Riddle Stables; we watch him hurtle to triumph in the first race of his career; we battle with him along the time-long backstretch, into the sweeping, careening turns, and then down "heartbreak highway"—the home stretch—as he smashes to the epic achievements that stamped him the greatest of all.

Big Red was a winner, I will always maintain, because he wanted to be a winner. He had more brains, more class, more speed, more desire to win than any other horse that ever sported silks. He had personality, and the dignity of a king. He was a great actor. Every race was a show for him, and, like all great actors, he never let his public down.

He set five records, one of which stands to this day. His average winning margin—and facts, cold facts, back me up —*was nine and a half lengths!* He was extended but once.

And there was more to Big Red than that, too. The authors of MAN O' WAR have delved into the glorious genealogy of the wonder horse, and traced him back to the storied Godolphin Arabian, with the million and more blood combinations—innumerable strains of great horses that combined to produce the super-son of Mahubah and Fair Play. Remember, too, that Man o' War went on to become a tremendous sire of other magical thoroughbreds. These, too, are in the story.

Thus, for the serious student of horses, for those who must be familiar with the family backgrounds of great racers, this book is invaluable. And for those who never saw Big Red, but who know the legend, the authors recreate the greatest of them all.

But Big Red remains "the greatest of them all." For my money no horse has ever touched Big Red.

Earl Sande said it another way, when he dismounted after riding MAN O' WAR for the first time:

"This horse," said Sande, "gallops faster than other horses race."

So here you have Big Red. If you knew him, you will be happy to meet him again; if you never saw him thundering to racing glory, you will see him now. Every reader of this stirring and warm and human book will have found a friend.

BOB CONSIDINE

Chapter I

IT WAS NEAR MIDNIGHT. The watchman thrust his hands into his pockets to warm them from the evening mist. He sniffed the air, heavy with the smells of leather, soap, hay, manure and the warm bodies of horses, and, fainter—drifting in through the mist—the scent of new grass in the meadows and yellowing birches. It was almost April, and all over the big Kentucky stud farm he could feel the languid stir of spring.

Pushing himself upright with a thrust of his shoulder against the side of a stall door, he began the rounds again, shuffling quietly past the stalls of the yearlings, the mares with foals nuzzling against their sides, the barren mares, to the end of the stables set apart for the stallions. Fair Play was restless; the watchman heard the horse rustling his straw and pawing at the clay. Listening for a minute, he peered into the stall where he could see the splendid outline of the stallion blacked in by the moonlight. Fair Play flicked his ears and turned toward the door; then he lifted his head and snorted as though in his dream he had heard the bugle.

"Whoa, boy, whoa!" called the watchman softly. "This ain't no Pimlico. Go to sleep."

He waited while Fair Play shifted to the other side of the

stall. His tail drooped and his small pointed ears relaxed.

When the watchman returned he heard a commotion in the stall of the mare, Mahubah. For several days they had been waiting for her to foal. She had been treated like an expectant princess, examined by expert hands, bathed and brushed and rubbed, her eyes and nostrils sponged in warm water. He padded back along the path, looked into her stall, then ran across the yard to the house of the superintendent to tell him that the mare's time had come. The date was March 29, 1917.

In a few minutes the night was full of hurrying feet. Lights flashed in Mahubah's stall. The grotesque shadows of Mr. Kane, the superintendent, the vet, and half a dozen grooms and stable boys criss-crossed against the wall.

"It's a colt," the superintendent said.

"Chestnut," the vet added as he wiped off the foal with a handful of clean straw and sacking. "And he's got his grand-daddy Hastings' star on his forehead."

After they had cleaned the stall and taught the baby colt to suck his mother's milk—he was bigger than most foals and so strong that he scarcely wobbled when he scrambled up on his feet for his first meal—Mr. Kane went home for a cup of coffee. He needed it. This was no routine foaling; these colts of Nursery Stud represented years of careful planning and the investment of more money than he liked to consider. Major August Belmont (and there were many horse lovers who agreed with him) considered the colt's sire, Fair Play, the best horse he ever had owned. The golden stallion had won more than $86,000 for him and had been the only horse to threaten the fabulous Colin. If it had not been for Colin, Fair Play would have been one of the great racers of all time. He had been foaled at Major Belmont's own Nursery Stud, a son of the devil, Hastings, and grandson of the famous Spend-thrift. The Major always liked Hastings in spite of the fact

2

that he was a hellion. He fought the saddle and bridle so fiercely that he exhausted every exercise boy on the place. At the post he was so eager to run that he worked himself into a frenzy.

"He was born mad," one of the rail owls said, "and never got real happy. He stayed mad at the world because he couldn't run fancy free, hard as he tried. There was a broad streak of bum in him and, like every bum, he longed to hit the open road." After winning twelve races, many of them famous stakes, Hastings developed "the cough," and Major Belmont sent him to Nursery Stud to share honors with the imported stallion, Henry of Navarre.

At the Kentucky farm Hastings was almost overlooked by everyone except the Major. Henry of Navarre was the top stallion and he got the first choice of the mares, but his children were almost worthless. Hastings' first crop, on the other hand, included seventeen winners, many of them brilliant. By the end of the second year, with only two crops on the track he had become the leading American sire. That year his children won sixty-three firsts; no other horse ever had led the sire list so young, with only two- and three-year-olds running.

Fair Play did not have his father's ungovernable temper, but there came a time when he hated the training and refused to run his heart out for anyone; he did not sulk, but he was cold and aloof—he was through with the vagaries of men. They were a proud-necked race, these sons of Spendthrift, but they could carry tremendous weight, and when in the mood they could run away with any race, the jockeys dragging on the reins.

Mahubah's lineage was just as royal; she was the daughter of the magnificent English Rock Sand for whom the Major had paid $125,000, the highest price that ever had been paid

3

for a stallion. Rock Sand had everything, a classic lineage (he was the son of an English Derby winner and grandson of St. Simon, the most highly prized stallion of his time), a gentle, even temperament, and intelligence. The seal brown colt won five out of six starts when he was a two-year-old and next year romped home in the Derby and the St. Leger. The Two Thousand Guineas completed his triple crown. When he retired with sixteen victories he was one of the most valuable stud horses in the world. Major Belmont was attracted to him especially because he believed that Rock Sand mares with their sire's gentle temperament would make a perfect combination with the fiery blood of Hastings. So he shipped Rock Sand to the United States in a padded stall built amidship in the *S. S. Minneapolis* accompanied by four round-the-clock attendants as well as his personal veterinarian.

When the ship docked, Rock Sand, no giddy-headed adventurer, refused to go down the gangplank. For more than two hours the grooms coaxed him, but not until a mounted policeman rode his horse up and down to show the royal stallion that it was safe would he venture from the hold.

The little chestnut colt that dragged Mr. Kane out of his bed on that chilly spring night in Kentucky was an experiment in the mating of two illustrious lines. By every augury he should be a prince of the American turf. As he trudged home in the first dawn, Mr. Kane wondered. In the morning when he forced open his eyes, he went into the office and wrote in the "Nursery Stud Day Book."

"Mahubah foaled chestnut colt by Fair Play, narrow stripe from right of star down center of nose. Height 42", girth 30"." Later in the morning he telegraphed to Major Belmont in New York, "Mahubah foaled fine chestnut colt."

The Major had been waiting for this. He as well as his father, who had founded Nursery Stud twenty years earlier, had been lifelong students of blood lines. They had experimented, discarded, rebuilt their stables again and again. To them the sport was not so much in the winning of high stakes as in breeding the perfect horse. They were both horse lovers. August the elder had taken great pride in the four-in-hand that he drove at Saratoga. In Belmont's time his was the handsomest foursome that trotted down Broadway under the elms of a summer afternoon. When he returned from his ambassadorship to the Netherlands he retired from public life and devoted his time to horses. Nursery Stud, which he started at Babylon, Long Island, with four sons of Lexington, became one of the most famous stables in the country, and the Belmont Stakes and Nursery Stud Stakes were named in its honor.

The elder Belmont considered racing a gentleman's sport, to be controlled by the same rules that governed his personal conduct. He was the first president of the American Jockey Club, which was organized the year after the close of the Civil War, an elect group of fifty turfmen, among them Winston Churchill's grandfather, Leonard W. Jerome, James A. Bayard, James Gordon Bennett, who was as great a sportsman as he was a publisher, Francis Morris, M. H. Sanford, William Travers, and William K. Vanderbilt. It was a self-perpetuating organization, its members serving for life.

August Belmont II inherited his father's point of view. Although he was keenly interested in seeing his horses win, he never bet on a race, and he took success and defeat with the same good-tempered equanimity. Like his father, he dominated the American turf. Indeed he had controlled it ever since that day in 1891 when Pierre Lorillard gave his famous dinner to twenty-five leading breeders and presidents of jockey clubs. Lorillard was ill. He had spent his life and his tobacco fortune making his stables almost unchallenged in America, and had then invaded England and the Continent. But in America racing was in an unhappy state; the public was shouting "corruption" and with some justification, for a disreputable element had edged into the sport. Lorillard proposed a committee to amend the racing rules and to super‹ vise more closely the licensing of jockeys and trainers. At his right sat August Belmont, with whom he had waged a feud so bitter that the two had not been on speaking terms for years. At this dinner Lorillard, sweeping away the past, suggested Belmont as chairman of such a committee. Belmont accepted in the same spirit. Two years later the functions of the committee were taken over by the Jockey Club, of which Belmont was president. It was a totalitarian system of ruling American racing, performed as a public service, high mindedly but arbitrarily, owing an accounting to no one. And August Belmont dominated it as befitted a man who at the age of twenty-one had become American representative of the Rothschilds.

His interest in horses and his experiments in breeding had been an absorbing means of relaxation from international banking. When he retired Fair Play to stud he said to a friend, "Now, at last, I believe I have found the perfect formula; breed Fair Play to the daughters of Rock Sand." He remembered Fair Play's half brother, Friar Rock, produced by one of Rock Sand's daughters, a horse which had won the Belmont, Brooklyn, Suburban, and Saratoga Cup; and Tracery, another grandson of Rock Sand, whom Belmont had sent abroad to skyrocket in England when Governor Charles Evans Hughes forced through the New York legislature a law against betting on horse racing and evil days fell upon the sport. When a French syndicate offered Mr. Belmont $125,000 for Rock Sand, he sold the stallion. After all, the horse had sired fifty fillies at Nursery Stud; he would breed them to Fair

Play. He knew that there is only one good sire in ten thousand stallions and he believed Fair Play was one of these; there was something unconquerable about the Hastings, Fair Play blood.

Mahubah, the rangy young mare whose Arabic name meant "good greetings, good fortune," was one of the most promising of these Rock Sand mares. When she had been mated with Fair Play two years earlier she had produced the filly, Masda, who made Sam Hildreth, the trainer, doubt his stop watch. If this new colt should happen to have the fire of his grandfather Hastings without his viciousness, the intelligence of Rock Sand, and the courage and perfection of Fair Play, they would have a horse to reckon with. As he re-read the telegram, the Major wondered if his theory had been correct, if the chestnut colt would turn out to be one of the great horses, or just another disappointment.

But no such doubts bothered the colt as he explored his mother's stall, his clean-cut little ears quivering with excitement at the strange noises in the yard. In a day or two one of the grooms fitted a halter to his head and led him out into the lane while the other grooms and stable boys paused in their currying and sweeping and washing down to watch.

"He looks like Fair Play," they said, seeing that he was a solid chestnut except for the white on his face that was half a star and half a blaze. Even through the baby fur his coat glowed a rich reddish copper.

"He'll be red, that one," they said, "redder than his father."

"And man, look at his stride," they said as he stretched out his legs to catch his mother.

Soon the colt was turned out into a paddock with Mahubah and the other mares and foals. The grass was greening, the redbuds and dogwood were bursting in the little woods beyond the fence. Mahubah grazed sedately while the colt tried

7

to imitate her, spreading his awkward legs and rubbing the grass with his nose. He worked his baby lips, but he could not eat grass yet, not for a couple of weeks. He kicked and rolled and chased the other foals, feeling the strength of his muscles and the intoxication of the wind in his mane as he raced in the sun. His legs were long and unmanageable, he did not get off as quickly as the others, but on a fair stretch he could show his heels to any of them.

The foals lived to themselves, protected by their mothers. They never saw a saddle or a bridle and had no notion what went on at the race track where the two-year-olds exercised in the early morning. And they rarely saw the stallions, Hastings and Fair Play. These were the only two left at Nursery Stud; Henry of Navarre and Rayon d'Or were dead and the others had been eliminated, so these two, father and son, were kings of the farm.

Occasionally, when Sam Hildreth had finished clocking the track work of the two-year-olds and watching the yearlings come from the pasture, prancing down the lane, too full of life to walk sedately, he leaned on the paddock fence and looked at Mahubah's colt with speculative eyes. Mr. Belmont had met Hildreth in Paris where he had migrated after the blight fell upon American racing in 1911, and asked him to undertake the training at Nursery Stud. Sam Hildreth was homesick for the United States so he agreed. He was one of the outstanding trainers in America. Horses were in his blood; he had begun by training a mule when he was little more than five years old and had spent his childhood roaming with his father and his father's horses over the south and west, from Kentucky and Missouri to Kansas and trailing along with the caravans to Texas, backing their horses against all comers. No one in the United States knew more about race horses than Sam Hildreth. When he was not training them for one of the large stables he was racing them himself.

He knew about August Belmont's theory of breeding Fair Play to the Rock Sand mares and believed in it. Mahubah's colt might well be the one. He had clocked Mahubah's filly, Masda, and she had shown amazing speed, but she was temperamental, a "morning glory" better at an early workout than in a race. So he watched this long-legged colt running in the pasture and smiled to himself.

The days grew longer, the yearlings and the barren mares did not return to the stalls, and soon the mares and foals stayed out too, grazing until it was too dark to see, then lying down to sleep, the foals close to their mothers while the moon drew disturbing patterns on the black grass and the birds rustled in the dogwood trees.

One midsummer afternoon when it was so hot that the foals and mares were kept in their stalls during the day to avoid the flies and were let out to pasture at night, grooms put halters on the colts and led them down the lane. A group of people were standing in the shade in front of the house, the superintendent and his wife, Elizabeth Kane, and Sam Hildreth, looking tall and loose and rangy beside an exquisite woman in a linen duster and a broad hat tied with a motor veil. Farther down the drive a chauffeur was wiping the dust from a long black car. The woman was Mrs. August Belmont, the former Eleanor Robson, who even in her dusty veil managed to give the group the air of a garden party. Even when she was motionless she had the grace of the beautiful actress who is accustomed to being admired. This time she was alone. Sam Hildreth missed the familiar figure of the Major, small, compact, always cool and detached in white linen and a hard straw hat. Everything about him was so perfectly appointed from his immaculate shoes to his precisely trimmed moustache, that he made Sam feel as though he were falling apart. Now the Major was in Paris engaged in the unbelievable war in which the United States had so recently become involved.

Eleanor Belmont held out a lump of sugar on her perfumed hand and, singling out Mahubah's colt, laughed at the inquisitive quiver of its nose.

"What do you think of him?" Hildreth was saying. Mrs. Belmont examined the colt a long while, measuring with her eye his chest, his legs and the length of his muscular body.

"I must remember everything about him to tell the Major."

"What will you name him?" Elizabeth Kane asked curiously. It was Mrs. Belmont's prerogative to name the horses of Nursery Stud. She looked thoughtfully at the white blaze on the colt's face, remembering the horseman's adage, "There never was a good horse with a bad name."

"It must be something full of power. How about Man o' War?"

Thus Mahubah's colt had a name, a proud name, but few used it. That autumn when his flaming coat began to emerge in all its glory one of the grooms said, "He's redder than his his daddy, Fair Play," and the adjective stuck. He was "Red" or "Big Red" to all the boys who watered and brushed and combed him and told tall tales about his speed in the pasture.

Chapter II

AUTUMN CAME, the seedling grass was green in the pastures and Man o' War was growing up. Like the other almost-yearlings who were separated from their mothers, he was given a stall of his own, sweet smelling and newly clayed. He did not miss Mahubah. There were so many interesting things to learn! He was eating grain and hay like a grown horse. During the winter when frost and sometimes snow lay on the meadows he ate like a savage and shot up a hand taller than his fellows.

When spring came and the yearlings were let out to pasture, Red spurted about the meadows with an excess of high spirits. He was still slow at the start, but on a stretch he could show them all his heels.

Again it was a time of feverish activity; almost every night the watchman ran for Mr. Kane to help at the birth of a foal. Among the young ones that wabbled after their mothers to the pasture was Red's young brother, Playfellow, and in Mahubah's womb was the germ of My Play. For a few months her three great sons were close together.

This was the summer of 1918, of the great war in Europe and the scourge of influenza in the United States. In the Blue

11

Grass country there was no terror of bombs and submarines, but there was influenza. The disease swept over the stables at Nursery Stud, one horse after another came down with it, but most of them recovered. Man o' War was last, in midsummer he was listless and scrawny, fighting to throw off the germ.

Major Belmont was in Paris and the end of the war seemed very far away. It appeared useless to keep the yearlings at Nursery Stud in hopes of racing them under his own colors when the fighting might go on for years, so he decided to sell them all except the chestnut colt that he had never seen. His interest in the son of Fair Play had been increased by reports from the Kanes and his wife; he was beginning to believe that Man o' War might be the answer to his "perfect formula." He would keep this one in hope that the war might be over soon enough for him to run under the scarlet and maroon of the Belmont stable. For the rest—the Major could begin the experiment again; he would have Fair Play—God willing —and the Rock Sand mares.

So he cabled to Nursery Stud, "Sell twenty yearlings." The price tag was $60,000 for the lot, a bargain even in this the darkest year of racings, so interested breeders sent their trainers to look over the horses at Nursery Stud. Samuel D. Riddle of Philadelphia dispatched Louis Feustel, his trainer, and Mike Daly, a groom who had an unerring eye for horse flesh. Feustel had worked at Nursery Stud and, like everyone who knew Fair Play well, had a lasting admiration for him. But these yearlings—he and Mike agreed that there was not sixty thousand dollars worth in the lot. So they reported to Mr. Riddle that even at Major Belmont's low price the yearlings were not a good buy.

Mr. Riddle accepted the judgment of his trainer; he was a novice at organized racing although he had been a sportsman, rider, huntsman and show horse owner all his life. He had grown up in Delaware and Chester Counties in Pennsylvania, where he had followed the hounds from dawn to sundown before the superhighways drove away the foxes. He was one of the founders of the Rose Tree Hunt Club, the oldest in the United States, a rugged group of sportsmen who gathered at the Rose Tree Tavern for horse racing, cock fighting, even dog fighting, and sampling the charred kegs of mine host. Soon he became master of his own pack of hounds and began to enter jumping horses in the big shows. Early in the century he owned a hunt trio, Major Treat, Willow King and Virginian, which were never beaten in competition. Persuaded by his wife and his niece, Mrs. Walter Jeffords, who with her husband owned a fine racing stable, Mr. Riddle bought a few steeplechase horses at the Maryland races and won with them. The year Man o' War was born he bought a beautiful two-year-old filly named Yankee Witch, and when she won for him he saw that, in comparison with flat racing, steeplechasing and the show ring were dull entertainment, so he looked around for new runners to carry his colors, black and gold.

When his trainer reported unfavorably on the Belmont yearlings, Mr. Riddle, his wife and Mrs. Jeffords decided to go to the meet at Saratoga and the annual yearling sale which had been moved from Sheepshead Bay to Saratoga the year before. To Saratoga also went Major Belmont's yearlings, for when he had found no private buyers the Major had cabled the Kanes to send them all to Saratoga including Man o' War. Why the major changed his mind about keeping Mahubah's colt no one will ever know. Perhaps he did not want to risk the criticism of holding out the best and selling only the culls, so in an impulsive moment he sent to the auction block the best colt he would ever raise.

Saratoga was feverish that summer, gay on the surface but uneasy underneath, haunted by the spectre of war. At the

United States Hotel the guests of Charles A. Stoneham (later the owner of the New York Giants) drank all the champagne in town, and the steward garnered a five-hundred-dollar tip with a hundred dollars each for the waiters. There was money in Saratoga, plenty of it, almost as much as in the old days when John D. Rockefeller sunned himself on the verandah of the United States, but now veterans rocked on the verandahs of the mammoth hotels that line Broadway, while in the sanctity of their offices the managers mopped their fevered brows. There was a rumor that the Government was planning to take over the States and the Grand Union with their acres of bedrooms to use them as hospitals.

Powers-Hunter and Fasig-Tipton, the two great firms of horse auctioneers, had moved up from Sheepshead Bay and established themselves in spacious quarters with shady paddocks and stalls for visiting yearlings. William B. Fasig, the picturesque old horse dealer, was dead; his firm no longer operated by hunches such as stopping all deals when one of the managers chanced upon number 13 or met a red-haired, cross-eyed girl, but the organization that the flamboyant, superstitious old man had carried to success by his spectacular advertising still divided the business with Powers-Hunter. To these two firms came the yearlings from the famous stables of the East, from the great Kentucky stud farms and those of New Jersey and Maryland. During the race meeting famous trainers and prospective buyers strolled about the paddocks. Captain Arthur Hancock was there with twenty-six yearlings, and so was John E. Madden, who was retiring from breeding and selling his famous stables. Sam Hildreth was in charge of the Belmont string, Man o' War, Fair Gain, Royal Coinage and the rest. It was unusual to name yearlings, but the major had not originally bred these for sale.

To Hildreth, Saratoga had an atmosphere of unrest and

sadness. It was good to meet old friends, size up the three- and four-year-olds, take a flier or two on the races, and gossip about the chances of this horse and that, but the place was changed. Canfield's old casino was closed, the clubhouse where Lillian Russell, she of the gold bicycle fame, and Diamond Jim Brady had dined at the height of the season, where William K. Vanderbilt lost a hundred and thirty thousand dollars when he stopped for a few minutes on the way to dinner. The great days had vanished along with the marble furniture of the casino and the biggest rug in the world that Canfield had brought to Saratoga on a couple of flat cars. The raucousness of easy money was still there, but it was not gilded with romance as it was in the spacious days when Victor Herbert led the orchestra in the salon of the Grand Union and composed "Mlle. Modiste," humming "Kiss Me Again" as he walked through the gardens in the dusk. For where was there another E. Berry Wall, "king of the dudes," who could wear his favorite's ribbons with such elegance on his walking stick? And where were the glamorous Flo Ziegfelds and Jim Corbetts and Anna Helds?

Those were the days. Sam Hildreth sighed a little when he thought about them. When he passed the casino he seemed to see the ghost of "Bet-a-Million" Gates who lost two hundred and fifty thousand dollars and won a hundred and fifty in a single day.

It was here on the avenue of elms that he had met his wife, a Saratoga girl who had never passed through the gates of a race track. She told him legends about the carriage parade that ever since she could remember had begun at three o'clock every fair summer afternoon and in the old days had been resplendent with coachmen in scarlet and brass buttons, high-stepping carriage horses with white kid harness or monogrammed leather mounted in gold and silver. Sam took her

15

to the race track and watched her fall in love with the horses.

Now Hildreth was back on his own. For he had bought a few horses from Major Belmont, Mad Hatter and Lucullite and old Stromboli, who had carried the scarlet and maroon ever since Sam had been training for the Major. Stromboli had won many victories for them. Hildreth did not intend to do anything with him except to use him as a saddle horse; the trainer just liked the old fellow. When this meeting was over he intended to have his own farm and race his own horses for a while. Meantime, he saw that Big Red and his stablemates were curried and rubbed and polished to look their best in the ring. Red could not be groomed properly, for there had not been time after Major Belmont changed his mind. If Hildreth had not wanted to get horses in training he would have bought Big Red from the Major, for he believed in the yearling.

One morning Samuel Riddle strolled about the Fasig-Tipton paddocks looking over the horses that were coming up for sale. He passed the long succession of Belmont stalls with only mild interest, remembering the report that he had received from Feustel and Daly. At the last stall he met Feustel staring at a red colt that was much larger than the others. As Riddle stepped closer, the rangy body moved toward the stall door and a magnificent chestnut head reached out with sharp ears flicking toward him and intelligent eyes looking him over. The colt seemed too large to be a yearling, but there he was entered in the catalog, "Man o' War ch.c. by Fair Play-Mahubah by Rock Sand. Breeder Major August Belmont."

Feustel was watching the muscles rippling down Big Red's sturdy legs.

"This," he said to Mr. Riddle, "is a horse! We didn't see him at Nursery Stud. You can tell by his rough coat that he

16

hasn't been made ready properly. Belmont probably didn't intend to put him in the sale."

"He's by Fair Play from a Rock Sand mare," said Mr. Riddle, consulting the catalog. Feustel squinted his eyes at the red yearling.

"Then I trained his full sister, Masda. She's a three-year-old now. Belmont sold her to Waterbury last year."

"How good is she?" asked Riddle.

"A lot of foot, but erratic and temperamental. Hildreth didn't think she'd ever make a racer. It's the Hastings in her. When she wants to run she can show her heels to anything on hoofs, and when she doesn't she flies into a tantrum. But this one—I think he's got sense."

"You think I ought to take a chance?"

Feustel nodded.

"He'll run with that blood in him. And if he won't you can always make a jumper out of him."

Mr. Riddle came nearer. Red poked out his inquisitive muzzle with the flaming hairs in the nostrils, and Riddle smiled.

"Very well," he said, "but don't let it get around."

Later Sam Riddle said that he never had known such excitement as he felt on the Saturday morning when the Belmont yearlings were put on sale under the ancient trees of the picture-book paddock. It would have been an amusing crowd to watch if he had not been so nervous. He was prepared to buy about a dozen yearlings and this was his first major venture in the auction ring. Fashionable women in picture hats loaded with daisies and grasses, sportsmen in flat straws with fancy bands around them, trainers and traders, swaggering jockeys conscious of the adulation of the crowd, and everywhere gold braid and khaki were to be seen. On the fences swipes and grooms perched, listening eagerly to the bidding.

Old William Fasig once said that Americans have a distinctive way of bidding; they always ignore their competitors and keep their eyes on the auctioneer, while foreigners, especially Latins, ignore the auctioneer and glare at their competitors, advancing a step with each bid until they are within stabbing distance of each other. Just as you expect one of them to murder the other, the horse is knocked down, and half an hour later you see vanquished and victor drinking cosily together.

In spite of Feustel's report, Mr. Riddle had been persuaded by the comments of other breeders that the Belmont yearlings were good, so he bid $12,000 on Fair Gain, another chestnut colt, but was topped by Joseph E. Widener, who paid $14,000. For Rouleau by Tracery he offered $11,000, but the yearling went for $13,600.

When the groom led Man o' War to the auction block Mr. Riddle scarcely heard the auctioneer recount the horse's lineage and extol his fine points. He kept his eyes fastened on the man's expressive hands. Somehow he felt that to glance at the yearling would be to shout to everyone that he was going to buy. Although Man o' War was not as sleek and shining as the others, he was a beautiful sight to those who knew horse flesh; he entered the ring with a free, rangy, imperative stride, his head up, his proportions magnificent. As he stood in the circle, interested, confident, setting his ears forward and distending his nostrils to sniff the exotic scents of humans, it seemed apparent to Mr. Riddle that everyone who saw him would want the horse.

But the bidding was slow, nobody seemed particularly interested, the only competitors were Mr. Riddle's friends. At last the gavel fell on his bid of $5,000. The horse was his, and he beamed with satisfaction, for he had been prepared to pay twice as much. Later he said that he believed he could have bought the yearling for a little more than half the amount if Mrs. Plunkett Stewart and Mrs. Robert Gerry had not overheard him discussing the colt before the sale and reported his interest to their husbands.

The meeting was over, the grooms and stable boys gathered together their buckets and sponges and curry combs, and the yearlings stepped gingerly up the gang planks of box cars. Soon they were rumbling away to new pastures where they would train for their spring appearances as two-year-olds. Mr. Riddle had bought eleven yearlings for $25,000. "Ten were blanks," he commented years later, "the eleventh was Man o' War."

>>

THE BREAKING

>>

Chapter III

IT HAD BEEN a big season at Saratoga with Roamer, the great old campaigner, breaking his own record in the Saratoga Handicap, Harry Payne Whitney's Johren winning the Saratoga Cup, and two-year-old Billy Kelly breezing to glory. The weather was perfect; the course, girdled with thousands of blooming rose bushes and sparkling with pools and fountains, had been a brilliantly designed setting for gold braid and khaki as well as the costumes of the belles who sat in the boxes or leaned over the clubhouse balconies. The subscription steeplechase had raised almost $20,000 for the Red Cross, and the fashionable world had drifted home to open bazaars and sell war bonds in New York or Chicago or Pittsburgh.

But Mr. Riddle stayed on. Feustel was breaking the yearlings and every day Mr. Riddle went down to the paddocks to watch them, especially Man o' War. The colt had been well handled, but now the kind grooms and exercise boys of Nursery Stud to whom he was accustomed had gone home to Kentucky and left him among strange people. Feustel began to make friends with him by rubbing his legs gently and lifting his feet one by one, always talking to him in a quiet voice.

The Breaking

After giving the colt two or three days to settle into his new surroundings Feustel came into the stall one morning and asked Harry Vititoe, a former jockey who had been engaged to break him in, to put a halter around Man o' War's neck and lead him into a paddock. The colt did not mind a halter, for he had been accustomed to it at Nursery Stud, but when Harry began gently to rub and pull his ears Red backed off, snatched his head away from the hands that held him, and jerked the stableboy across the ground as though he were as light as a dried leaf. While the boy got up, Harry waited until Red stopped quivering, talking to him all the while, then, with two boys holding him on a close halter, stroked his neck, his haunches, and his ears again. Very few colts like to have their ears touched and Red was no exception. Every time the man touched his ears he jerked away dragging his procession of stable boys across the paddock. The colt did not have the devil Hastings' hatred of people nor the cold disdain of his father, Fair Play, but what he disliked he fought with all the intensity of his fiery nature.

For several days Harry kept working with the colt very gently, very patiently. When he finally slipped the rubber bit into Red's mouth and pushed the training bridle over his ears, the colt put up such a fight that the stable boys scampered to the fences.

Mr. Riddle, who had come down to watch, gloried in the big colt's movements, quick as chain lightning, and his mental reactions that were just as instantaneous, but when he saw Red fighting so devilishly hard to get free from the irritating bit and the straps around his head, he knew that the colt was going to be a terror to break. They never would do it if a single one of the grooms who handled him was rough or short-tempered or cruel or fought back. Mr. Riddle was a novice in racing, but he knew about horses; he impressed on everyone

21

around the stable how easy it would be to ruin the fiery colt.

"Do you think we'll ever break him?" his wife asked one day when he told her that Vititoe had spent an hour trying to put a surcingle around Red's body and attach side straps to the bit rings. The straps had elastic ends so that the colt's head was not restrained, but Red had fought like a tiger, screaming with rage and thundering around the paddock trying to shake it off.

"Yes," Mr. Riddle answered, "if we all have patience enough. That colt has brains. When he sees that we are too many and too strong for him and that he will make more by submitting than by fighting, he'll submit."

For several days Red was such a demon that it was dangerous to go near him. Finally after he had been schooled to the reins in the ring behind the stables, with Harry spending infinite time and patience waiting until his tantrums were over and then gently persuading him to walk for a few yards or back up, the jockey began the most difficult part of all, persuading him to accept a rider. Saddling him was a two-hour battle. The saddle had no stirrups to irritate or frighten him, but he distrusted it. After Red had fought it in the paddock for an hour or so and realized that he could not shake it off, Harry patted him and, while a couple of grooms held him, partly leaned his weight on the saddle. Red jumped and whirled, every nerve quivering. But he was tired; after a while Harry leaned again, then put one leg over the saddle. In the flicker of an eyelash Red tossed him on the grass. It took the stable boys fifteen minutes to catch the colt and take him to his stall.

That was enough for one day. Harry slit a few carrots lengthwise with his pocket knife and gave them to Red who gobbled them happily. He did not hold rancor; all he wanted was to be let alone. As the stable boys said of him, "He's

22

nice and he's smart, but don't ever try to force him or you'll come out second best every time. Ask him and he'll do what you want, push him and it's all off."

It took almost a week to persuade Red that he might as well submit and let Harry ride him. Sometimes he fought until he was worn down, outwitting the stable boys and running them breathless, twisting and squirming so that it was impossible to saddle him, but always in the end Harry rode Red. He never made it a battle of wills between himself and the horse, and after the struggle there was a reward, a carrot or a lump of sugar from Mr. Riddle. But Red never liked the saddle. Never in all the time that he was saddled for a race did he forget these first struggles and submit without a token battle.

It was a little easier when Harry rode the colt on the track following a groom on a pony (the stable term for any steady wise old horse that is used for training). Sometimes Red trailed behind with the pony setting the pace, sometimes he dashed ahead, but the example of the older horse steadied him a little.

At the end of September when Mr. Riddle sent Red to his training farm in Maryland he was still a rebel. He felt at home in the palace car, one of the de luxe box cars that the railroads switched from one road to the other without the need of changing. It had his stall in it, and always in his stall he was manageable. They never had to pad its walls to keep him from hurting himself. There he was "quiet as an old cow," the stable boys said. It was the outdoors, the chance to stretch himself and gallop with his tail fanning the wind, that excited him.

His new home, Glen Riddle, the training farm on Maryland's gentle, flat spreading eastern shore, was one of the most modernly equipped farms in the country. In the decade following Man o' War's arrival on that bright October day in 1918 it grew to include fifteen hundred acres and stables for sixty horses. Here Mr. Riddle had built a one-mile track of standard width for the training of his own yearlings and those of the Jeffords who owned the adjoining farm. In this climate the horses could work outdoors almost all winter, and the farm was so convenient to Philadelphia that the Riddles and Jeffords could come down for week-ends or even for the day to see special trials.

That autumn was a busy time for Mr. Riddle who had become so fascinated with racing and breeding that he had very little time for following the hounds when they met at the Rose Tree Tavern. He now had three establishments to super-vise: his deer park, his thoroughbred breeding farm, Glen Riddle, and another farm, Glen Helen, near Lexington, Kentucky, where he kept a stable of mares. That autumn he con-centrated on getting his yearlings ready for the opening of the spring racing season.

Man o' War also was busy; there were his new stables to explore and new lush pastures, different from the rolling hills of Kentucky. And there were new acquaintances to make. Red decided that he liked Frank Loftus, his groom, and Clyde Gordon, the exercise boy. They were his retinue. There was still a month of golden autumn weather, the grass had not yet turned brown, and the sun was still warm on the pastures. Every morning Clyde rode Red out to the track, where he was paced by Major Treat, one of Mr. Riddle's unbeatable trio of hunters. The Major was ten years old at this time, a sedate wise old horse retired to training the impetuous yearlings. Immediately he and Red struck up such a friendship that they were inseparable. For a month the colt galloped first on one side of the Major then on the other, or followed him when the Major set the pace. With the old horse Red was manageable, indeed he gave very little trouble except at saddling time. He still resented the restraint and had a habit of holding in his breath while the girth was tightened and then exhaling to leave it loose and comfortable. After saddling him Feustel led him around for a while before attempting to tighten the girth again.

There were many things to learn; things to do and things not to do; never to break into a canter from a trot, how to get off on the right foot when he broke away, and how to break from any position.

On the track the two stables of colts were worked every day. At first they merely jogged along the track; then they were taught to walk up to the rail and back straight away from it, and then to gallop straight and gallop on the rail.

After their workouts and rubdowns Red and Major Treat were turned into the pasture together, Red prancing, snorting, full of fire, the Major quiet and reserved but always around when his young friend wanted him. When Red had worked off his high spirits they stood under a tree together contentedly brushing away the late flies with their tails. If the Major was not around, Red was morose and impatient. His friend's stall was next to his own and when the yearlings came in from a workout he expected to find the Major waiting for him.

Although he hated the saddling and bridling, Red loved to run. The very sight of the race track set him aquiver. In the fall trials in which the yearlings from the two farms were matched together in sets of two, the red colt drew Golden Broom, the young star of the Jeffords stable. Mrs. Jeffords had fallen in love with him at the same sale in Saratoga in which Mr. Riddle bought Man o' War. He was a French-bred colt of such amazing beauty that she paid the highest price in the sale for him and immediately changed his name from Switch to Golden Broom to match his coat.

Golden Broom was very different from Man o' War. He was short-bodied, compact, and his powerful short legs drove his white stockinged feet so rapidly that he seemed to churn up the surface of the track. Man o' War, still awkward and long-legged, never could get started until Golden Broom was a length or more away. At the end of their sprints the golden colt was always ahead, but the red one was catching up with him at every stride.

As the two trainers hung over the rail with their stop watches in their hands they each had reason to be encouraged. Golden Broom broke fast, but when Feustel saw how his colt was going at the end he was not worrying. Given a longer distance in which to show his tremendous stride, the colt, he was certain, could outrun any yearling that was tried against him.

Winter was the time for short workouts and fattening in the stables. Man o' War had a mighty appetite, a fact that delighted Feustel, for no trainer likes a finicky eater. The colt rattled his feed tub and gobbled in such haste that Feustel had to teach him better manners by feeding him with a bit in his mouth.

On January 1st the yearlings celebrated their second birthday. It does not matter whether they were born in May or December, on their first New Year's day they are officially declared one year old and on their second they are two-year-olds, grown up and old enough to race. So it is an unlucky colt that is born in the autumn; he does not have much of a chance as a racer. However, January and February are not such good birth months as one might expect. Foals born so early in the year make no faster progress than April babies whose dams are nourishing them on fresh green pasture grass instead of dry winter fodder.

Thus in the spring of 1919 Man o' War was a two-year-old,

a sleek strapping fellow standing a head higher than most race horses. By this time his coat was a fiery red bronze, as beautiful as that of his father. There is something dramatic about a bright chestnut that catches the imagination. And Red was dramatic, not only in color but in every lightning movement. He was born to be the idol of the spectators.

All winter Red worked with Golden Broom on the training track, running a furlong, two, and finally three, and, with each increase of the distance, he had closed up on Golden Broom. Mr. Riddle was not discouraged; he knew that he had a good horse.

"When the time comes," he said, "Man o' War will take care of them all."

Chapter 4

IN THE SPRING of 1919 when it was time for the final tightening up of his string, Mr. Riddle spent most of his time at Glen Riddle supervising the training of the two-year-olds. This had become his absorbing interest, and to conserve his time for it he had given to the Jeffords his famous pack of American fox hounds, old black-and-tan Pennsylvania stock that he had bred to music as well as to speed and conformation. Such packs are rare, and the music of these hounds was the special pride of the huntsmen of the Rose Tree Club.

Finally in May the Riddle and Jeffords strings moved to Havre de Grace, which was practically next door, perched on the bluffs at the mouth of the Susquehanna. The eight-year-old track of farm land loam was in the middle of hunting and horse breeding country and the stables were full of two-year-olds getting ready for the season.

Man o' War went into rigid training with the rest of them, up at five in the morning to see how Major Treat had slept (the stall of the old campaigner was always next to Red's), then breakfast, three quarts of cleaned and carefully sifted oats. After breakfast Frank Loftus removed the night bandages from the colt's legs, looked them over for possible

28

bruises, rebandaged them, and then rubbed and brushed the horse until he gleamed like polished copper.

After the token battle with the saddle and bridle, Clyde Gordon rode Red out to the training track. It was still dark at five o'clock and almost every morning as they warmed up they saw the mist rising from the river and the sun coming through pale and golden. Red felt the enchantment of the early light and the hush on the meadows, he was tingling with well-being, and if he had had his head he would have raced to the horizon. But that was not the schedule. One morning Clyde held him down to a slow jog, then a canter for a mile or so, and that was all for the day. On the next, the boy let him out a little, never to the limit, and he would run the distance for which he was being prepared. These were the mornings he liked best. Gordon never had to drive him, he did everything with his whole heart and always, even when walking, he was up against the bit.

After the workout Red returned to the stable, where he was walked for an hour while he cooled slowly. Sometimes he was given a few sips of water measured almost with a medicine dropper, then his feet were cleaned and scrubbed and the bandages of cotton and surgical gauze were wound again about his legs. On warm days the perspiration was sponged from his coat with a solution of alcohol, arnica and witch hazel.

At last he was back in the stall newly carpeted with sweet smelling rye straw and he was left alone for a few hours to loaf with Major Treat. George Conway, the stable foreman, and Frank Loftus, his personal groom, did not disturb him while they scalded his feed box and tended to the minor chores. One of them was always within hearing and, preferably, within seeing distance of the stall.

At a little after eleven Mrs. Riddle came to supervise Red's lunch of bran, oats, and cracked corn, with a lump of sugar from her pocket for dessert. After the meal the horse's door was closed and he had four hours to himself for a nap or communion with Major Treat. Later he was taken out to walk for thirty minutes to limber up his muscles, then to the pasture for fifteen minutes of grazing, no more, no less, timed by Conway's watch. This fifteen minutes was the best part of the day, the grass was young and the mid-afternoon May sun caressed his shoulders. He snorted with disapproval when Gordon led him back to the stables.

In the stall Red's bandages came off again and his legs were inspected and rewrapped. Loftus made him a fresh bed of straw while he was brushed, rubbed, and prepared for the night. Supper was his cooked meal of the day, bran, oats and flaxseed meal salted and cooled to the exact temperature. Finally Loftus put on the sleeping blanket, Red stuck his muzzle across to see that all was well with Major Treat, and then to sleep.

In spite of this regimen as closely supervised as that of a prince royal, Red caught the flu. For several days it had been sweeping the track and many horses were so ill that they had been destroyed. At first Red escaped, but one afternoon the germs attacked him. His temperature skyrocketed to 106. The Riddle stables were filled with consternation. Feustel ran to phone the vet, but the overworked man was not to be found. There was no other nearer than Baltimore, and that was too far away—he would be too late. Feustel and Conway were helpless, they could do nothing except keep Red quiet. The stable boys walked on tip toe; not a bucket clanked or a chain rattled.

One of the grooms wanted to give Red "Dr. Green," an old Kentucky remedy for almost any of the ills of horses, a piece of sod cut out with the roots and earth attached. When it was put in the stalls, horses ate it, roots, earth and all, and, according to stable lore, the cures were marvelous. But nobody wanted to take a chance, so all night long Feustel listened to Red's troubled breathing. The Riddles and Jeffords made anxious visits to the stall.

It seemed an endless night, but gradually the dawn began to break and in the early light Feustel peered into the stall, afraid to see what ravages the germs had made. Man o' War was resting, his breathing was regular—he had beaten the fever. By mid-morning he was demanding his breakfast as impatiently as ever.

As the training period neared its end, Feustel concentrated on starts from the barrier. There were no stall gates in those days, but a barrier that stretched across the track and snapped up when the starter sent the horses away. Because of his size and the length of his stride it was difficult for Man o' War to get off to a quick start. Johnny Loftus, who was to ride him, worked to stir him up; and Johnny knew his business, for he was the outstanding jockey in America. The year before he had ridden War Cloud to win the Preakness and he had headed the column of percentages. By June he had Red outbreaking them all, but the colt was so excitable that he spent too much energy fighting at the barrier. He never did like to wait.

Already the sharp-eyed rail birds, the hangers-on of the race tracks who perch on fences like drabbled crows in the early morning and clock the horses in hope of selling a few tips to betting fans, had noted both Man o' War and Golden Broom and were passing the word along the grapevine that here were a couple of thunderbolts.

Mr. Riddle had hoped to have Man o' War ready for Pimlico, but that meeting was too early, so he waited for Belmont. By the last part of May, Man o' War, Major Treat, and their retinue started on the journeys that were to take them so many triumphant miles.

The stables and paddocks at Belmont were strange, and Red was nervous. He was not overpowered with awe at making his debut on a race track that proudly claimed to be the world's best. The course, its spacious acres—650 of them, not naturally so beautiful as those of Saratoga but carefully landscaped to give it an artificial charm—its well-kept track and its steeplechase course were planned by William C. Whitney, who had revived racing at the Spa, and its development was the work of Joseph E. Widener. Its name honored August Belmont the elder, whose son was president of the New York Jockey Club.

On the May night before the opening in 1904 August Belmont celebrated with a dinner at the Turf and Field Club, which had been the old Manice Mansion adjoining the field, and afterward with a ball at the stand. The list of guests was an international roster of distinguished turfmen. Indeed, it was such a fashionable event that at the luncheon which August's brother Perry gave next day, Lord Suffolk and Sydney Paget arrived in toppers. Thus inaugurated, Belmont rivalled Saratoga as the most fashionable racing meet. On its famous velvet lawn before the clubhouse New York's international sporting set watched the outstanding races of the season. Belmont had inherited the classic races of old Jerome Park in Fordham, the Withers, the Belmont, the Juvenile, the Nursery and the Metropolitan, and later from the Coney Island Jockey Club the Suburban, the Futurity and the Realization Stakes.

When racing fell into the doldrums Belmont fared better than many of the other courses. At Sheepshead Bay a squad of mounted police patrolled the infield. Saratoga, according to the noted sportsman, Harry S. Page, "looked from a dis-

MAHUBA, DAM OF MAN O' WAR

FAIR PLAY, SIRE OF MAN O' WAR

Man O' War with Louis Feustel, his trainer

Man O' War being given a rub-down at Belmont in June 1920

tance as if the New York Yacht Club had decided to stop there on its annual cruise. Sail cloth was run up on long poles placed along the fence enclosing the grounds so that the pool room men could not spy the winning horses from afar and wire the results to their rooms." Patrons were not allowed to leave the grounds between the first and last races of the day and no wire connections were allowed. Both the Jockey Club officials and a group of Pinkerton detectives were determined to keep the returns from the pool rooms.

Finally both Sheepshead Bay and Saratoga folded up, but Belmont kept going by turning its beautiful lawn into a horse show ring and using its stands for watchers of air craft races.

In 1917 after racing had returned, Belmont was wrecked by a fire, but temporary stands were put up to seat more spectators than the old ones. 1918 was a good season, and 1919 was expected to be the best in many years. The races were still run "the wrong way" (clockwise), but this did not bother Man o' War, nor was he impressed with the exalted company in the stalls on either side of him and Major Treat. In them were the best of the Whitney and Widener strings and of every other famous breeder from California to Kentucky. An outstanding group of three-year-olds were running, Billy Kelly, Sir Barton, and Hannibal, as well as a promising crop of two-year-olds.

Red gave them no more than a passing glance; he had little time for striking up acquaintances. The early morning workouts on the training tracks were even more sensational than those at Havre de Grace. The rail birds, who pulled up their collars in the early morning Long Island fog, clocked him again and again at a half mile in 47 seconds with Clyde Gordon holding him in so hard that he almost choked the horse. Indeed, Red looked so good that Mr. Riddle and Louis

Feustel never left him alone for a minute day or night. Always Gordon or Loftus or some other equally trusted groom was near his stall. Only a few days before, a horse had broken down and hemorrhaged on the track, stifled by a sponge that had been inserted in one of his nostrils.

On that June 6th, 1919 everyone who was anyone in the racing world was at Belmont. The beautiful saddling paddock, shaded with wide-spreading chestnuts and oaks, was gay with the spring costumes of fashionable women mingled with the bright silks of the jockeys. By the time Man o' War made his debut they were beginning to relax and visit in the boxes. Women were gathering their gloves and summer furs and the top sports writers collecting their notes, leaning back to gossip with one another, for the last race in the afternoon is never written up except to give the bare results for the benefit of the "investors." That is, unless something extraordinary happens.

And then it did happen. Even Man o' War himself knew that there was something unusual in the air as he followed Major Treat to the paddock to join six other two-year-olds, Lady Brighton, American Boy, Devil Dog, Gladiator, Neddam and Retrieve. He flicked his ears inquiringly at Mr. Riddle and Louis Feustel talking in his stall and at Johnny Loftus dressed in white riding breeches, a black and gold silk blouse, and a peaked cap. Feustel threw a saddle over Red's back and tightened the girths. After Red had made his usual protest, Johnny Loftus settled in the saddle and put his feet in the stirrups. In the other stalls other boys in bright colored blouses were being tossed up on the other two-year-olds. The saddling paddock looked like the setting for a medieval pageant of vivid silks and prancing horses.

"Hey, Red," Johnny whispered in his ear as he lined up impatiently behind Retrieve, following in single file a pony mounted by a man in a scarlet coat. As they paraded toward the starting post Red pointed his ears toward the buzzing of thousands of voices and the exciting rhythm of the band. People hung over the rail and pointed at him, the chestnut youngster who was going to the post with odds of 3 to 5. Red wanted to dance, but Major Treat, plodding along beside him, kept him steady.

At the barrier far down the straightaway stretch Major Treat left him, and Red felt his bridle grasped by a groom. All seven of the young horses were held by their bridles. They danced with excitement, jockeys rapped with their whips and kicked with their heels, trying all their tricks to be sure they would get away without interference. For two minutes the nervous youngsters pranced and wheeled, then at exactly 5:08 for a fraction of a second they were in line, standing correctly, facing the right direction. The barrier disappeared, and the crowds in the stands roared, "They're off!"

The horses sprang away, churning the dirt as they exploded down the track. Man o' War was on the outside with Johnny Loftus holding him in, pulling on the reins. Johnny was following the instructions of Feustel who had been afraid of an accident at the post.

"Wait until they get out of your way, Johnny," he had said, "then let him go after them. He'll catch them at the furlong pole and win galloping."

So Johnny Loftus let all the others get away and then eased up on Man o' War's mouth. Red shot forward as though he had been released from a catapult. In less than a hundred yards he had caught the pack and passed them. For a furlong Retrieve kept beside him, giving every ounce of strength he had. A hush fell over the stands, as though the crowd held its breath, then exploded in a roar as Red streaked out ahead. As they passed the field stand, Johnny looked over his shoulder. He glanced to the right but no one was in view, then to the left to see if Retrieve was sneaking up on the rail, but the rest of the field was so far behind that he could not even find them.

This was what the crowd had come to see. They screamed, they jumped to their feet, and pounded on the rails. Johnny tightened the reins. Red resented it, he was just beginning to run; tingling with the excitement of the crowd, he could have run straight to Long Island Sound. But Loftus stood up in the stirrups and pulled so hard that at the finish he had slowed Red down to a canter. Even fighting against all of Johnny's muscle power Red had won by six lengths. He had run the five furlongs in 59 seconds under a choking pull.

As the roar of the crowd shook the stands and rolled down the track, Loftus turned Red back to meet Clyde Gordon on Major Treat. Clyde caught Red's bridle and led him into the tiny enclosed winner's circle in front of the judges' stand. As Red stood there, quivering, magnificent, his wet satin coat gleaming bright copper, his ears flicking, trying to understand the roar of sound, the crowd stared at him with hoarse delight. They did not want to leave even after Red had been led away; they trickled out of the stands reluctantly, looking back over their shoulders, feeling that they had been lifted up into a great moment, that they had been part of an exalted experience such as one does not encounter often in a lifetime. The judges, the breeders, and the veteran racing fans had a glow in their eyes. Racing had not regained its popularity since the blight. This dramatic red colt that had so assaulted the emotions of the crowd might bring it back.

Chapter V

At the stables where Red was cooling off with the other horses in their gay hoods and blankets there was a buzz of excitement. To Red it seemed like any other afternoon, the yapping of dogs, the smell of hot mash cooking in the out-door pits, the splashing of water for the evening baths, the shouting and bustle of swipes and grooms going to dinner in relays; but to Louis Feustel it was an afternoon shot with glory. As for Mike Daly, the groom who had first seen Red at Nursery Stud, his smile split his face like a slashed water-melon as he proclaimed, "We've got ourselves a champ."

While the grooms were reliving the race with Clyde Gordon and Frank Loftus, Mr. Riddle's friends were congratulating him under the judges' stand, laughingly accusing him of "ringing in" a four-year-old. No colt could be so large and good as Man o' War. As the turf editor of the *New York Morning Telegraph* said, "He made half a dozen high-class youngsters look like $200 horses."

For three days Red loafed and rested. He became more accustomed to the strange stables and the mascots that snarled or squawked or bleated in the neighboring stalls. In one a fierce dog growled at strangers, in another a rooster cocked its scarlet comb and occasionally screamed at the passers-by—he was tethered to the door of the stall by a long, thin chain and a ring around his foot. Farther on a goat sardonically chewed an old corn cob. There were several goats; they were such favorites as mascots that it was an old racing custom for the stable boys to discomfit their rivals by stealing their mascots—hence "getting the other's goat."

Man o' War did not need a goat, a parrot or a rabbit. He had Major Treat. On the third day after his first appearance had set the racing fans afire the Major led his protégé again to the track. This time Red was to run in the Keene Memorial Stakes (from then on he ran in none but stake races). Five other youngsters were entered in the race: Ralco, Anniversary, My Laddie, Hoodwink, and a colt named On Watch, a son of Colin. Old-timers who remembered the great races in which Fair Play had run the unbeaten wonder-horse, Colin, to the limit of his strength and more than once had come within "a swollen lip" of the victory, wondered if Man o' War could avenge his sire.

This time Red was not so nervous and inquisitive as he waited in the saddling paddock for Johnny Loftus to be tossed up in his black-and-gold blouse. He knew where he was going, and he was quivering to get started. Again the band played music that made his heels dance as he held his place in the parade. This time the horses were only a minute at the post. Loftus used the same strategy that had won Red's first race; he held back until the final eighth of a mile, then gave Man o' War his head for a breath-taking burst of speed. He shot by Ralco and My Laddie so fast that the fans swore these two stopped to watch him pass. He romped home with Loftus standing up in the stirrups to keep him from running out of the field. On Watch, his only competitor, pounded across the line three lengths behind. As the *Daily Racing Form* recorded

in its classic style, "Won easily; second and third driving."
Fair Play had been avenged.

On a slow track Man o' War had run the five and a half
furlongs in 1:05⅗ and he had won $4,200. Both he and On
Watch had carried 115 pounds, the last time Man o' War
would carry so light a weight.

Two weeks later when Red was entered in the 5½ furlong
Youthful Stakes he met On Watch again along with St. Allan
and Lady Brummel. This time he paid for his early victories.
To insure a close race the Jockey Club attempts to equalize
the chances of the horses by adjusting the weight they carry.
In the scheme of measurement each pound represents a length
at a mile. The handicapper of the Jockey Club had decreed
that Man o' War carry 120 pounds, the weight of Johnny
Loftus plus his tack (which could not exceed 110 pounds) and
the little lead plates that he wore under his saddle.

After his spectacular defeat On Watch had been dropped
to 108 pounds, but it made no difference in the running of
the race. Again it was Red "won easily; second and third
driving," and the public happily collected one dollar for
each two it had invested. As one of the sports writers said,
"It was nothing more than an exercise gallop for Man o' War."

The next day Red with Major Treat and the rest of the
Riddle string moved to the Aqueduct course to be ready for
the opening day of the meet. Here many of the famous races
were run, among them the Brooklyn Handicap and the Great
American. The one in which Red was entered was the 5-fur-
long Hudson Stakes. It was an opening feature and he had
been given only two days of rest. This time he was given a
heavy handicap, 130 pounds to carry, giving 15 pounds to
another Riddle colt, Rocking Horse, 15 to Shoal, 18 to Evergay and 21 to Violet Tip, a pretty filly who would have been
his half sister if he had been a human. She was a daughter of

Fair Play and a Rock Sand mare, but in horse lineage only foals by the same dam and different sires are half brothers and sisters—those by the same sire and different mothers are not related. Violet Tip was running light partly because of the five pound "sex allowance" granted to mares and fillies.

Again Man o' War was an odds-on favorite. The Glen Riddle entry opened at 1-10. (When an owner, or trainer, has more than one horse entered in a race the horses are coupled as a single entry.) Rocking Horse, the second Riddle colt, was not expected to do anything and didn't; he ran dead last. Violet Tip and Shoal opened and held at 15-1 and Evergay at 40-1.

Red was nervous and hard to manage; he held up the break for three minutes. Perhaps it was not entirely his fault or that of Johnny Loftus—the other jockeys might well have tried to delay the start, hoping Red's high weight would fret him and wear him down—but when they finally broke away it was the same old story, "Won easily, second and third driving." Violet Tip tried; she finished a length and a half behind, but she never had a chance.

These races were beginning to be repetitious; the results all read alike with the exception of the entries. Red was entered next in the Great American, but he was prevented from running by an attack of colic after wolfing down a heavy meal. He had to wait a few days for the Tremont Stakes. On that day he did it again, carrying the same 130 pounds. His reputation had now become so formidable that only two stables entered colts against him. Ralco, with 115 pounds, carried hopes for second place. Red ran the six furlongs under a strangling pull. "Won easily, second and third driving." The spectators were sure Loftus could have cut many seconds from the unimpressive time of 1:13 if he had let the colt out.

For the rest of July Red rested and worked a little, while the stable hands cut out pictures of him from the sports sections of the daily papers, and feature stories about this phenomenal new colt who had such a heart for racing that he was reported to give Johnny Loftus a reproachful eye when the jockey held him in at the finish. He hadn't really run yet, they said, for no horse had given him a race for the money. Five furlongs was nothing to him; he needed more to stretch out in. The fans were speculating about what he would do at Saratoga.

In 1919 the Saratoga Meeting was still the most important racing event of the year. The track at the Spa was the oldest in the United States and the second oldest in America, second only to the Woodbine track in Toronto. From its earliest days Saratoga had been a racing town. Three years before the half way mark of the 1800s trotting horses were racing for purses of from $50 to $200 on Horse Haven, the new track out Union Avenue in the pine woods. In 1863 the first running races were held on the track. John Morrisey, "Old Smoke," the gambler who built the Clubhouse and had a quiet hand in almost all the business of the Spa, promoted the Saratoga Association. He never appeared as a member, his name would have shed no luster on the list of those whom he interested in the idea, such men as William Travers, who became the president of the Association, and luxuriously moustached, dashing Leonard W. Jerome.

That first season the Association put on eight races with twenty-six entries, but the track was too narrow, so they left Horse Haven for a training track and moved across the avenue to 125 acres of woodland which they started to develop into the course that is today unrivalled in its landscaped beauty. The Travers Stakes is the second oldest turf classic in North America, bowing again to the King's Plate in Toronto, but scarcely less famous were the races open to the two-year-olds, the United States Hotel Stakes, the Hopeful and the Grand Union, for all of which Red was to make a bid.

Here in that summer of 1919 were gathered the best two-year-olds in America, the greatest trainers and the most famous jockeys. Harry Payne Whitney's trainer, peppery Jim Rowe, snorting at the challenge of the sensational Riddle color bearer, had readied two youngsters to carry the Whitney colors, Upset and Wildair, and had another, John P. Grier, not quite ready but said to be the best of them all. A filly named Bonnie Mary arrived with the winner's share of three important races, the Fashion, the Juvenile and the Great American Stakes. She had beaten On Watch and Upset, and had lowered by a full second the record in the Great American. Rouleau, the son of Tracery from Nursery Stud, was there as well as Carmandale, David Harum, Donnacona, and the Jeffords' Golden Broom, to whom Red had lost so many times on the track at Glen Riddle. This was the stiffest competition Man o' War had met. Now he might be pressed to show what he could do.

The Spa was an ideal place to work in the sultry late July days. Red thrived on the routine, the parade to the training track in the early morning, trailed by grooms with their sponges and blankets, the cooling down under the avenue of elms, and the rolling in the sand pile before morning grooming. By August he was rested and fit.

When he came to the saddling paddock to enter the United States Hotel Stakes on August 2nd he was, as usual, the odds-on choice at 9-10. He was the idol of the crowd; the others, promising as they were, did not have a chance against him in the minds of the betting fans. Upset was quoted at 6-1, Bonnie Mary at 9-2, By Golly at 10-1, Feodor and Rouleau at 20-1, Homely and Carmandale at 25-1, David Harum at 30-1 and Sandy Beal, 40-1. Although they were all over-shadowed by Man o' War, several of them would write turf history.

As they moved about in the saddling paddock adjusting their gear or waiting to be tossed up, the jockeys represented the Who's Who of the track. Eddie Ambrose wore the Whitney brown and blue, spectacular Buddy Ensor stood by the bridle of Bonnie Mary, "Pony" McAtee was stroking the head of David Harum, and with them were Bill Kelsay, Robertson, and Laverne Fator who was said to have a clock in his head and could gallop a horse a mile without varying more than a fraction of a second from the time the trainer set. Seldom were so many outstanding riders entered in one race and all of them with one thought—to beat Man o' War.

This was a six furlong race. At the barrier Man o' War was in eighth position with Upset on the rail and next him Bonnie Mary. At the break Red shot away at such a pace that within a few hundred yards both the fans and the jockeys knew the race was over. Fator in an impotent gesture drove Carmandale for a quarter, but at the end of two furlongs the horse was reeling. None of the field came close, although Upset, Homely, and Bonnie Mary came on in a late drive that gave the spectators a thrilling moment. The race was Red's from the first, and he finished it, as usual, fighting Loftus for a chance to run. As one of the sports writers put it, "During the last stage of the race Loftus was complacently admiring the scenery."

That night Saratoga went wild about Man o' War. At the palatial Riddle residence where the celebration went on until morning, the guests compared Red with Colin and St. Simon, with Spendthrift and Eclipse and Herod, but not one could remember such a glorious two-year-old.

Eleven days later Man o' War was entered in the Sanford Memorial, until that day a comparatively minor event but since immortalized in racing history. There were nine entries (only seven of which went to the post), among them the best of the year, Red's old training comrade, Golden Broom, and Upset, the chestnut Whitney colt. The last four entries, The Swimmer, Armistice, Captain Alcock and the imported Donnacona, were "maidens" (they had not won a race). This was their first entry and the odds against them, 100 against Alcock and 50 against the others except Donnacona, who was quoted at 30, showed what the fans thought about their temerity in challenging the top three.

Golden Broom had grown even more beautiful in the year since Mrs. Jeffords had fallen in love with him at the yearling sale. "The picture colt," the fans called him, because of his peculiar golden shade and his superb head with the white blaze that made him the darling of artists. In contrast with the magnificence of Man o' War he had a neat perfection and a symmetry that were a delight to the eye. And in his movements he had a smoother rhythm than Red, he ran closer to the ground, but Red made up for his bumpy gait by his tremendous stride.

There was no question that Golden Broom was a perfect colt. As Mrs. Jeffords said to the handicapper, "Don't you handicap my colt on his looks. If you do, he will have to carry more weight than any colt of the year."

Moreover Golden Broom's performance matched his looks. Indeed, he was so good that Mike Daly, who was training him, suggested to Feustel that he and Man o' War should be entered in alternate races instead of competing with each other, for they were so obviously the two outstanding youngsters of the year. Instead, they arranged, in their workouts together for the Sanford a private match at three furlongs. Now, though, Red could cope with the blinding speed of the golden colt. Running even furlongs in the amazing time of 11, 11, and 11, Man o' War had edged out Golden Broom by nearly a length.

Red went to the post odds-on as usual at 11-20 and carrying 130 pounds. On the morning of the race, when it was known that Golden Broom also would be handicapped at 130 pounds after his smashing victory over the Whitney colt, Wildair, in the Saratoga Special, Mr. Riddle offered to withdraw Man o' War to give Golden Broom a better chance, but Mrs. Jeffords refused to consider such a hollow shot at the trophy. Golden Broom was fit, the quarter crack of one of his hoofs that he suffered earlier in the season (he had thin soled hoofs as do most white stockinged horses) no longer bothered him. She wanted him to meet Man o' War and let the better colt win.

It was a typical languid August racing afternoon. To the call of the bugler's "to boots and saddle," the pageant started, the parade of velvet-groomed horses and jockeys with their gay silks shimmering in the light. The fans got out their glasses and leaned on the rails, waiting for a thrill. The horses reached the barrier with no mishaps. Mars Cassidy, the regular starter, was replaced that day by C. J. Pettigill, a retired starter who had been acting as Placing Judge and had aroused much resentment among the fans by his decisions on close finishes in those days before the camera took the guessing out of judging. Actually Pettigill was a good and experienced starter, but he was the victim of a malicious fate that ticketed him in racing history as the muddler of the start of this race and the starter of the notorious American Derby of 1893 in which the horses were an hour and a half at the post.

What happened at the post on that August afternoon of 1919 always will be a matter of dispute. This is the version of Bill Knapp who rode Upset, as he told it years later to James Donn, president of the Gulfstream course at Hallandale Park, Florida.

"There were seven horses in the Sanford with Man o' War held at 11-20 odds, but when the field bounced away it was Golden Broom settin' the pace, with Upset on the outside just a neck away. Man o' War didn't make his bid till we hit the turn, and then he churned up along the rail till his head bobbed into the corner of my eye. There he was, tossin' those twenty-eight foot strides of his and tryin' to squeeze through on the inside of Golden Broom and Upset.

"If I'd given so much as an inch, the race would've been as good as over, but jockeys don't ride that way. I could have breezed past Golden Broom any time I took my feet out of the dashboard, but that would also have let Man o' War out of his mouse trap and he'd have whooshed past us in half a dozen strides.

"When Johnny Loftus, ridin' Man o' War, saw we weren't goin' to open up, there was nothing left for him but to pull up sharply and duck to the outside. That's what I'd been waiting for. That same moment I gunned Upset with my bat and galloped to the top in a pair of jumps. Man o' War then had to come out around the two of us, and it cost him all o' two lengths. From there to the finish he was chargin' again like a jet plane but Upset had just enough left to push his head down in front.

"Sure, I win the race all right—it was the biggest thrill o' my life—but lookin' back at it now there's sure one horse which shoulda retired undefeated. Never was a colt like him! He could do anything—and do it better than any horse that ever lived. If I'd moved over just an eyelash that day at Saratoga he'd have beat me from here to Jaloppy. Sometimes I'm sorry I didn't do it!"

The crowd that watched the defeat of Man o' War on that history-making afternoon agreed with Bill Knapp. When the horses returned to the stands a roar of adulation greeted Red —he was the hero, greater than ever in defeat. The noise fell ironically on the ears of Johnny Loftus as he unsaddled Man o' War and slumped in his wet silks to the weighing in. Already he felt the scathing verdict of the sports writers and he could hear the bettors muttering "a fix."

He was right in anticipating the indignation of the press. As W. C. Vreeland, the veteran turf reporter, wrote, "Man o' War is the champion. He never was so great as he was in defeat. That he failed was due entirely to his rider, Johnny Loftus. If Loftus had been a stable lad instead of the premier jockey of America, he could not have ridden a poorer race. Loftus made three mistakes, all costly. Man o' War overcame two and would have made amends for the third if the error had not been committed so close to the winning post. He stood a drive such as no other colt has been asked in the last twenty years, without flinching. . . .

"A horse can be beaten in a race and still gain glory. Such was the honor that Man o' War achieved. Never will his courage be questioned henceforth. It was an unknown quality for he was never before put to the test. When the test came he was not found wanting. 'Semper Fidelis!' Let that be placed on his resting place when his day comes to pass over to the Elysian fields where great race horses graze."

Chapter VI

O<small>N THE NIGHT</small> of the Sanford while the Riddle stables grieved, the strategy boards of the other stables met late, trying to estimate the significance of the defeat of Man o' War. They had picked up hope. Once beaten, the colt might be beaten again. No one of them truly believed he could be out-run, but perhaps he would get another bad start or Loftus might go rail-happy again and give them the chance to outwit him. Jim Rowe, particularly, believed he had a chance. It was wormwood to him that he, one of the great trainers with the resources of the Whitney stables behind him, had not been able to defeat this colt from a comparatively unknown stable. For nearly two decades his horses had brought home the prizes, at first for James R. Keene's famous stables and later for Harry Payne Whitney. That night, as he and his cabinet sat under one of the great elms smoking away the mosquitoes and enjoying the cool night breeze, they considered how the Whitney stables could snatch another victory. Bristling with confidence they decided to enter Upset in the Grand Union Hotel Stakes to challenge Red again.

Ten days later, on a clear, bright afternoon with the sun so strong that the spectators had to shade their eyes with fans and racing cards, the Grand Union was run. None of the trailers in the Sanford were entered—they had had enough, but it was a good field; Rouleau, Red's playmate at Nursery Stud, Evergay, Blazes, Gladiator, Peace Pennant, The Trout, Hasten On, and the Canadian, King Thrush.

Johnny Loftus was up again on Red. Legends which have grown up about the Sanford have it that Mr. Riddle was so indignant with Loftus that he refused to speak to the jockey, but the fact is that Loftus rode Man o' War consistently for the rest of the season. This day as the horses paraded to the post he was alert and confident, more so than the spectators who watched tensely, wondering whether the defeat had some-how psychologically tipped the scales against the magnificent red strider. They need not have been disturbed for the start was clean, Loftus made no mistakes, and after coasting for two furlongs he took the lead with Upset driving furiously behind and Blazes keeping in third place. Not for a mo-ment was there any real competition. Through the last eighth Loftus pulled with all his might to slow Red down. The time was 1:12 on a fast track and could have been much better.

One of the spectators who had watched Man o' War prance home with mixed emotions was the Texas oil tycoon, Mont-ford Jones. At the sale of yearlings the year before he had paid $13,000 for Rouleau and now his colt had come in a sorry eighth. As he watched Red being led away to the stables and listened to the thundering of the crowd he knew that he wanted the fiery chestnut no matter how staggering the cost. He sought Mr. Riddle and made him an offer of $100,000. Mr. Riddle laughed. Montford Jones raised it to $125,000, to $150,000, but Mr. Riddle was not tempted. He did not need the money and he had no intention of parting with Man o' War.

The season was almost over, Red had a few days of rest

before the Hopeful, the big event for two-year-olds that was run on closing day. This, the gala event of the racing year, opened under a blistering sun. By afternoon when the first spectators began to drift into the stands the air was so heavy that programs stuck to the fingers; women sweltered under their flowered picture hats, and the white linen coats of their escorts were wet between the shoulders. While they placed their bets and languidly fluttered their fans, the heat was so intense that they could scarcely breathe. It pressed down on them like a sultry weight. By the time for the running of the Saratoga Cup, one of the most highly coveted of American sweepstakes, they were so wilted that only the dramatic victory of Exterminator brought them to the edges of their seats. As he shot over the finish line the sky began to darken, a thunder cloud rolled up, and the park grew dark and hushed with the stifling airlessness of a storm before the thunder breaks.

In the saddling paddock waiting for the Hopeful to be called, dripping grooms hung on to the bridles of the two-year-olds, skittering nervously, excited by the electricity in the air. In the half light they got away for the parade, Man o' War, Upset, and Constancy the favorites, and Cleopatra, Dr. Clark, Hasten On, Ethel Gray, and Captain Alcock, lightly weighted and lightly regarded by the fans. Constancy, who had just won the Spinaway Stakes, was the entry of Commander J. K. L. Ross, whose three-year-old, Sir Barton, ranked with Exterminator in public favor. Dr. Clark was an entry of the Whitney stables. Rowe had made up his mind that if he couldn't beat Man o' War with one horse he might with two. His strategy called for Dr. Clark to run interference for Upset, set an early pace to tire Red out, and give Upset a chance to come in at the finish. Every jockey was riding to beat Man o' War any way he could.

Horse of the Year

As they reached the post the thundercloud burst, stinging and blinding the horses, and making the track a river of soup. Around the take-off post the horses milled. Everyone seemed to be interfering with Man o' War. Several times he kicked out and once hit Ethel Grey, who should have been in number seven, four spots away. Mars Cassidy almost lost control. Time and again when the field seemed to be within a split second of alignment, a horse would break; it looked as though the field had conspired to wear down Man o' War.

Finally he got off in a start that was called "good" by the trackman for the *Racing Form*. Constancy flashed to the lead in the blinding rain, her wet flanks streaming, with Dr. Clark beside her, doing his best to set a murderous early pace. Next came Captain Alcock and behind him in a leisurely gallop was Man o' War, waiting for Loftus to let him run. As they rounded into the home stretch, Red loped ahead of Captain Alcock and Dr. Clark, but he let Constancy keep her lead until he was straightened away for the final drive. Upset was trying to move with him but the strategy had not worked, the pace set by Dr. Clark had killed off both him and Upset. Red was fresh, he leaped ahead with two or three mighty strides. One moment he was behind Constancy, the next, he was five lengths ahead. The race was over. Without looking up the form man typed, "Won easily; second and third driving." On the slow track, almost ankle deep in mud, the time was 1:13.

While Johnny Loftus jauntily weighed out, his silk blouse plastered to the skin, Mr. Riddle was enjoying himself under the judges' stand. He was engaged in needling "Exile," Dr. M. M. Leach, the English sports writer who was inclined to believe that the victory of the American bred horse was in the nature of an accident. Before the race he had been confident that both English fillies, Constancy and Cleopatra, would take the measure of Man o' War in spite of his misplaced

51

confidence in Donnacona, who had finished far behind Man o' War in the Sanford. But he was an honest sportsman; when he saw Mr. Riddle's colt carry 130 pounds (for the sixth time) through a driving rain after twelve minutes of conniving at the post and then go out and lose the rest "like a jack rabbit running with a field of over-stuffed pigs," Leach acknowledged that Man o' War was good. And he said so handsomely when that night he sent a note to Mr. Riddle in which he wrote;

"Please accept my congratulations. I am convinced that Man o' War is as good a two-year-old as I ever saw."

The Saratoga meet was over. Again the fashionable summer people scattered, and the old Spa settled down to its autumn calm. Man o' War had a few days of vacation with Major Treat before they returned to Belmont for the running of the Futurity. This six-furlong* race on the straight away course at Belmont was the richest and one of the oldest stakes for two-year-olds. When J. G. Lawrence had established it thirty-one years earlier at Sheepshead Bay he had intended to make it the richest purse in the world for two-year-olds. And so it had been; the first winner, Proctor Knott, who beat the famous Salvador, won $40,900 and this sum remained high until in 1929 Whichone took home $105,730. In Man o' War's year the prize was only $26,650, but the prestige was great.

Despite all that, the owners entered their best youngsters with some misgivings. There is a superstition around the tracks that the best two-year-old seldom makes the best three-year-old and that the winner of the Futurity is somehow hoodooed for the next season. It is a fact that until Citation

* Today the Futurity is six and one-half furlongs.

came along no winner of the Futurity ever won the Kentucky Derby.

However, the owners and trainers of 1919 seemed to be particularly free of superstition, for the lists were crowded with top ranking two-year-olds, all out to beat Man o' War. Jim Rowe still boasted that he could do it. This time he entered three colts under the Whitney blue-and-brown, John P. Grier, the colt that he had been keeping in reserve, the one that was rumored to be best of them all, with Upset and Dr. Clark again to run interference. Around the stables it was whispered the Grier really had a chance, he might run Red straight out of Belmont Park. Another entry that the railbirds predicted would give Man o' War a real race for the money was Dominique, son of the famous Peter Quince, a brilliant colt who had won seven of nine starts his first season. Cleopatra, who had run second in the Hopeful, was entered, and also Paul Jones, On Watch, Captain Alcock, and Miss Jemima.

Again Man o' War was an odds-on favorite, this time at 1-2. He was full of dynamite that afternoon. George Conway, the stable foreman, walked with him to keep him from lunging out when he came onto the track, a habit that became so bothersome that later Feustel himself held his bridle.

It was all Conway and Loftus could do between them to hold onto the fighting plunging tornado. At the barrier he fought for eight minutes to break through and not until Mars Cassidy assigned an assistant to his bridle could he get the field in line. When they finally streaked down the track, it was another romp for Man o' War. Nothing could have touched him that day; he was over the finish by nearly three lengths with Johnny Loftus standing in the saddle. Officially for the ninth time it was, "Won easily, second and third

driving." The second and third were John P. Grier and
Dominique. Red had broken the record for the Futurity,
running the six furlongs in 1:11⅗ against a stiff wind and
he had not even been extended.

Then Mr. Riddle made a difficult decision. Man o' War
needed only $20,000 to gain the winning record of $100,000
which had been reached by only three two-year-olds, His
Highness, Domino, and Colin, and there were enough stakes
within easy taking. Man o' War, though, needed rest and his
owner cared more for his horse than he did for breaking
records, so back Red went to the pastures of Glen Riddle.
There was some talk of a match between him and the English
champion, Tetratema, but it never progressed beyond the
talking stage. Later the English champion's son came to the
United States and his children competed with children and
grandchildren of Man o' War.

That autumn the red colt was the hero of not only the sports
world but of all America; his picture, his biography, his
habits, his likes and dislikes, his training routine, were familiar to every newspaper reader in the country. They knew
how many carrots he ate a day, how many lumps of sugar,
how long he napped, what his grooms said about him, no
matinee idol was so often photographed. Almost unanimously
the sports writers named him the "Horse of the Year." So
dynamic was his personality that it overshadowed that of
another great horse who in any other year would have been
a public idol. This was the Canadian, Sir Barton, who had won
the Triple Crown—the Kentucky Derby, the Preakness, and
the Belmont Stakes—for the first time in American history.

No other horse since Lexington had so stirred the emotions
of an entire nation, even those who had never seen him. Both
horses had that indescribable quality of greatness which
lifted those who saw them out of their ordinary lives and

made them conscious that they had witnessed something that would stir their memories as long as they lived. Lexington, like Man o' War, had magnificent stamina. Like Man o' War he was defeated only once; Lecompte, a horse who set a new world record, beat him in a four-mile heat. The next day Lexington ran against that record and, paced by four horses, lowered it by 5¼ seconds. Two weeks later Lexington, tired and half blind, met Lecompte again and set such a terrific pace that Lecompte's owner withdrew him after the first heat.

But when Lexington broke his world records he was five years old, and his place in racing history was secure. What Man o' War would do as a three-year-old was a matter of speculation. The press was taking a long chance in proclaiming him one of the greatest horses in history. Year after year brilliant two-year-olds turned out to be only sprinters like Billy Kelly who in 1918 had been proclaimed one of the outstanding hopefuls of the year. As the conservative *New York Sun* said editorially:

"The thirtieth Futurity* has gone down into racing history and another wonder horse has joined the remarkable galaxy which includes Colin, Novelty, Domino and Artful. In Man o' War the racing season of 1919 has developed a colt which many declare to be without an equal in all the history of racing on this continent.

"In the calm of the day after, we are inclined to rest on the statement that 'Man o' War is one of the greatest horses that ever won the classic for two-year-olds.' As for his being the greatest, we are satisfied to permit time to tell the tale. We have had so many 'greatest evers' in racing the past few seasons that we believe it behooves the calm critic to sit back and let future performances, rather than present talk, place a horse in equine history."

* The Futurity was established in 1888 but it was not run in 1911 and 1912.

Chapter VII

Mᴀɴ ᴏ' Wᴀʀ loafed through the winter at Glen Riddle, eating tremendously and on pleasant days romping in the paddock, stretching his muscles, rolling, snorting and streaking from fence to fence, delighting in his strength, for, although he was approaching his full maturity, he was still very much a colt. By spring he had grown taller and thicker in proportions—he measured sixteen hands and more at the highest point of his withers. His shoulders as well as his quarters had developed so enormously that they almost seemed out of proportion to the perfect cylinder of his barrel. His forehead had widened above his extraordinarily delicate muzzle and his bright coat gleamed with the richness of perfect health. His lively senses kept him interested in everything; the clinking of water buckets, the whistling of grooms, the sound of voices on the path before the stable, set his ears to flicking and brought his inquisitive muzzle to the door of his stall.

While the amateur handicappers were busy making predictions for the coming season (C. C. Ridley of the *Daily Racing Form*, one of the most accurate judges of horses in America, listed Man o' War at the top of the three-year-olds, awarding

him a handicap of 136 pounds against 120 for Blazes and
116 for Upset) he unconcernedly munched his oats. He had
the assurance that belongs to perfect health and beautiful
physical co-ordination, and if he could have expressed an
opinion on the subject he probably would have said that it
was glorious to feel on top of the world and it mattered little
to him that he was conceded to be one of the most magnificent
looking thoroughbreds ever shown in America.

Mr. Riddle watched Red put on weight with satisfaction.
Now he tipped the scales at over eleven hundred pounds and
girthed about seventy-two inches. He had almost reached the
peak of his development, but Mr. Riddle was taking no
chances. He knew that the racing fans expected to see their
idol at the Kentucky Derby which, that year, was run on May
8th, but he did not enter the colt. The Derby was run at a
mile and a quarter, and Mr. Riddle believed the distance too
much of a strain for a three-year-old so early in the season
when he was not yet in top condition. The Preakness, then run
at a mile and an eighth,* he considered a more fitting distance, and many turfmen agreed with him.

So Red, who had been training since early spring, was
groomed until Clyde Gordon was almost able to see his re-
flection in the copper coat, Major Treat was brushed and
polished too, and the old campaigners set out for Baltimore.
This was home country, the same lazy, warm, caressing spring
air, the same slow voices that he had known in Kentucky and
on the eastern shore.

Preakness day at Pimlico—there is no other day quite like
it in American racing. From the very first Pimlico, "old
hilltop" (when the course was laid out on the old Association
fair grounds it was built around a hillock) has had a more
neighborly atmosphere than the beautiful track at the Spa,

* Since 1924 the Preakness has been run at one and three-sixteenths miles.

crowded with gamblers and spectacular members of the fashionable and would-be fashionable world, or Belmont, the international meeting ground. There was always something cozy about Pimlico. The old Victorian club house with its cupola and arched balconies was crowded with friends of sportsmen who rode their own mounts in the steeplechase races. Here General George Patton competed with General Billy Mitchell long before they won their stars, and the Long Island fox hunters Harry Page, the Hitchcocks, and the Sanfords brought down their favorite mounts.

In the horse and carriage era people made Preakness day a holiday, coming out from Baltimore with champagne and sandwiches for a picnic. Even Washingtonians declared a fiesta. Once Congress came to Pimlico in a body to see Pierre Lorillard's Parole win the black-eyed Susans.

Man o' War was making his first bid as a three-year-old in one of the great races of the American turf and one of the oldest in tradition; a tradition that goes back to the years immediately after the Civil War when a group of friends who wanted to bring racing back to Maryland met at a dinner party one night during the race meeting at Saratoga and subscribed to a Dinner Party Stakes that was to be the big event of the proposed Baltimore meeting.

In those days almost all Baltimoreans were horsemen; the Governor of Maryland was the president of the Jockey Club and the owner of the finest stock farm in the United States, including several imported English stallions. So the Jockey Club leased the old fair grounds of Pimlico. The first meeting was a great success; a thousand people came out to see Mr. Sanford's colt, Preakness, win the Dinner Party Stakes. Thus Preakness, named after the Preakness Hills of New Jersey, gave his name to the second race of the American triple crown.

Here Red was among genuine horse lovers. To be sure, the gamblers would be at the Preakness, for the new pari-mutuel machines were bringing large revenues to the Jockey Club, but a majority of those who came out to watch him run were genuine horse lovers. Racing was in the blood of Marylanders, they had bred fine horses since the state was a colony. Long before there was a race track they used the Baltimore-Annapolis road as a course. There were real endurance races in those days, four miles was the average, but these Marylanders would bet on anything connected with a horse, even the eighty-mile race from Frederick Towne to Baltimore and return, in which a large horse ridden by a man competed with a small mare ridden by a boy. The horse, so the legend goes, won by exactly eleven hours.

If ghosts come back to the scenes of their earthly adventures, Colonel Benjamin Tasker, lord of the Maryland turf, must have been in one of the boxes on that Preakness day to watch Man o' War run, or more likely he was down in the infield crowded against the rail, for on Preakness day the old stands bulge to overflowing and the infield is open to the fans. Not a living breeder would have been quicker to recognize big Red's magnificence than Colonel Tasker. He had an unerring eye for horseflesh and a fighting spirit to match. When his imported Selina met Colonel Bird's champion, American-bred Virginia Tryall, and won a smashing victory, and when his horses were altogether so successful that the Virginia Jockey Club excluded Maryland-bred horses from their purses, the Maryland breeder outflanked his adversaries by sending his mares to foal in Virginia.

But as a matter of fact, there was scarcely room for even the ghosts of old Maryland sportsmen on that day at Pimlico. Every horseman in the East was there, for the stakes were high and the interest in this first appearance of the three-year-old Man o' War was keen. Would he be one of those flashes in the pan, those sprinters who look like marvels as two-year-olds and at three are burnt out, used up, unable to stand the pace of the longer races? Nobody really believed it, but one couldn't help remembering Billy Kelly and all the other phenomenal two-year-olds that had faded out at three. Such a thing could happen, and more than one fan, who had backed Man o' War with all the long green that he could put his hands on, held his breath.

In the stables on the Pimlico track Red met several familiar rivals. Paul Jones, the winner of the Kentucky Derby, was not there, he was a gelding and ineligible for the Preakness, but Wildair was entered and in top condition. Jim Rowe was counting on him to bring home the black-eyed Susans. Wildair had just beaten Sir Barton and run third in the Kentucky Derby, so his stock was high. Upset also was entered. Rowe was relying again on his old tactics, using one to tire Red out and the other to make the final drive. Upset had been gathering laurels of his own; he had won the Latonia Derby and had run second in the Kentucky Derby. The other entries were Donnacona and his running mate, On Watch, Blazes, the great sprinter who was quoted at 30-1 in the longer distance, Commander Ross's King Thrush, and the outsiders, Fairway and St. Allan.

Man o' War was restless that day and not quite ready. His friend, Johnny Loftus, who had come down to the stable in the old days and played with him when they were not working, was no longer riding him. Loftus, always headstrong and sure of himself, as indeed who would not have been when lauded as the greatest horseman in America, had been suspended by the Jockey Club for an episode while he was riding one of Commander Ross's horses in Canada. He was continually getting into trouble with his employers; in 1918, when he was riding War Cloud for Mr. Macomber, he failed to ride according to the instructions of the trainer, and Mr. Macomber was so displeased that he refused to let Loftus mount the horse again. But Mr. Riddle, who did not blame the jockey for Man o' War's one defeat, was willing to engage him for the season of 1920. He had gone before the Jockey Club and asked to have Loftus reinstated but without success, so he had engaged Clarence Kummer, an excellent jockey who was fond of Man o' War and sometimes had exercised him at Saratoga when Johnny Loftus hadn't been around mornings.

It was almost time for the race to be called, and the jockeys were in the saddling paddock adjusting their gear and flicking the last speck of dust from their boots. Upset and Blazes had arrived, and King Thrush was getting a last polishing of his gleaming rump. As Red was led into the paddock he was dancing nervously at the end of his bridle.

"Scraped himself on the cars," the groom explained anxiously, "and he's as edgy as a cat."

Mr. Riddle put out his hand to try to quiet Red, but he could see the horse was ready to explode. He was worried.

"Clarence," he suggested, "don't you think it might be a good idea to let Major Treat lead him to the post?" But Clarence was impatient.

"Aw, gee, Mr. Riddle," he answered, "that ain't necessary at all; Red will be all right. Just you quit worrying."

Mr. Riddle did not press his suggestion, but he watched anxiously as Feustel tossed Kummer up. The jockey swung Red to his position seventh in the line; the colt was sputtering like a fire cracker ready to pop. The band struck up "Maryland, My Maryland." Red lunged out and bolted up the track, his head thrust out, his eyes blazing and his tail streaming in the breeze. Kummer stood in the saddle and hauled on the reins with all his strength, but to no effect; he might as well have been trying to stop a comet. A great shout went up from the stands as the fans recognized Man o' War. Hit by the roar of voices, Red pulled up of his own accord and pointed his ears to see what it was all about. Kummer had him under control again and back in the parade, but with a sickening fear of what this bolt might have cost the horse in freshness and stamina.

At the post there was a six-minute delay created by On Watch, St. Allan and Upset, all bent upon wearing Red down. Jim Rowe's jockeys, as well as brilliant young Earl Sande on King Thrush, had orders to take the big horse by the head and run him into the ground. Red surged out at the break, head up as he always ran, eyes blazing. King Thrush, with Sande riding like a fury, drove beside him. For six furlongs he kept it up, then fell back, done in. Then Upset tried; toward the finish he made a spurt, but the best he could do was to drive home a length and a half behind Red's tail, and that only because Kummer did not try to make the margin wider. Home they staggered, the cream of the three-year-olds, behind Red who galloped around the course in his twenty-five foot stride, never extended, never tired. As he stood in the winner's circle, his proud head held high in the statuesque pose that he always took as though he were royalty on exhibition, his gleaming flanks scarcely damp, his neck wreathed with the black-eyed Susans, the crowd went mad. He had done the nine furlongs in the fast time of 1:51⅗.

As Red was led back to the paddock to cool off, Mr. Riddle was surrounded with photographers wanting to snap his picture with the celebrated Woodlawn Vase, a work of Tiffany that Mr. Thomas Clyde had presented to the Maryland Jockey Club two years earlier as a prize for the Preakness. This famous old trophy of the Woodlawn Association of Kentucky, which Mr. Clyde had held since 1903, he had offered for the Preakness with the understanding that each winner should choose the track on which it was to be offered, but each of them had brought it back to Pimlico for the Preakness.

The reporters interviewed Mr. Riddle, they interviewed Louis Feustel and Clarence Kummer, who summed up his opinion in the memorable sentence, "Man o' War is sure a nice horse." They interviewed the grooms and the exercise boys, they described Man o' War so intimately and painstakingly that they might as well have given him words. Even the ultra-conservative papers burst into lyrical praise. The dry and factual *Daily Racing Form* exclaimed, "Individually, Man o' War is perfect. His peculiarities are those of equine sturdiness. He has been carefully and judiciously trained and raced, and has earned the popular esteem given to him. One hopes that Man o' War will never again be beaten and that he will go into retirement to father children as great as himself."

The Riddle stables were jubilant, even the lowliest swipe who filled the water buckets and cleaned out the stalls repeated what C. C. Ridley or John Hervey, the great sports writer, better known as "Salvator," said. The swipe might not be able to read, but he heard the comments all about him and repeated them with embellishments of his own. Everyone who worked with Red was already convinced that he was the greatest horse who ever set hoof on a race track, and now the world was saying so too. He had not been a flash in the pan. He was a stayer, and there wasn't a living horse that could hold a candle to him. Bring on your Sir Bartons and your Exterminators, bring Paul Jones, the Derby winner—Red could show his heels to every one of them.

So Man o' War's camp was beginning the season with high excitement. They were eager to get to Belmont, where Red would begin to pick up real money. Then on to Saratoga, where he had made history the year before. This year would be better with no flukes, no mistakes. The campaign was on. As they polished the harness buckles and put the saddles and blankets out to air, they carried on an endless discussion of strategy. And every night they cut another picture of Red or an editorial from the newspapers and passed it around. They were a proud lot, befitting the entourage of a champion, and they took no back talk from any other stable, not even from the Whitney grooms or the Canadian outfit that served Sir Barton. Red was on top of the world, and they were right there with him!

PROCESSIONS

Chapter VIII

MAN O' WAR was lauded, not only by the racing publications but by the newspapers and the general magazines read by housewives and children who should have been doing their homework. Red did not know that he was the most popular horse of all time, that pictures of him cut from the rotogravures adorned the dens of little boys and lone woodsmen's cabins from Maine to California, but he could hear the roar of the crowd at the races, and understood it. He liked it; he was a great actor, and he accepted the applause as his due, graciously, almost with a twinkle in his eye. He loved to run, and he ran best with the hoofbeats of other horses behind him and the shouts of the crowd in his ears. He did not even mind being rated once in a while, held behind with the dust in his nose and his eyes blinded by chunks of earth cut by flying iron shoes. These discomforts made him all the more determined to get ahead. He was a happy horse, he liked almost everything, even the rub-down and the currying; there was a gusto about him that gave a sparkle to everything he did.

After the Preakness, Man o' War, Major Treat and his retinue entrained for New York, bound for the Withers Stakes

at Belmont. So did the Whitney entries. Jim Rowe had not
yet given up hope. For him Man o' War was a tragedy. If it
had not been for the flaming super-horse, his Upset, Wildair
and the almost untried John P. Grier would have had better
than an even chance of sweeping all before them; indeed,
they did make an impressive showing in every race that was
not dominated by Man o' War. They were unusually fine
horses and had the makings of champions. Rowe had been
accustomed to victory; the season before Man o' War dark-
ened his horizon his stables had won fifteen out of sixteen
starts, and even during the last season the Whitney stables
had taken home the second prize totals of the year.

Rowe was starting only one horse in the Withers—Wildair,
who since the Preakness had won the Metropolitan Handicap.
It still did not look like much of a race, because Wildair had
already tried hard and had never come near enough to see
the throat latch of Man o' War. The only other entry was
W. R. Coe's David Harum, who was going along to pick up
third money; he was weighted at only 118 pounds, but everyone conceded that he had no more chance of winning than a
Missouri mule.

No one of Man o' War's competitors in the Preakness except Wildair had a wish to try again. Not since the days when
Pierre Lorillard's entries frightened off competition had
there been such a dearth of entries.

Man o' War had improved tremendously in the twelve days
since the Preakness. Then the turf writers had said he was
not ready. Now he was in splendid condition, trained to a
fine point and eager to get to the track. Earlier in the week he
had run six furlongs in 1:11, and, on the morning of the race
he was clocked for a furlong in the extraordinary time of
:10⅗. It was a pity there was no horse to test his mettle.

In spite of the lack of competition, Belmont was jammed

with racing fans on Withers day, not only the usual crowd of fashionable New Yorkers but clerks and office boys, janitors and bricklayers were there. Everybody who could get a day off had come out to see Man o' War run. In the stands the bookies were offering 6-1 against Wildair and 30-1 against David Harum, with 4-1 to place—he was the only entry carrying "place" betting. Red was odds-on, as usual, at 1-7.

As the cheers swept over the Long Island flats when Big Red appeared in the parade with Louis Feustel at his bridle (after the Preakness either the trainer or Conway always led him to the post), one spectator looked down with mixed emotions. Major Belmont held Red in his glasses and watched the smooth-flowing symmetry of his movements even in walking behind the pony. He remembered his wife's cable and how he had liked her name for the little red colt he had never seen, the colt who had the color and the fire of Fair Play. He thought regretfully that but for the war this blazing colt would be racing under his own scarlet-and-maroon instead of the gold-and-black. Man o' War was almost as magnificent as his father, and the Major always had considered Fair Play the best horse he had ever owned.

The horses were at the post. They were off. The Major leaned forward as he watched Red come away in a scorching lead. It was a procession; the other two might have been running individual races of their own. All the way around the course Man o' War struggled to get free, and for the last furlong ran with his head pulled into his chest. Yet even against Kummer's stoutest restraint he had done it again; he had chipped the American record of 1:36⅕ established at Saratoga three years earlier by Sunbriar. Man o' War had run the mile in 1:35⅘. The fans were confident that if he had been let out he could have bettered the world record of 1:34⅖ which Roamer had run against time.

67

But the crowds had seen a great show, and they were content. Major Belmont looked for Mr. Riddle under the judges' stand, and when he found the colt's owner to congratulate him the Major admitted that Man o' War was as good as Tracery, the famous son of Rock Sand, who had made history in Europe and whom he loved best because he had raced under the Belmont colors. Furthermore, he made the admission handsomely as was his custom. He said, "I will now concede that Man o' War is the best horse I ever saw."

After the Withers the chorus of adulation grew; everyone acclaimed Red as the best horse the world had ever seen. Even the *New York Sun* joined the snake dance editorially:

"When a great man appears we are naturally afraid of him and extraordinarily jealous and envious. We honor him, if at all, when he is safely dead, and pick poor sticks from among our contemporaries to set in high places. But horses are another matter, and we honor them when they deserve it. None has ever deserved it more than Man o' War."

There were very few days to rest between races in this, the height of the season. While Mr. Riddle's ears were still ringing with the bursts of extravagant delight that Red was winning from the press, it was time for the horse's next appearance, this time in the Belmont Stakes. If Red won this race—and it would be a national catastrophe if he did not—it would be the second of his races for the American triple crown. The third, the Kentucky Derby, he was never to win. Mr. Riddle did not start a horse in the Derby until seventeen years later, when Man o' War's son, War Admiral, carried away the roses.

The Belmont Stakes was not only a great traditional race of the American turf, one which was designed to conform exactly in both length and conditions to the English Derby, but it is one which had a particular significance for Man o' War. It had been more or less a family affair ever since Red's great-grandfather, Spendthrift, won it in 1879. His grandfather, the cantankerous Hastings, won it in 1896, and his father, Fair Play, ran a smashing second to Colin in 1908. If he could have looked into the future he would have seen that Mad Play, another son of Fair Play, would win the stakes in 1924 and two of Red's own sons, American Flag and Crusader, would be victors in 1925 and 1926. Chance Shot, a son of Fair Play, would take it in 1927, and War Admiral, Man o' War's best son, in 1937, to round out his triple crown.

Red was an impressive spectacle on that summer afternoon of the Belmont Stakes. When he was brought into the paddock the crowd was so dense that he scarcely could be seen a few feet away. There was only one other entry in the paddock, Donnacona, who had come out for second money. David Harum had been listed, but his owner, Mr. Coe, had scratched him. Mr. Coe could afford to lose the entry fee and he did not want the humiliation of seeing his horse in "a procession."

That is just what these races had come to be, processions, never contests, for there was no one to give Man o' War a real race. Still the crowds came just to see him run. Even without a shadow of competition, this was thrill enough, there was an excitement in watching Red in motion, the sun on his bright coat as he ate up the course in his unbelievable stride that gave everyone who watched a catch in the throat.

The Belmont Stakes was run on a track placed so that from the grandstand the horses came into view only on the stretch. There was a good deal of grumbling in the stands, but when the crowd saw Big Red and Donnacona parading to the post behind a red-coated rider on a black cob, they forgot their grievances. The start was without incident, Red was dancing, eager to get away, but he did not make trouble. The race was as before, no more than a fast canter for Red, but when the time was posted the applause from the stands sounded like a salvo of artillery; he had broken the record for a mile and three eighths, running it in 2:14⅕ with Donnacona twenty lengths behind. Without half trying he had shattered by three seconds Sir Barton's American record of 2:17⅗ set in the same race the year before. What he could have done if he had broken Kummer's strangle hold is anybody's guess. As it was, he had set not only an American but a world record which is still unbroken after thirty odd years.

This was getting embarrassing. Red was too good; he was driving every other horse from the track. He seemed to be on the point of disrupting American racing instead of reviving it, if one were to judge from the entries, but from the point of view of the box office the sport never had been so prosperous. Even if Man o' War could not find any one to race against him he was such a popular spectacle that every soul who could scrape up the entrance fee was willing to stand on somebody else's feet, even to offer his own as a sacrifice on the Long Island's sardine-packed special trains to Belmont.

And the fans were just as eager to go to Jamaica when Red was entered in the Stuyvesant Handicap ten days later, the race that had been named in honor of the first American-bred colt to run a mile in less than 1:40. The handicapper loaded Red with 135 pounds, six more than he had given to Sam Hildreth's Purchase the year before. This notwithstanding the fact that Purchase, along with Mad Hatter and Sir Barton, had been the brightest star the turf had seen for many a day.

Again it was a two-horse event, another procession. Yellow Hand came out, not for a moment to challenge Red but to take the second money. This time Man o' War was quoted at the astronomical figure of 1-100 and for those who wanted to take a long shot, the bookies offered odds of 60-1 against Yellow

MAN O' WAR WITH JOCKEY CLARENCE KUMMER

MAN O' WAR WORKING OUT BEFORE A RACE

SETTING A NEW MILE RECORD IN THE WITHERS STAKES AT BELMONT, MAY 29, 1920

WINNING THE MILLER STAKES AT SARATOGA, AUGUST 7, 1920

Hand although he was carrying 32 pounds less weight than Man o' War. Yet, for all that, Yellow Hand was not "just another horse." Before the season was over he won ten races and the next year he was the country's leading four-year-old.

On this afternoon Red delighted the crowd; he was feeling skittish and was determined to run. But Clarence Kummer had his instructions; he did not want to make the victory too humiliating for the other horse, so he held Red in firmly all the way, allowing him to win by a paltry eight lengths.

At Jamaica, as at Belmont, Red was hemmed in by swarms of admirers. The ordinary crowd could be kept away, but there were always famous sportsmen, many of them notables from abroad, who wanted to get a closer look at him, and even although Mr. Riddle knew that too much distraction was not good for Red he could not be so ungracious as to refuse such requests. These, plus the equally legitimate ones of photographers and sports writers, kept the Riddle stables in a continual state of activity.

Red was so busy having his picture taken, posing for his admirers, and keeping up his workouts that there was not much time for his old pal, Major Treat, but still Red never felt comfortable when he came back to his stall and failed to see the Major next door. On the few occasions that this happened he kicked his floor boards and whinnied in no uncertain tones of irritation. The Major was his safety valve, the steady old fellow who gave him a feeling of security. It was almost as though Man o' War depended on the Major to say to him; "Take it easy, Red. I too have known adulation in my day; not this great bellowing of the crowd, but the polite applause of the horse shows. But the applause doesn't matter too much. Your season isn't over and you never can tell what will happen. Even if you can outrun every creature on four legs, don't be too cocky.

"Remember when Upset beat you last year? It was a fluke, everybody knows, you couldn't do anything about it when Johnny Loftus made those stupid mistakes, but it might happen again. Don't get all wrought up with this hero worship. We horses have more sense and we don't get carried away by our emotions. What these humans need is a little horse sense. So calm down and take your nap. If they want to take another picture, let them wait."

All of which was good sound advice and it was lucky that Man o' War understood Major Treat better than he did the stable boys. They were agog with rumors of fantastic offers that Mr. Riddle had received for Man o' War; each day a new one went the rounds, and, even though they were rosily embellished by the time they reached the stables, most of them had a foundation of truth. By now Man o' War's value was almost astronomical.

The latest rumor was to the effect that Joseph L. Murphy of Philadelphia had offered Mr. Riddle for Red the highest price that ever had been paid for an American horse. This one was true. Mr. Murphy already had offered $200,000 for Red immediately after his victory in the Withers; he now increased his offer to $260,000 and this was indeed a top figure. The nearest was $256,000 that a wealthy Argentine had paid for Mr. Belmont's beloved Tracery.

Mr. Murphy was the son of an oil tycoon, one of the few who ever bucked Standard Oil successfully. The father had been a lover of horses and had developed a stable of trotters and racers which he campaigned all over the United States. His son had not kept his father's stables and did not care for trotters, but he liked racers and at one time had owned Flitter Gold, a half-brother of Fair Play. From the minute he first saw Man o' War he had a tremendous admiration for the horse. He was on fire to possess Red and dreamed of organiz-

72

ing a stud around him and exhibiting him at fairs from coast to coast to encourage the breeding of thoroughbreds.

But $260,000 did not tempt Mr. Riddle. He told Mr. Murphy that although there had been times when he would have sold Red for $200,000, they were past. He too was planning Red's stud career and preparing to select his harem. He had decided against racing the horse as a four-year-old, the races in which he could be entered would be limited, and besides he feared Red would be asked to carry such great weight that he might run the risk of losing to a mediocre horse. Mr. Riddle had asked Mr. Walter Vosburgh, the handicapper of the Jockey Club, what weight Man o' War might be expected to carry if he raced the following year, and Mr. Vosburgh had been frank about it.

"If he wins his first race I will put the heaviest weight on him ever carried by a thoroughbred."

That meant 145 or possibly 150 pounds, Mr. Riddle guessed. Red already was racing under the heaviest weight ever carried by a three-year-old, and that, Mr. Riddle thought, was enough to ask of any horse.

He had come to love Man o' War and expected to devote the rest of his life developing his stud career. He could imagine nothing so interesting as breeding and racing Red's sons and daughters. True, a wonder horse such as Man o' War does not appear every year, but it was possible that one of his children might match his record, and to own and train such a horse would be reward enough for any sportsman.

Chapter IX

Man o' War's parade of victories was a continual humiliation to Jim Rowe; every time he watched his best colts come back to the stables, dripping and winded, his blood pressure shot up. Wildair was a speedy horse with a proud ancestry and the best conditioning the most famous trainer in the country could give. And so was Upset. It was ridiculous that this son of Fair Play, who always had run second to Colin, should canter through two racing seasons breaking records right and left and not even breathing hard. It was unnatural—almost witchcraft. Man o' War could not be that good!

Jim Rowe did not believe for one minute that Man o' War was unbeatable. And if anyone could stop the colt, he was the man. He looked upon every race in which Red was entered as a special challenge to him. So far he had met with bad luck except in the Sanford—he still fumed when he heard it referred to as a fluke—but the season was not over, and he had not exhausted his bag of tricks.

In the Whitney stables Rowe had one horse in reserve, the shapely young chestnut, John P. Grier, not massive and spectacular like Man o' War but compact and full of power, one of the fastest horses at a mile that Rowe had ever clocked.

Grier was a son of Whisk Broom II and he lived up to his illustrious parentage. Both Rowe and the handicappers had considered Grier a sure winner of the Kentucky Derby, but the colt had suffered a minor injury and had been withdrawn. The same injury plagued him at the opening of Pimlico, so he had not met Red in the Preakness. Ever since early June Rowe had doctored and pampered and worked on the colt, who was now in prime condition, ready to meet Man o' War in the next race for which the Riddle colt was entered.

This event was the Dwyer, to be run at the Aqueduct on July 10th. There was no other entry; as usual Man o' War had frightened away competitors. None even ventured out for "place"; the other owners found it uncomfortably humiliating to see their best horses come staggering home, their eyes popping and their hearts pounding, while Red broke another record without even working up a lather. If Jim Rowe wanted to stick his neck out, let him. He was welcome to the chance.

So Rowe did just that. He succeeded in getting Grier entered in the Dwyer weighted with only 108 pounds as against 126 carried by Man o' War. And he spread the news around that this was it; now he was ready to take Man o' War. His boast ran like wildfire through the circles where he was looked upon as the top man in racing, the oracle of the stables. The grooms watched the two horses at their workouts and compared their performance, clocking them and speculating whether Grier, who was unquestionably one of the fastest sprinters that ever limbered up in the early Long Island mist, could stay beyond a mile. Maybe he could, they decided. Maybe Rowe had something. Grier was a mighty good looking horse and he was fresh. Man o' War had been racing steadily for a month and he might have lost his edge.

The sports writers heard the rumor almost as soon as it

reached the stables at Aqueduct. They interviewed Rowe, who was breathing confidence and defiance; they interviewed Feustel, who was not impressed by the challenge, and they did not neglect Clarence Kummer, who probably knew more about the comparative merits of the two horses than anyone. Kummer had not only ridden Red in all of his three-year-old victories but had also ridden John P. Grier in the two races in which he had been entered, both of which he had won. What chances did Grier have, the sports writers asked? Was he a sprinter or a stayer? That was a long home stretch at Aqueduct, and only a stayer could hold out against Man o' War. Kummer undoubtedly had a warm admiration for Grier, he acknowledged that the Whitney colt was remarkably fast, one of the fastest he ever had ridden, but he didn't believe any horse alive could beat Man o' War. Was he only being loyal to his employer? Maybe so. That was a likelihood to be taken into consideration. All told, it looked like the most exciting race of this or many seasons.

As the sports writers speculated on the outcome, the fans, reading and understanding that Red was going to face a real challenge at last, rushed for tickets. Even the bookies reflected the general excitement by dropping Man o' War from 1-100 to 1-5 and quoting Grier at 18-5.

In Man o' War's camp the excitement was intense; Gordon, Conway, and the rest watched Red as though he were the Hope diamond. They had done all this ever since Red won his first race, but now their vigilance was redoubled, and their anxiety. They had become a bit complacent and these ministrations had assumed the aspect of a ritual, the palace routine, but now that Man o' War was threatened it would be a catastrophe if he sprained a tendon or caught a cold.

Man o' War may have felt the undercurrent of anxiety. He was not tired physically, he could not have been in better condition, but nervously he was a bit on edge—too many people, too much adulation. Mr. Riddle wanted to give him complete rest and quiet for a few days. When the 10th came around he had been at Aqueduct for several days and had held up well in the workouts. The stable hands agreed that Mr. Riddle had nothing to worry about. But Louis Feustel was not so sure. He did not say anything until the horses were in the saddling paddock. It was a tense moment, twenty-five thousand fans jammed the stands, fought for standing room and crowded around the paddock like hounds on the scent of drama. Jim Rowe stood in front of John P. Grier's stall holding court.

"Today Grier will trim Man o' War," he assured everyone within earshot.

Louis Feustel and Mr. Riddle stood talking in front of Red's stall, waiting for the moment to toss up Kummer. Gordon was putting the finishing touches on Man o' War's toilet and the colt stood quietly enough, with his head stretched toward Major Treat. They were taking no chances, Major Treat was going to accompany Red to the starting post.

"I'm worried," Feustel said to Mr. Riddle. "Man o' War isn't screwed up as tight as he might be." Mr. Riddle looked concerned, but at this late moment there was nothing they could do, with Jim Rowe waiting to crow over him and twenty-five thousand people counting the seconds until the band would strike up the signal for the parade.

The rider on the pony gave the signal; Feustel tossed up Kummer, who felt Red's muscles tighten under him, and laid a quieting hand on the horse's neck. Red fidgeted for several moments, and then quieted down as Mr. Riddle held his bridle while he gave Kummer his instructions.

"Lay along with Grier all the way, and if you find you can win don't try to ride him out, but win by a length or two lengths. I don't want more made of Red than is necessary."

He looked over to the neat chestnut colt that was dancing under Eddie Ambrose. A good jockey and a good horse. Rowe too was giving his last instructions.

The bugle sounded, the horses came out of the paddock, Man o' War, nervous and inclined to be skittery in spite of the quieting influence of dignified Major Treat, and John P. Grier, lively but manageable enough under the firm hand of Eddie Ambrose. Eddie did not hurry, taking advantage of every extra moment that helps when your opponent is carrying weight. This time the crowd did not let out such a mighty roar as the horses paraded down the stretch; the fans were too intent on examining John P. Grier, trying to estimate the power of this much publicized challenger of Man o' War.

Even though there were only the two entries, Mars Cassidy had trouble at the gate; both horses were lurching and kicking, and it took him two minutes to get them off. Stop watches clicked, the crowd let out a mighty roar as Man o' War, following his custom, shot away from the barrier to set the pace. He was on the inside and it looked for a minute as though he had left Grier at the post and was running alone. The crowd gasped when they saw that Grier was sticking so closely to the champion that they were locked together and he was hidden by the greater bulk of Man o' War.

As they raced down the long back stretch the fans, who always love a challenger, were so electrified by the performance of Grier that they shouted for him almost as hoarsely as they did for Man o' War. The watches clicked at the quarter pole in 23⅘. On they thundered toward the three sixteenths. Racing like a team, they clocked 46 seconds at the half mile and 1:09⅗ at the six furlong pole.

As they neared the turn for home Grier was still hanging to the champion's throat latch. The crowds went mad. As the horses started down the long stretch with both jockeys driving furiously, Clarence Kummer lashed Red with the whip. He responded, but he could not shake off Grier. It looked as though this was going to be another of the famous dead heats of history. Then with a mighty sprint Grier pulled up. He was at Red's throat latch, he was looking Man o' War in the eye, his black muzzle showed in front.

"He's got Man o' War!" went up a frenzied cry.

Harry Payne Whitney stood on a chair in the box of Walter J. Salmon and clenched his fists, shouting until his voice broke and he could only croak. In the box of Mrs. Payne Whitney, the financier, John P. Grier, for whom the colt was named, was beyond shouting, limp and exhausted from the thrill of his life. Mr. Riddle stood against the rail of his box frozen, his eyes riveted to the track. Whatever the outcome, this was racing, this was what Man o' War was intended for. At last he had met a horse worthy of his best.

Grier was still in the lead. A great sigh arose from the stands. Red was extended, giving all he had; he pulled up, gained an inch, another, by the time they reached the next pole the two horses were neck and neck again, so the record did not show that for a bright moment Grier had taken the lead from the greatest horse in America.

Then a sixteenth of a mile from the finish line Grier cracked. He had given his last ounce of strength in his final burst of speed. Ambrose, knowing that he was beaten, did not punish him. Man o' War drew away to finish a length and a half in front.

It was a race of a thousand thrills. Even those spectators who were seeing their first one, who were unable to make comparisons, and had come out only to see the champion, realized that they had just seen a race that would go down in history as one of the greatest ever run on American turf. As for the fans, they compared it with the race in which Henry of Na-

varre and Domino finished in a dead heat, the struggle between Irish Lad and Broomstick for the Brighton Cup, or the
match between Hour Glass and the immortal Omar Khayyam.
Two records had been broken. Red's time of 1:49⅖ for the
nine furlongs was a new American record for the distance, and
both he and Grier had tied the record for six furlongs at
1:09⅗.

That evening John P. Grier was a hero almost as fervently
acclaimed as Man o' War himself. He was undoubtedly the
second best horse in America. For the first and only time in a
true race, with Man o' War clear and in his stride, Grier had
caught and headed him for a fleeting second. He had forced
Man o' War to finish driving. Even Louis Feustel paid him
honor.

"From the way Red was leveling off," he commented, "I
knew he was fighting a buzz saw."

Red was exhausted, his withers soaked and flecked with
foam. When Gordon sponged him down he was quivering as
though he had the ague. When he was taken back to his stall
at last he stuck his muzzle against Major Treat and then he
lay down on the fresh straw and closed his eyes. Victory was
sweet, but at that moment he was too tired to care. Dimly he
knew that Louis Feustel was watching him and that Clyde
Gordon was breaking out a sweet smelling bale of hay, but
he wasn't interested. Tomorrow or the next day he would want
to run again, but now he only wanted to rest.

RETURN ENGAGEMENT

Chapter X

Man o' War was still the champion, his luster brighter than ever, but for Jim Rowe the defeat of his colt had been so glorious that it was almost as sweet as a victory. Grier had been so good, so very good, that Rowe was not discouraged. What the colt had done once he could do again, and maybe Lady Luck, who often favors a gallant loser, would tip the scales ever so lightly in his favor. That was all Grier needed, just one lucky break. As he read the accounts of the race, Rowe stiffened his resolve. He would take Red yet. Not now— his colt needed rest and time to recover from the state of complete exhaustion into which he had run himself. Rowe would send Wildair to take first money at the Empire City Derby. Man o' War had been entered in it, but Rowe felt confident that Mr. Riddle would scratch his horse (which he did), for Red too needed a rest. Both of them must be content to wait for Saratoga.

Man o' War revelled in the few days with no work, taking to a holiday with the same gusto with which he pranced to the starting post. He and Major Treat ate and loafed and rubbed noses, and Clyde Gordon pampered them. He did not bother them with elaborate toilets; it would not hurt to go a few days without the polishing and currying.

Then came the familiar trip to the Spa. The holiday was over and Red was back on the old routine, beginning with the morning workout at pine-scented Horse Haven. His first race was the Miller Stakes. Mr. Riddle had entered him with some misgivings, for this time, although he would have no more formidable competition than Donnacona, he would be mounted by a new jockey. Clarence Kummer had taken a spill from a filly appropriately named "Costly Colors" and was laid up with a fractured shoulder.

Trainers are always nervous about a new jockey no matter how good he may be, for horses have likes and dislikes as strong as those of people, and if there is no sympathy between the horse and the rider the horse's chances are greatly diminished. Old timers still repeat the tale about King Edward VII and his famous horse, Diamond Jubilee, that carried his colors to glory when he was Prince of Wales. The horse hated "Morny" Cannon, who was chief jockey of the royal stables and was considered the best rider of his day. Diamond Jubilee would have none of him, and fought so hard that he had to be blindfolded until Cannon was in the saddle. Even with all his skill Cannon could do little with the horse. Finally the trainer mounted Diamond Jubilee with Herbert Jones, the exercise boy whom the horse loved, and Jones rode him to victory after victory, soon becoming the first jockey of the Prince's stable.

Man o' War was not an unfriendly horse; while he had none of Fair Play's temper which, according to Joe Palmer of *The Blood Horse*, "was better than a cobra's but not as good as a wild cat's," he was sometimes temperamental and liked his own way. It was a question what he would do under a new jockey, especially one who might make the mistake of trying to drive him. Mr. Riddle wondered who was the best choice. He decided on brilliant young Earl Sande, who was under contract to Commander J. K. L. Ross but free for the Miller Stakes, and engaged him to ride Man o' War. Only three horses were entered, Man o' War, Donnacona, who had tried so many times to take his measure, and another named King Albert.

As soon as the horses came out on parade it was evident that Man o' War liked Earl Sande. He loped cheerfully around the course and even under a strong pull came within ⅗ of the track record of 1:56⅗. The crowds had enjoyed themselves even though the only interesting thing about the race was Sande's comment as he slid down in the winner's circle.

"I never felt anything under me like that colt in my life. Why, he is the greatest horse I've ever ridden." Sande was far more exhausted than Man o' War from trying to restrain him.

Sande's opinion was particularly significant because he had been riding Sir Barton, who had been performing tremendous feats and was considered by many shrewd turfmen the most under-rated horse of all time. As one of the sports writers said to his fellows in the press box, "What that British nag needs is a course in a charm school." He just didn't have the personality to compete in the hearts of the fans with the spectacular and magnificent Man o' War.

But granted he did not have the charm, did he have the speed and the stamina? Many fans believed he had. A year earlier he had been not only the first horse to win the triple crown, but he had won the Withers also, all against competition of the highest order. This season he had started as well; on opening day he had won the Saratoga Handicap against the spectacular Mad Hatter (a son of Fair Play), the Whitney

Wildair, and his most serious rival, courageous Exterminator. Carrying 129 pounds, four more than Exterminator and eleven more than Mad Hatter, Sir Barton had not only outraced them but also had broken the world's record for a mile and a quarter with 2:01⅖.

Immediately after Sir Barton's great race in the Saratoga Handicap there had been clamor for a match race between him and Man o' War. If Exterminator were included, the fans insisted, it would be the greatest race in history and would arouse national interest second only to the Presidential election. Mr. Riddle was almost honor bound to do it, they felt, for, until Man o' War met horses of all divisions as well as his own contemporaries, he could not rightfully be considered the greatest horse of the year. But his owner could not consider such a special event until Red had completed his schedule for the autumn. He had plenty of work ahead and must have time to rest.

Mr. Riddle's most immediate concern was the Travers Stakes, in which Jimmy Rowe was making another bid to "take" Man o' War. He had come to Saratoga with his best three, Wildair, Upset, and John P. Grier, and had entered both Grier and Upset in the Travers. Both had been rested and conditioned for more than a month, saving their energy while Man o' War broke records. For the week previous to the Travers, Man o' War and the Whitney pair electrified the early birds with their workouts. Rowe's strategy was fairly obvious, he was playing two against one, and the rumor spread that this time Red would more than meet his match.

"Now," Rowe boasted, "I've got him." Added fuel to his hopes was the news that Clarence Kummer was still unable to ride Man o' War; he had made a few tries, but his shoulder was so sore that he was unable to control the big strider. Mr. Riddle would have liked to employ Earl Sande again, he and

Red worked excellently together, but Sande's contract with Commander Ross took him to Canada. The next choice was Andy Schuttinger, who was considered an excellent judge of pace. This was a hard decision to make, for by all the advance intimations the Travers was going to be Red's toughest race. Certainly the fans and the bookies thought so for the Whitney pair was being offered at 4-1 with Man o' War at 2-9.

For the first time Mr. Riddle had the pre-race jitters; he could not keep away from the stables and he redoubled precautions for fear something might happen to Man o' War. Later he said of that week before the Travers:

"I will own that this was the only time I was ever nervous, really nervous, about the outcome of a race that Man o' War went into after he had shown us what he was. It was not so much that I had any doubts of his ability to win. Of that I was entirely confident. But I knew he had the two best three-year-olds, aside from himself, to beat. I knew that John P. Grier had just about as much speed, for a mile, as horses ever have. I knew that it was to be two-pluck-one, that Grier was to carry us just as far as he could, and then Upset was to come along and finish the killing if possible.

"I had watched them in their training and knew they were both as fit as the man called the greatest living trainer could make them. I knew of the boasts that he had made, that the day of the downfall of Man o' War was at hand. I knew that this was believed by a lot of people who passed for very smart, and that they were backing the Whitney pair down to the shortest odds laid against anything that had started against him since the Preakness, his first start of that season.

"Over and above that, what worked me up to a very nervous state was the fact that people kept coming to me and warning me that 'something is going to happen' and for me to watch out for it.

"I knew, of course I had nothing to fear from Mr. Whitney or from Jimmy Rowe except the gameness and speed of their entries. But what might come from some outside quarter—that I couldn't tell. So we watched Man o' War night and day, every second of the time, until he was saddled for the race itself. I gave Andy these instructions: 'Take him out in front the minute the flag falls. Keep him going. Don't let either of them get near you. Just show them up if anyone thinks they can beat him. That's all. He will do the rest.' "

The excitement was running high, even higher than it had been at the Dwyer, for now it looked as though at last the cards were stacked against Man o' War. Everyone who could crowd into the track came out to see Red put up a fight for his championship. After the Dwyer this should be the greatest race ever run at Saratoga. The track was bursting with the largest crowd it ever had seen; the gates were thrown open to the infield and several thousand lined the rails almost the entire circuit of the track.

As the horses came to the post that August afternoon, Man o' War was first, carrying 129 pounds, with Andy Schuttinger on his back, his third rider in three consecutive races; next was John P. Grier ridden by clever Eddie Ambrose and carrying 115 pounds. Ambrose had his orders; "Break on top and do the mile in 1:35. Go as far as you can and then Upset will take over. But get on top at the break and run his heart out." Rodriguez on Upset, who was carrying 123 pounds, was briefed: "Trail them to the mile. Grier will run him dizzy, then you come on to win."

Man o' War was breathing fire, but there was no nonsense at the post. Off they went in one minute, Ambrose whipping and driving furiously to get on top and win the rail, to run a mile as it never had been run before. But John P. Grier never had a chance. Man o' War, when he felt that he had his head, surged out two or three space-eating strides and was a length in front before the other two were fairly in stride. When Schuttinger took hold of him, Ambrose was driving Grier mercilessly and losing ground. The pace was blistering. Schuttinger hit the quarter in 23⅕, did the second in 23⅖, and the third in 23⅖, which was ⅖ below the fastest time ever reached in the history of Saratoga.

As they hit the stretch John P. Grier, running a full second slower, dropped back. He had been under a strong drive all the way and he had nothing left. Ambrose refrained from punishing him—there wasn't any use. Upset had been pushed so hard to keep from getting too far behind that, even although he passed Grier easily, he had nothing for the final spurt. Big Red shot by the nine furlong pole, beating his own record for that length by ⅖, and was over the finish line two and a half lengths in front, with Schuttinger standing in the stirrups trying to slow him down. Although the jockey had been applying the brakes for over a furlong, Man o' War had beaten the record that the older Sir Barton had made under a drive, and had equaled the track record for the distance. Moreover, in the years since, Red's time has been bettered in only one running of the Travers, and then, with Lucky Draw in 1946, by only one-fifth of a second.

As Roy Dickerson, assistant starter who had led Man o' War to the post that day said thirty years afterward, recalling mellow memories, "There never lived a horse that was more horse than he was that afternoon. He was so beautiful that it almost made you cry, and so full of fire he made you thank your God that you could come close to him. No horse ever lived who could have beaten him that afternoon."

The Travers was Red's last race at Saratoga. It would have been appropriate if his career had ended at the Spa where it had begun two years earlier, here under the eyes of many of those who had seen the long-legged red colt in the yearling sale and thought he might make a hunter if he could not run. But in these two years he had run, some said, as no horse ever had run before. He had gathered laurels almost nonchalantly at all the great races except the Kentucky Derby, and his triumphs were not yet over. He and Major Treat had still the fall campaigning ahead. He was entered for the Lawrence Realization, the Jockey Club Stakes, and the Potomac Handicap, three gruelling distance races, so there was no time to loiter at the Saratoga track where his morning workouts furnished entertainment for his admirers breakfasting on the clubhouse verandah.

The month at Saratoga had been hot and the flies annoying. The heat accentuated the odors of the stables. Everything smelled rank, the grass, the hay, the close stalls, the horses, the dripping stable boys. At night it was better when a little breeze came up and swept away the staleness of the day. Then Red nickered to Major Treat and the two of them stood at the stall doors with their heads stuck out in the moonlight.

Or sometimes Red dreamed as he slept and made quiet little snorts as though the dream were pleasant. The stable boy on watch looked in to see that everything was well and wondered what the big horse was seeing in his sleep. Was he back at Glen Riddle cooling his muzzle in the dewy wet grass of his paddock, or had he gone farther back to Kentucky and the Nursery Stud? Was he a fuzzy red foal again trotting after Mahubah to the pasture? Perhaps he was dreaming of the races he had won, but the groom thought not, for if he were Red would be tossing his head and quivering with excitement. You could tell, too, that these were gentle dreams by the way his ears lay back peacefully and his spine relaxed. Certainly Red was entitled to pleasant dreams.

Chapter XI

AFTER SARATOGA it was back to Belmont for Red. The big purses at Belmont were outstanding; its average purse ran higher than those of any track in the United States or, for that matter, in the world. If Man o' War was to be the leading money winner of the year he would need to win the two races for which he was entered at Belmont as well as the Potomac Handicap, the big autumn stakes race at Havre de Grace. And it was natural that Mr. Riddle should want Man o' War to head the list, not particularly for the money but because it was fitting that the greatest horse of this or many years should bring home the fattest purse.

Red was an old campaigner now. He knew the Belmont, Pimlico, Saratoga and Aqueduct stables; he knew Peanuts, Exterminator's pony mascot, and all the goats and cats and chickens that made the Eastern tracks; he even knew the rail birds, those nondescript, rootless creatures who followed the horses around with the season, from Churchill Downs to Pimlico, Belmont, to Saratoga and back again in the fall. Wherever Red was, there they were, on chilly mornings, hunched on the rails, like crows, holding their stop watches in numb hands, waiting to see him work.

At Belmont Red settled down to training, the old routine, out to the tracks with his old friend, Clyde Gordon, then the cooling and sponging and grooming. He had not escaped without a few marks of Saratoga's skin disease which scars most of the horses who have been at the Spa and drink the mineral waters, but there were only a few spots on his neck, and Feustel was not worried.

The Lawrence Realization Stakes, the first race in which Man o' War was entered on his return to Long Island, was a taxing mile and five eighths for three-year-olds, but Red liked the longer distances, which gave him a chance to let himself out and really loosen up. In spite of the long season he was in good shape. In his final workout over the longer course Clyde Gordon sent him a mile and a half. Without tiring or driving he did it in 2:29⅗ and that was ⅖ faster than the record for the distance at that time.* The astonished clockers looked at their watches and, believing they must be wrong, consulted each other; but that was the time; they could not all be mistaken.

Before Red was out of his blanket and properly rubbed down, the news had spread over the course and by afternoon every owner who had a horse at Belmont raised his eyebrows. What was the use? they thought. But this was only a confirmation of their earlier decision that it was foolish to enter a horse against Man o' War. Nobody had listed one except George A. Widener. He had entered a lively youngster named Sea Mint, but when he learned about Man o' War's time at the workout he sacrificed the entry fee. Better to scratch his horse than to suffer the embarrassment of seeing him make a sorry spectacle of himself.

While Red champed his oats with satisfaction, unconscious of the crisis that his workout had caused, Mr. Riddle was in a

* The record now is 2:27⅗, made by Bolingbroke in 1942.

quandary. The race seemed doomed to be a walkover. To run Red once around the track raced by his own shadow was no race at all. It would disappoint the fans, who would feel cheated if they didn't see a real race, no matter how poor a chance a competitor might have against Man o' War. There was no drama in seeing a one-horse parade. Then, too, a walkover would reduce Red's winnings by $2,500 or half the $5,000 given in the stakes, according to the rules of the Jockey Club. It was getting to be a problem racing a horse so good that nobody would enter one to run against him.

As Mr. Riddle said to an admirer who asked him how it felt to own a horse like Man o' War; "It feels fine, but I don't believe I want any more like him. That may sound strange," he added, "but Red is too much of a responsibility. I always have tried to regard him as an ordinary horse, but my friends and the public won't let me."

No, Red was never an ordinary horse and the difficulties that he created took on his own heroic proportions. However, in this situation raised by the Lawrence Realization Stakes, Mrs. Walter Jeffords saved the day by entering Hoodwink, a colt of hers. His chances of winning were those of a barnyard pig against a deer, but at least by this unhappy chance he would go down in history as the sacrificial offering who saved Man o' War from a walkover.

Before the start Mr. Riddle instructed Clarence Kummer, who was again in the saddle, to hold Red in. After all, it was only fair to avoid showing up Hoodwink too badly. Kummer nodded. At the post he took a strangle hold on Red and let Hoodwink break in front. For the first three quarters he threw every ounce of his weight against Red's determination to stretch out and run. Red was in high spirits that day and fretting to go; he had come out to run and run he would in spite of Kummer hauling on the bridle. When they passed the clubhouse he had taken the lead. From that minute it was good-by to Hoodwink. Kummer had Red under control again in the stretch, but in spite of all he could do Man o' War pranced home a hundred lengths in the lead. A time-browned old photograph of the finish shows Hoodwink peeking around the stretch turn as Man o' War is crossing the finish line. Until the time flashed up no one realized what had happened; Man o' War had galloped over the course so easily, getting his head for only a few seconds in rounding the lower turn, that it was hard to believe he had done it in 2:40⅘. He had broken a couple of records again, the American record of Fitz Herbert, 2:45, and the world record of English War Mint, 2:45⅖.* And he had done it so nonchalantly that, as one of the sports writers said, "He was not breathing hard enough to put out a candle."

As he rubbed his aching arms Clarence Kummer knew that he had just ridden the fastest horse America had ever seen. Mr. Riddle glowed with pride as he received congratulations. Nobody gave a second thought to poor Hoodwink.

Red was enjoying himself. He liked Belmont and never felt lonely there. The night noises were comforting. Red was no recluse who hankered for solitude, he was a gregarious horse who always liked to have something going on. When he waked at night he liked to hear the rustling of hay in the other stalls and once in a while an inquiring whinney when another horse was awakened by an unfamiliar sound.

The weather was pleasanter than it had been in Saratoga, the sticky August heat had given way to paler suns and in the morning there was even a hint of autumn in the air. The people who crowded around Red at the saddling paddock on the day of the Jockey Club Stakes had come out in tweeds.

This was to be Man o' War's last race at Belmont, but, even

---

* The record now is 2:39⅘, made by Ace Admiral in 1949.

if he had realized it, Red no doubt would have scorned any nostalgic regrets. Such sentiments were for old-timers dreaming about their past glories, and Red was little more than three years old. He did not know that Mr. Riddle was planning to retire him at the peak of his glory and that he never would see the tracks as a four-year-old.

Again it looked like a "no contest" affair. Mrs. Jeffords did not make a second sacrifice, but Harry Payne Whitney, who had such good reason to smart from Man o' War's victories, sportingly entered a colt of his, Damask, a good horse but not a likely contender against Man o' War. The bookies quoted Man o' War at 1-100. This was the third time he had carried these astonishing odds.

Major Belmont also was concerned about the effect that Man o' War was having upon the entries. Even though Mr. Whitney had saved this one from being a walkover the Major was afraid that these continual processions would dampen the popularity of racing. To make the Jockey Club Stakes more interesting he offered to double the winner's share up to $10,-000 if Sir Barton would accept the challenge at weight for age. He would have liked to include Exterminator, but the gelding was not eligible. His plan did not materialize, however, because Sir Barton had other commitments. However, the Major need not have worried, for in spite of the fact that they had no hope of seeing a real contest the fans swarmed to the track as usual.

It was, as everyone expected, another procession although Damask did not do too badly, finishing only fifteen lengths behind. He was a good colt; a few days later in the Autumn Gold Cup race he ran Exterminator a close second and made the veteran extend himself to win. But against Man o' War he made no showing. Red was racing not against him but against the clock. Although he was under strong restraint all the way and seemed to have done nothing sensational, when the time was announced the fans gasped. He had run 2:28⅗—he had broken the American record for the mile and a half.

Down in Kentucky at Nursery Stud the stable boys who followed the races to watch the fortunes of their great stallion restricted now to winning his laurels second hand through the victories of his sons and daughters, were jubilant. Man o' War's winnings that day had made Fair Play the leading sire of the year.*

The race in which Damask ran Exterminator ragged would have been the logical place, according to the fans, for Red to meet the great gelding and settle once for all time the speculations as to whether he could outrun Exterminator. However, Mr. Riddle did not consider the purse, $2,500, enough for the strenuous demands the race would make on Red, so he decided to hold his champion over for the Potomac Handicap at Havre de Grace in the middle of September.

It was a disappointment, for Exterminator had been second to no other horse than Red in the affections of the fans ever since "Uncle" Henry MacDaniel had picked the awkward ugly duckling for Willis Sharpe Kilmer just before the Kentucky Derby of 1918. Nobody believed that the gelding had the faintest chance to win, but he did, and he kept on winning. He was probably at his peak the day he won the Saratoga Cup just before the thunderstorm in which Red made history in the Hopeful Stakes, but he had done well also in 1920, winning over $90,000 in spite of the fact that he had been debarred from some of the races that carried the highest purses. There was something appealing about the horse that kept right on winning in spite of his stepchild looks, and the

---

* Man o' War won $5,850. The race is now worth $50,000, and since 1920 has been known as the Jockey Club Gold Cup.

fans would have liked nothing better than to see him run against the magnificent Red.

Still they had to be content with the Potomac Handicap, scheduled at Havre de Grace a week later. At least it looked more like a race than the past two or three in which Man o' War had run, for there were three other horses of high reputation entered. These were the Whitney Wildair, with which Jimmy Rowe was making his last try, and the coupled entry of Blazes, the sprinter, and Paul Jones, the Kentucky Derby winner.

Rowe made no boasts this time. He had not much hope, or perhaps he had become philosophical about Red. His reputation had not been harmed. In spite of the defeats of his colts by Man o' War they had done exceedingly well for the season. He expected Upset to be high on the list of money winners, certainly within the first three or four, and the total for the Whitney stables would be among the winning half dozen. So he was amiable about the stables and made no fiery predictions.

Everybody in the racing world was at Havre de Grace that autumn afternoon, the clubhouse was crowded with the Who's Who of turfdom, breeders, owners, promoters. Commander Ross was there, everybody except Colonel Matt J. Winn. Red was in a particularly good humor according to the grooms, perhaps because he felt like a great actor coming back to play before a home town audience. It was here that Red had learned to break away quickly at the post and all the other racing techniques that Feustel and Johnny Loftus had taught him before he set out on his two-year-old campaign. He had begun here at Havre de Grace and here he would run his last scheduled race, for Mr. Riddle had made no other entries for the season.

As the horses filed out of the saddling paddock there was a ripple of excitement in the stands. It might not be such a walkaway for Red. Anything could happen. The bookies reflected this expectation of drama by reducing the odds to 15-100 as against 10-1 for the other entries, figuring that Red's tremendous burden—he was carrying 138 pounds, as against a top weight of 114, the highest load a three-year-old had ever carried in America—might at last be tiring. In addition, the track was cuppy and would prove a hindrance to a long strider. Feustel was so worried about the condition of the track that he said to Mr. Riddle, "If the colt were mine I wouldn't start him," but Mr. Riddle did not like to scratch Red at the last moment so he let the horse go ahead, believing he would pull through.

The crowds who jammed the stands held their breath as the horses broke evenly. Then Red burst out like a golden flame but this time under great odds. His hoofs fought the heavy loam, until he was a length and a half ahead. He held the lead against Blazes, who challenged him for six furlongs, then exhausted, fell back, giving way for Wildair, who made a gallant effort through the stretch, but could not gain an inch.

It was over—Red wheeled into the winner's circle with no prompting from Clarence Kummer, accepting it as his rightful place. The crowds were splitting their throats as they watched him pose. He had broken Sir Barton's record by nearly two seconds.

Mr. Riddle gave a sigh of relief. The season had gone off with no flukes, no accidents. This in many ways had been the most difficult race of them all, not the competition but the cuppy track and Red's tired condition; for he had been in training too long and had lost his keen edge. When Mr. Riddle looked back on these two campaigning years, he always considered this Man o' War's greatest race.

Perhaps it was his greatest, but it was also the one in which he suffered his first mishap. Physically Red had been a marvel, never sick, never lamed or injured. Not since his bout with the flu at this same track when he was an untried two-year-old had he caused Louis Feustel the slightest worry. It seemed that luck had a special weakness for the handsome colt and spent overtime looking after him. Now he had struck himself when he ran in the Potomac and a tendon had begun to bow. It was not a serious injury, but any injury was a reason for concern, especially since the air was thick with rumors of a match race against Sir Barton. At one moment the grapevine said it was all settled, even the place and the date, at another that Mr. Riddle would not run the colt again now that he had finished his career in a blaze of glory. But the speculation seemed to be in favor of a match, a spectacular one with a purse that would be a stretch to the imagination.

Whatever the plans might be, Man o' War needed a rest and he needed time for the tendon to heal. So he stayed on in Havre de Grace while Feustel and Conway worked on the leg. The pain was slight, and Red, as usual, enjoyed himself, stuffing all the oats that Conway would give him and loafing through the short autumn days. What these humans were concocting for his future was no concern of his. Match or no match, the rest was good, and if they asked him to run again he would be ready.

MATCH OF THE CENTURY

Chapter XII

As a matter of fact Mr. Riddle was listening to the clamor for a match race and considering the offers that began to pour in, because Red needed only $24,000 to make him the top money winner up to that time, and what owner could resist such a temptation? It was fitting that Man o' War should go down in history with this additional crown. So while the suggestions were being thrashed out in the press, even some which as yet had not been made, Mr. Riddle waited. The offers that he had received were attractive, but there was no need to be in a hurry about accepting them.

At the Saratoga meeting in August Colonel Matt J. Winn, the impresario of Churchill Downs, had made a tentative proposal for a special race, offering $25,000 and a gold cup to be added to a sweepstakes in which both Sir Barton and Man o' War would be entered. He suggested that it should be run either at Latonia or Louisville; he personally preferred Louisville, believing that since Red had not run in the Kentucky Derby and had never been seen by the majority of Kentucky horse lovers who could not afford to follow the races to the northern and eastern tracks, such a race would break all attendance records at Churchill Downs. However, he did not press the idea then, for both horses had many commitments for the rest of the season.

At the Belmont race meeting Mr. Riddle and Commander J. K. L. Ross talked the matter over and decided to accept the first purse of $50,000 that they were offered for a match race between Man o' War and Sir Barton. It was not long until they received it. The Laurel track in Maryland offered $30,000 and Kenilworth in Windsor, Canada, just across the river from Detroit, upped the bid to $50,000.

Mr. A. M. Orpen of Toronto, the promoter of the Windsor match, was determined to get it. Hearing that Colonel Winn was going to over-bid him, he arranged a conference with Commander Ross and Mr. Riddle, who at that time were both at Havre de Grace. At a meeting in the directors' room of the Jockey Club he raised his bid to $75,000 plus a $5,000 gold cup. As this was the largest purse ever offered for a match race in America and both owners had already agreed that they would accept less, they were willing to sign then and there. According to Colonel Winn they were a trifle hasty. His own offer of $75,000 and a $5,000 gold cup reached them both by wire and telephone a few minutes after they had affixed their signatures. Colonel Winn said somewhat reproachfully that he was prepared to go to $100,000 and would have done so as he had been promised the final bid, "but" he said mildly, "something must have gone wrong."

At first it was planned to include Exterminator in a three-cornered race, but Mr. Kilmer did not agree to a mile and a quarter, the length of the Kenilworth contest; the Binghamton sportsman wanted it to be a mile and a half or more, a real test for distance runners, so Exterminator was dropped and the match was set for October 12, "rain or shine, mud or dry." The conditions were that if either horse should fail to appear on account of injury, the other would get the cup, but not the stakes, for galloping once around the track.

This match race was a return to a long-standing American custom that had fallen almost into disuse. In the early days match races were common and there are nearly a hundred recorded in our turf history. Among the most famous of them was the one in which the American Eclipse defeated Sir Charles in Washington on November 20, 1822. The immortal Lexington won two matches. Marathon and Geranium split two contests and for some unknown reason never met again to settle the issue; the great Domino ran dead heats against both Henry of Navarre and Dobbins, and there were many other famous matches, but none in which the purse was so large; indeed, the Kenilworth purse has been topped only twice since, when Zev met the English Papyrus for $85,000, on October 20, 1923 at Belmont, and again when Armed beat Assault, on September 27, 1947 at Belmont, for a purse of $100,000.

In spite of the fact that the Kenilworth match was ballyhooed as "the match of the ages," it was not entirely popular among sportsmen, especially Canadians, who felt that promoting racing as a business enterprise, and a big business enterprise at that, was not in the best interest of racing. But Mr. Orpen paid no attention to the old-fashioned sticklers for racing as a sport. He was putting on a big time show, and he and the committee were making elaborate arrangements; there were to be six timers and three extra placing judges, and each owner was to have a steward in the stand as well as the representative of Kenilworth's Jockey Club. Every provision was made to guard against knavery, for scandal was in the air; the Chicago Black Sox story was still a baseball stench, and rumors were flying that several outstanding horses had been "nobbled" and pulled in recent races.

Windsor was a gala city on the day of the race. Both owners had arrived with an entourage of guests, Major August Belmont was there and John E. Madden, who had bred Sir Barton, as well as most of the leading sportsmen of the East, mingling with Canadian officials and well-known sports writers from the whole continent.

On the morning of the race Commander Ross was nervous. His trainer, Guy Bedwell, advised him to cancel the race, postpone it or transfer it to Louisville, Laurel, Saratoga, or Belmont, where Sir Barton would have a chance. King's Park, this new Kenilworth track, had a hard adobe surface which would be agony for the Canadian horse. Like nearly all the get of Star Dust, Sir Barton had tender feet; even on soft tracks it was necessary to put pads of felt between his shoes and his hoofs in order to lessen the pounding on his tender feet. Bedwell, who had nursed Sir Barton through so many physical handicaps including a long siege of blood poisoning, and always had high faith in the colt even though he was difficult to keep in good condition, wanted him to have at least an even chance. He had nursed Sir Barton doggedly through his second year when his record was not too good, and in his third year Bedwell had been rewarded for the many nights that both he and Commander Ross had sat up with the colt. Sir Barton was a great horse, the only one that had won the American triple crown, and Bedwell could not endure to see him beaten, humiliated, without a chance to show what he could do.

But Commander Ross, being a Canadian, was determined to have the race on native soil. All that morning the Commander was jittery. At noon he sent to the press stand a startling message saying that Earl Sande was not in good form and would not ride Sir Barton.

"My action is taken without prejudice to Sande," he added, "and I am only exercising my prerogative as the owner of Sir Barton."

While the sports writers were speculating as to what this might mean—there never had been a breath of scandal against Sande—the brilliant young jockey was in tears, almost in a state of shock. No doubt he minded losing the fifteen-thousand-dollar fee, but even more he minded the humiliation, the stinging and unwarranted slap to his pride. He had no choice but to ask for a release from his contract.

Bedwell interceded for him.

"Sir Barton hasn't a chance in the world to win this race," he urged boldly. "By this insult you are throwing away the best young jockey in saddle history." But Commander Ross would not listen. A second jockey of his stable, Clarence Kummer, he had released to ride Man o' War, so he settled on Frank Keogh, a top-ranking jockey who had ridden many of his horses to victory.

Everybody in the racing world was in the stands on that autumn afternoon—owners, breeders, trainers. Thirty thousand fans paid the five dollar admission fee and fed greenbacks to the mutuel machines, although the returns were predestined to be only $2.10 for each $2.00. Sir Barton's loyal fans had kept his price at 11-2, although it was fairly common belief by race time that he could win only if Man o' War were struck by lightning or should refuse to run.

Red was in excellent form; his leg, which had filled up while he was in training for the match, had healed. On the track that morning he had worked a quarter in record time. After the three preliminary races had been run Sir Barton was brought out on the track and jogged a mile. Man o' War had no warming up gallop; he was led to the paddock where he was walked around the ring. As Louis Feustel groomed him the crowds gathered and circled him hundreds deep. As they increased they became such a danger in their very numbers, all pushing to get a glimpse of Man o' War, that the committee sent a call for special police to keep them back. Red was unconcerned as Feustel decorated his mane and tail with tiny gold and black ribbons.

Finally he was ready and Sir Barton had returned from his gallop. The trainers gave their instructions. To Keogh, Bedwell said, "Shake him up all the way. Give him the whip hard and often and keep him going at his best all the way. If you can get him to the front, do it. The colt is game and will do his best if you urge him."

Feustel's instructions were, "Ride as you would in any selling race. Go to the front if you can, but don't get excited."

The two started to parade to the post, Sir Barton carrying 126 pounds, conceding Red six as weight for age. A third horse, Wickford, had been entered to comply with Canadian rules which did not allow match races, but he had been scratched as was intended.

Sir Barton was in the lead, a compact, short-bodied chunk of a horse in blinkers—restive, straining, stepping gingerly on the hard track with his tender feet. Man o' War sauntered indolently behind him as though this were just a part of the day's routine. As they passed the grandstand a great shout went up for both of them, the small gallant horse in front and the enormous bright chestnut with the white blaze on his beautiful face.

At the post, the starter waited until they were both standing still, then pressed the button. The webbing flew up, they were off, Sir Barton in the lead, flying. At seventy yards Clarence Kummer eased up on Man o' War and he shot past

Sir Barton to take a lead of two lengths. Sir Barton tried to close up, but the best he could do was to keep the distance from widening, running stretched out to the breaking point, each step an agony. As Red swung around the far turn, Kummer let him out for a few yards and the distance widened by seven lengths. Keogh was flailing Sir Barton in a desperate effort not to catch up but to keep Red in sight. The track was slow, it did not look like much of a race; Red had taken the last quarter of a mile at an easy lope, yet when the time went up he had broken the track record by 6⅖ seconds.

To Mr. Riddle and Commander Ross it had been a disappointing race and one full of unpleasant overtones. The atmosphere about the track and expectations of foul play had gotten on their nerves. They were both sportsmen of the highest type who loved racing, and the faintest suspicion of corruption in any way connected with the match was offensive to them. They had taken every precaution, guarded their stables every minute; actually there was no proof of any unsavory practices except that when Red was unsaddled Louis Feustel found that someone had cut the stirrup leathers, but it was such a badly done job that they had held. Yet as a spectacle the meet had been a great success. The crowds had come to see the wonder horse, the greatest horse in America, and he had broken a record for them.

One of the spectators who was not a racing man but who was there to see the show was Harry F. Sinclair, the oil magnate. His interest was baseball, but it happened that someone introduced him to Sam Hildreth, who was bursting with pride because he had known Red "when" and full of stories about Nursery Stud. The two spent the afternoon together in Sinclair's box, Hildreth pointing out good horses in the other races and telling the oil man something about the sport.

Mr. Sinclair was so moved by the performance of Man o'

War that he decided he must have a stable. As a result of that afternoon he acquired the Rancocas stables in New Jersey that once had housed the winners of Pierre Lorillard, and he engaged Hildreth as his trainer. So was the racing tradition carried on. Big Red in his last race so impressed his image on the imagination of a stranger that he took away with him the dream of owning and breeding a horse as magnificent as Man o' War.

THE CROWN JEWELS AND THE TAJ MAHAL

Chapter XIII

AFTER THE KENILWORTH MATCH Commander Ross, who had been first to congratulate Mr. Riddle, urged that he take Man o' War to England and enter him in the Ascot Gold Cup. This was a tempting idea, much more tempting than Colonel Winn's telegraphed offer of $50,000 for a match between Red and Exterminator, and vastly more tempting than other proposals that poured in: schemes to exhibit Man o' War at Chicago's World's Fair, to put him in the motion pictures, and a hundred others. Making money with Man o' War was not a consideration, especially now that he had won his laurels as the greatest money maker of the time, but the honor of winning one of the most coveted English prizes and of exhibiting Man o' War in the country that considered itself "the cradle of fine horses," would have been a fitting climax to Red's career.

Mr. Riddle, however, decided against risking the hazards of an ocean voyage and taking Red to a strange climate. The same objection held against the suggestion of a friend whose imagination was inflamed by the possibilities Red offered. His idea was that Mr. Riddle issue a challenge to race any horse in the world in 1921, the stakes to be $25,000 or

$50,000 a corner and the place to be decided by the toss of a coin. It was a fascinating idea, but Mr. Riddle did not consider it seriously.

"No," he commented, "that would never do. It would not be possible in my opinion for an English or French horse to become acclimated in less than a year and the same would hold true if we had to go abroad. That would mean the loss of a year to the breeding industry of this country. The year in which the race would be run would take another twelve months. I wouldn't like to accept the responsibility of keeping the horse out of the stud for two years."

Mr. Riddle's plans for Man o' War's stud career so occupied his thoughts that he continued to refuse fantastic offers to buy the horse, even sums as high as a million dollars. The figures had risen spectacularly since Red's two-year-old triumphs. After Mr. Murphy's bid of $260,000 a syndicate offered $500,000 and this was soon topped by a million-dollar offer by Louis B. Mayer, then a newcomer to racing. But the most persistent bidder was the late W. P. Waggoner, who liked to have his picture taken looking at a silver dollar and whose casual remark that everything has its price did not endear him to Mr. Riddle. Mr. Waggoner offered $500,000, then $1,000,000. Each time he was told that the horse was not for sale. Finally when he came into Mr. Riddle's office one day and threw on the desk a blank check with his signature on it, Mr. Riddle enjoyed giving him this answer which he often repeated with relish in later years.

"Go to France and bring back the sepulchre of Napoleon from Les Invalides, then to England and buy the Crown jewels, then to India and buy the Taj Mahal—then I'll put a price on Man o' War."

Now that his racing career was over, sports writers and sports lovers tried to evaluate Man o' War, put him in his special niche in the hall of equine fame. Probably no horse in the world had been the subject of so many eulogies, from the de luxe three-hundred-dollar book of photographs recording many of the great moments of his life to books, magazine articles, and newspaper comments galore. Even editorial writers of the nation's leading dailies turned their attention from world affairs and local politics to write a tribute to him. And what a subject he made! He had everything; he could sprint; he could run a distance; he could carry weight, such weight as no other horse had carried; he could run in the rain and the mud or on a hard-baked track that was torture to more sensitive hoofs, he could be rated and controlled, and all these things he did superlatively. Add to these virtues his superb appearance, and you have the well-nigh perfect horse.

Indeed he had about him none of the placid conventionality that one associates with a perfect specimen. Red broke long-held theories about racing as easily as he shattered time records. The motion picture record of the Kenilworth race gave sports writers a shock as well as fresh ammunition for their pens, for these showed that Man o' War had toppled into the discard long-established ideas about motion. It always had been held that the fastest race horse was the one which raced closest to the ground and thus covered space with the greatest economy of motion, but Red had never heard of this theory and he ran to suit himself.

The accepted ideal of the race horse was well expressed by the distinguished English turf writer, "Touchstone." "Give me good hind quarters and sound forelegs and I am satisfied, I want an animal built low before and high behind, with plenty of length and stride, good hocks, an open chest and a well-set-on head and then I know that I have a 'goer,' (provided always that his pipes are in order). . . . The horse who works long and low and shaves the turf in his stride is the animal for me."

Red answered Touchstone's specifications as to build, although he might have considered the horse's legs too long, but he would have been profoundly disturbed if he had seen the motion pictures that showed Man o' War taking tremendous bounces, arching far above the ground in his enormous strides, with his four feet almost drawn together. Bounding along in this unconventional way, he had shattered records so easily that, if horses had been able to read all the amazed comment, they would undoubtedly have started a new style in racing.

But even when the motion pictures disclosed just how Red did it they did not answer the question why he should have been so superior to every other horse who raced against him. For it is the great lament of the fans that he never had to fight for his victories. Except for his one brush with John P. Grier, the only horse who ever extended him, Red's fame rests not on beating other horses but on beating the clock.

"Actually," champions of Exterminator, Seabiscuit, Equipoise, or Citation ask sometimes, "whom did he ever beat?" The answer is that the horses which he sent back with their pride crushed and their hearts broken were not mediocre. Had it not been for Red, John P. Grier and Upset, Paul Jones and Wildair would have been remembered as exceptional three-year-olds, and Sir Barton as one of the great racers. But super individuals such as Man o' War always outclass their contemporaries by a tremendous span. He not only beat them, but conceded them many pounds of weight, running always with much in reserve. The ultimate of power and speed in that majestic body could have been brought out only by a twin horse of his superb ability, and such a one he never met.

Mr. Riddle once said, "We do not know to this day how fast Man o' War was, as we were afraid to let him out; knowing his intense speed, we feared he might harm himself."

As for the actual figures; one of his speed records still stands, thirty years after his thundering hoofs raced under silks. He still holds the world's record for one and three eighths miles which he did in $2{:}14\frac{1}{5}$ in the Belmont Stakes, and his $2{:}40\frac{4}{5}$ for the mile and five eighths which he ran in the Lawrence Realization stood for many years until it was tied by five-year-old Historian in 1946 and lowered by Ace Admiral in 1949 to $2{:}39\frac{4}{5}$. The mile record which he ran in the Withers has been lowered several times, most recently by Citation and Noor. His mile and an eighth in $1{:}49\frac{1}{5}$ was lowered by Hot Toddy in 1929 and again by Indian Broom in 1936 to the phenomenal $1{:}47\frac{3}{5}$. His $2{:}28\frac{4}{5}$ for the mile and a half fell to Handy Mandy who held the mark until Bolingbroke, son of Eclipse, lowered it to $2{:}27\frac{3}{5}$ in 1942. Those who champion Man o' War emphasize the fact that the record which still is credited to him is a world as well as an American record. And, furthermore, with the exception of the Dwyer Stakes, all these records were set by Red under restraint throughout most of the race.

Even faster than some of his official records were a few that Man o' War set in training. There was the half mile he worked at Saratoga in 45 seconds flat with the 137 pounds of Clyde Gordon up; the three furlongs in 33 which he made on the same track with 130 pounds in the saddle; and the two furlong spurt at Windsor which was clocked at $20\frac{1}{5}$, probably the fastest bit of spot running any horse ever has done.

What he could have done if he had been extended is one of the speculations that will intrigue racing fans and horse lovers as long as Man o' War is remembered. Even if we as a race should disappear into the limbo of time, some archaeologist of a race as yet unborn would, no doubt, excavate our kitchen middens and then the speculation would be revived. For such an archaeologist would be sure to attack with gusto the mountains of printed matter that he would find regarding Man o' War. If he should happen to come across the pen picture of John Hervey—or "Salvator," he would have an excellent idea of the flaming colt.

Summing up his racing career, Salvator wrote, "Man o' War in training was a thoroughbred of extremely high nervous organization—a necessity to any animal of such feats as he performed.

"His nervous excitement on race days was always extreme. He was at times restive at the barrier, and once or twice was held there for the break-away by an assistant starter. The tumult of a large crowd affected him and he was especially sensitive to the music of a band, which never failed to arouse him to still greater excitement. The charts of his races show, however, that as a rule the delay at the post was very brief, and on two occasions when it was longest it is admitted that it was due to the tactics of opposing jockeys, who hoped to keep him there so long that his heavy burden would tire him and cause his defeat, and this might have been the case had he not been a colt of such Herculean strength.

"Man o' War was, however, the reverse of such a horse as, for instance, St. Simon, who wasted away and tucked up during a campaign, was almost unmanageable in and out of the stables, and whose tantrums made the life of his groom well-nigh unbearable, while on one occasion it required four hours to load him into a railway car.

"Such antics were not in the repertoire of Man o' War who was without viciousness or any traces of the man-eater, who finished both his campaigns better and stouter than when they began, who was a good shipper, and gave his caretakers no more anxious moments than accompany the training and campaigning of any high-strung thoroughbred.

"His intelligence being so great, it contributed constantly to his tractability. Nor was he, like St. Simon, given to taking the bit between his teeth and rushing around the course with blazing eyes and mouth wide open, refusing to be taken back and running his races to suit himself, finishing with his jockey in such a state of exhaustion that he had to be helped from the saddle.

"While Man o' War ran mostly in front, he showed on repeated occasions that he could be rated, restrained, or kept in back of other horses at his rider's will, not making his move until the chosen moment.

"Such was the race horse, Man o' War—an altogether different creature from the one so often 'written up' by sensation-mongering scribes who pictured him for their own purposes as not merely a high-mettled racer but a cyclone in equine form in and out of his races, wild-eyed and ungovernable, whose training and management were tasks of the most formidable difficulty.

"It has been written that 'a great man is made up of qualities that meet or make great occasions'—and this is supremely the definition of a great horse. Of such, few have exemplified it more consistently than the son of Fair Play and Mahubah, and in concluding the description of his turf career nothing may be more fitly placed there than the old poet's words commemorative of the deeds of Oliver Cromwell on the field of battle: 'He nothing common did, nor mean, upon that memorable scene.' "

Even if he had been able to read them, Man o' War would have been unimpressed by such eulogies as that of Salvator. He always had known that he was a super horse; one could tell it by the confident way he looked at his admirers, the way he carried his head and the way he held himself like a gleaming bronze statue in the winner's circle. He had the good-natured, easy assurance of a popular monarch who accepted the adulation of the crowds that came out to feast their eyes on him as one of the attributes of his supremacy. There was an aura of greatness about him that gave a feeling of elation to all who saw him. Always, under every circumstance, he conducted himself like a prince of the turf.

Red loved this adulation, it was one of the major satisfactions of his life, as great a pleasure to him as the race itself, his delight in the actual physical experience of running, using the power in the muscles of his smoothly geared body.

Around the stables his court felt some anxiety, the grooms and swipes wondered if he was going to miss the adulation now that his life was going to be restricted to the paddocks of a stud farm. Was it going to be hard on Red to settle down to the quiet monotony of a stallion's life even though wherever he was he always would be a one-man show?

Chapter XIV

IN LATE OCTOBER when Red and Major Treat bade farewell
to their last race track, to the familiar confusion of horses
and trainers and grooms, and to the enticing scent of mash
cooking in the field pots and bales of fresh hay broken out
after the last race, the details of their future had not yet been
decided. When sports writers asked Mr. Riddle where he
would locate his stud farm he could only say "Wherever Mr.
and Mrs. Jeffords decide. They love the horse quite as much
as we do. He always has been a sort of party horse—we all
have a claim on him and have shared him together. As Walter
Jeffords is a Kentuckian and Kentucky is the birthplace of
Man o' War, it is only natural to suppose that he will be retired to that state." Nothing definite had been planned, except
that Walter Jeffords would manage him.

Man o' War's immediate destination was Glen Riddle in
Maryland, but it was a slow journey south, for it had no
sooner started than it was transformed into a triumphal procession. At every stop along the way crowds gathered to see
the champion, and he obligingly stuck his proud head out of
the van door in answer to their cheers.

At last the caravan reached Pennsylvania. Before going to

The Rose Tree Inn

Glen Riddle, Red and Major Treat stopped at the Rose Tree Hunt Club in Media, where Mr. Riddle's neighbors and friends had planned a welcome befitting royalty. As the van drew up at the club track, the thousands of people who had been waiting ringed around. Philadelphians had come en masse and with them many visiting celebrities, including Jack Dempsey and Olympic oarsman Jack Kelly, who wanted to see Man o' War come home. And Red gave them a good show —when the van door was opened and the ramp put down, Major Treat walked sedately to the ground and stood aside to wait for Red.

"Here he comes," the crowd breathed as Red stood posed in the doorway looking over his audience. Spurning the ramp, he gathered his feet together like a cat and sprang lightly over the rail.

"My God!" exclaimed Mr. Riddle, and the words were echoed through the crowd, shocked to realize how easily the leap might have snapped a regal leg.

This to Mr. Riddle was the high moment of Red's career, for the clubhouse in which he received the congratulations of his friends had been the scene of many of his pleasantest hours. This was the oldest fox hunting club in the United States. At that time Mr. Riddle was honorary president and for many years he had been master of hounds. He had known in his youth some of the original members, sportsmen so robust that they looked upon the use of the hunting horn as an affectation. A man who couldn't raise his voice and call a hound five miles away was not counted much of a fox hunter. In those days there was no need of a M.F.H., for there was not a single member so unskilled that he could not be trusted with the hounds.

Mr. Riddle had helped to preserve the old inn with its wide porch and its faded sign of a rose tree hanging from one of the windows, and to see that the new clubhouse in the rear did not detract from the homely charm of the original building that suggested the hospitality of an old English tavern. Here the Riddles and the Jeffords had enjoyed many a "full moon supper" under the stately trees within hallowing distance of Piney Ridge, where a fox was most likely to awaken the music of the hounds.

Now Mr. Riddle brought his triumph home to share it with his life-long friends. In the afternoon after the luncheon in his honor at which many a toast was drunk to Man o' War, the horse was led out to the club track past the gravestone of Slasher, the club's most famous hound "whose like we ne'er hope to see again," and with Clyde Gordon up in colors was given a chance to run. He shot along the track, his red coat gleaming in the October sun. Never had he looked more like a champion.

From the Rose Tree Club the caravan rolled over the hills of Pennsylvania to the flat meadows of the eastern shore. At Glen Riddle again Red had a short vacation, four months in which to fatten on the lush grass and prance in the paddocks where he had grown to the stature of maturity. But it was not all play, for Red could not be let down too quickly; every day he was worked a while by Clyde Gordon who took him out for a canter or a gallop, sometimes on the old race track where he had first tried out against Golden Broom and again along the country lanes where the trees were turning gold.

Man o' War had almost reached his full growth—not quite, for his teeth and bones were not yet fully developed. When he first raced at Saratoga he had weighed 975 pounds and by the time he went home to Glen Riddle after his two-year-old campaign he had reached 1,020. By spring he weighed 1,150 and had grown to 16½ hands. Even during his three-year-old season he grew a little. He was a magnificent hunk of horseflesh quite different from the leggy yearling of the Saratoga sales. But otherwise he had not changed; even when he was a colt he carried himself with the haughty assurance of an emperor.

That winter S. H. Chubb of the American Museum of Natural History visited the Riddles at Berlin to take Man o' War's measurements and preserve them for comparative studies in which the director, Mr. Osborne, was interested. Man o' War was intrigued and held still while Mr. Chubb passed the tape measure and calipers about his flanks and head. He measured Red's limbs and body, his deep chest, his legs and bone structure, and recorded his weight—Big Red had gained a hundred pounds since his retirement—and he took photographs from various points of view to illustrate the measurements.

The purpose of the measurements was to arrive at some conclusion about the proportions and bone structure that make a great racer. But when all the scientific data is assembled and we are able to view the diagram of the hind leg of Man o' War as compared with that of the prehistoric midget horse or the old farm dobbin, we are tempted to agree with James R. Keene's old stable boy. Mr. Chubb tells how the old Negro shook his head when he heard his master and a group of sportsmen discussing what are the characteristics of a great race horse. When Mr. Keene asked the groom what he thought a good horse needed to have, he answered positively, "Speed, Mr. Keene, speed."

"Of course," agreed Mr. Keene, "but what else, Tom?"

"More speed, sah, more speed, dat's what makes a good hoss."

By this time Mr. Riddle and Mr. Jeffords had made their decision about the future of Man o' War. In January they planned to send him to Lexington, Kentucky, and put him under the management of Miss Elizabeth Daingerfield, whose distinguished record as a manager of stud farms was second to none, making no allowances for the fact that it is a difficult profession for a woman. Miss Daingerfield had grown into the profession naturally, for she had inherited her father's love of horses and his skill. She had spent her life with horses and she knew as much about them as any breeder.

Her father, Major Foxhall Daingerfield, of Virginia, had been the manager of Castleton, the beautiful stud farm of his brother-in-law, James R. Keene. Here on the historic acres that had once belonged to the Breckinridges, her father developed one of the greatest racing stables in the country. As a child Miss Daingerfield made friends with the great Domino and Spendthrift, she played with the English brood mares, Cinderella, Pastorella, and the others of the harem for which Mr. Keene paid half a million dollars, and she helped raise their colts and fillies. Kingston she knew and the remarkable Sysonby, and she was familiar as any groom with the habits and peculiarities of Ballot, Peter Pan, and Cap and Bells who won the English Oaks in 1901. It was an establishment with a proud record. Behind the high iron gates and in the spacious halls of the old Breckinridge mansion no one thought or talked of anything except champions, and how to breed and how to train them. Miss Daingerfield needed no formal instruction, she had learned all there was to know about a stud farm by actually growing up with one, and one that was managed according to the old English maxim, "Breed the best to the best and hope for the best."

When the Keene stud was broken up in 1911, the blue year of racing, and Castleton became a stud for trotting horses, Miss Daingerfield acquired her own farm, Haylands. There Colin, who was under her management, finished his stud career and there she bred such thoroughbreds as Walter J.

Salmon's Step Lightly, who had just won the 1920 Futurity. There was scarcely a racing day at Saratoga or Belmont or Churchill Downs that she did not receive a prize for the breeding of a winner.

In addition to Haylands Miss Daingerfield had under lease Hinata Farm and here she built a new stallion barn in preparation for the coming of Man o' War and Golden Broom. She expected them in the early spring. Man o' War already had been advertised for public service to outside mares at $2,500, the same figure that had been charged for Friar Rock, but it was not an excessive amount for Willis Sharpe Kilmer was asking $3,000 for the services of Sun Briar. Mr. Riddle was not anxious for business; he did not intend to give service to many outside mares, for he expected to have his own collection.

Selecting mares requires a high amount of skill and knowledge and is one of the most difficult problems of a horse breeder, because upon his wise choice depends the success of his establishment. There are many theories of selection, almost as many as there are experts on pedigree. Some breeders, among them the late August Belmont, consider it unnecessary for a mare to have made a name on the race track, they prefer one who has not exhausted herself to win records but who was foaled by a champion sire. Man o' War's mother, Mahubah, who was raced little, is a case in point. But however much they may disagree about racing mares, stud experts are agreed that a good brood mare should belong to a proud family tree and be built on the proper lines, not short-barrelled but long-legged and roomy.

The pedigree expert usually is not content with a study of the mare's immediate ancestors but will examine her pedigree to thirty-two or even sixty-four quarterings. One English stud manager has a way of arriving at an approximate picture of the mare's background by underlining each classic animal on her family tree with a blue pencil, each handicap winner with red (not counting selling races), and the remainder with brown. Then he counts them up, and if the brown predominates he does not buy the mare.

One of the most complicated but popular theories of breeding is known as that of nicks or guides to lucky mating, the theory being that certain strains which have combined favorably in the past will have established themselves and can be depended upon to produce good results in future unions. The Aga Khan is a great believer in nicks and he has one of the world's most illustrious stables. In the case of Man o' War it would be necessary to determine what strains combined best with the Fair Play line.

Thus it was necessary to study not only the performance of the ancestors of the mares considered as mates for Man o' War but also their personalities, for horses do transmit not only their appearance, their smoothness or hardness of hair and "feathering" in odd spots, but temperament, mannerisms, immunity or proneness to certain diseases and particularly longevity. Abilities acquired in training also can be transmitted. One has only to remember the famous Kentucky trotter who was put to stud before he was raced and proved a dismal failure as a sire in spite of his illustrious pedigree. Failing at stud, he was put into training and broke many a record on the track. When he was returned to stud after his success on the track he sired many of the best trotters in Kentucky.

All of these maxims and a hundred others Miss Daingerfield remembered as she selected Man o' War's harem with the assistance of William Allison, the English pedigree expert. Good mares were hard to find and harder to buy since racing had recovered from the doldrums of the anti-betting laws and the sports depression of the war years. Of the fifteen that she selected, six were imported from England. For one of the English mares, Batanoa by Roi Herode, Mr. Riddle paid $15,000. Bathing Girl by Spearmint, Colette by Collar, Gambardia by Bayardo, Lady Comfey, also by Roi Herode, and Santissima by St. Angelo were proportionally costly. Among the American mares were Florence Webber, a daughter of Peep o' Day, and Miss Starlight by Watercress.

They began to arrive during the late fall and winter. The English mares stood the trip well and they made a pleasant sight romping with their American cousins in the roomy paddocks of Hinata. The new stallion barn was completed, all was in readiness. Miss Daingerfield had engaged Man o' War's special groom, John Buckner, better known as Buck, who had cared for Domino, Spendthrift, and Colin. Christmas had come and gone, and Red's fourth official birthday; it was almost time for the stud season to begin.

Thus it was time for Red to leave Glen Riddle. When they put him in the van to take him to the railroad, the grooms and exercise boys broke into tears. His triumphs had been theirs; there was not one of them who had not followed every race with a catch in his throat, who had not gloried in Red's homecoming as though he had been their own. Or rather, it was the other way around, they belonged to him and with his going they felt as though the meaning of their days suddenly had been snatched away. Plenty of fine colts were training at Glen Riddle, but they felt it in their hearts that there never would be another Man o' War. Clyde Gordon was lucky—he was going along.

In late January of 1921 Man o' War and Golden Broom set out for Kentucky. On the night of the 27th they slept in Colonel Bradley's barn at the old Association track. The next afternoon Clyde Gordon in the Riddle colors brought Man o'

War out for a canter past a cheering crowd. This was his last exhibition, and that afternoon he went to Hinata Farm to begin his stud career.

He had come home to the place where he was born. Hinata was not many miles from Nursery Stud, where Fair Play still lived with Mahubah, "his wife" as the manager of the Belmont farm called her, for she never had been covered by another horse. Man o' War sniffed the same crisp winter Kentucky air that had made him rattle his feed tub in the yearling barn at Nursery Stud, and the pale sunlight of the first warm January day may have reminded him of the spring only three years earlier when he had run free in the pasture before he had known the meaning of a saddle or a bit or a chilly early morning workout. In three years he had become one of the most famous creatures in the world, vying with princes and prize fighters and aviators. Perhaps he had some dim realization of what fame means on that afternoon when he travelled out the Russell Cave Pike and watched the children who lined the road to wave and shout his name.

Chapter XV

Man o' War remembered this country. He knew the rolling hills, the paddocks with mile after mile of white fences, with here and there an entrance flanked with boxwood and a glimpse of a white house screened with wisteria or a vista of a flower garden. In every direction on every pike were the great stud farms where the most famous horses of the American track had learned to nibble the sweet Kentucky grass.

Many of these farms were connected in some way with Big Red's ancestors, his immediate family, or his more or less remote cousins. The city of Lexington had surrounded and almost smothered the oldest of them all, "the Meadows," where Dr. Warfield, so the legend goes, built a race track before he finished his own house. As he sipped mint juleps on the side porch he could watch the antics of a chestnut foal that he named Darley after its illustrious English forebear. This colt, later re-named Lexington, was Man o' War's great-great-great-grandfather, through his maternal line, and perhaps the only horse to rival him in his prodigious feats on the track and as a sire.

Not far away, at Belair on Walnut Hill Pike, Red's great-grandfather, Spendthrift, was foaled. Dan Swigert, whose name stands high in Kentucky horse breeding, here divided his affections between his stud and his old-fashioned flower gardens blooming on land granted by his English Majesty to Kentucky's first governor. He had an unerring eye for horseflesh. One morning he said to his wife, "I have a couple of fine colts in the pasture and I'm going to name the best one 'Spendthrift' after you."

"Very well," answered his wife, "we'll name the other one 'Miser' after you."

What happened to Miser has been forgotten, but Spendthrift made a sensational record on the track and later sired Hastings, the hellion who sired Fair Play.

And the farms that were not directly connected with Man o' War and his kin were all entwined with the life of which he was a part: Dixiana, for instance, the famous stud farm of Major Thomas, the "Nestor of the American turf." Major Belmont prized the sign that once hung on the gate, "Lightning rod and book agents keep out. Only a good horse wanted. All lovers of dogs and horses and all who will remain to dine with me are welcome." A later owner gave the sign to the Major, who brought it to Belmont Park and hung it on the gate that separated the track from the Turf and Field Club.

On John E. Madden's Hamburg Place the famous turfman had bred three Derby winners, two of them rivals of Man o' War—Paul Jones, Sir Barton and Old Rosebud. Four years later he was to make it five with Zev and Flying Ebony. Few breeders could place over their stable doors as proud an inscription as that which hung over the foaling stalls of Hamburg Place:

IN THIS BARN WERE FOALED

	Kentucky Derby
Old Rosebud	1914
Sir Barton	1919

Man o' War Comes Home

Paul Jones	1920
Zev	1923
Flying Ebony	1925

Madden, they said, was such a keen judge of horse flesh that when he was judging at Madison Square Garden he could pick the winner as the horses came through the gate; he didn't need to wait and see them in the ring.

At Greentree, Mrs. Payne Whitney's formal and beautiful farm, had lived many winners of the Whitney stables, and at Idle Hour, where the green and white barns and fences of Colonel Bradley were painted the racing colors of its owner, were housed the racers of the three-time winner of the Kentucky Derby. Here the Colonel exhibited to his friends his cups and trophies and the portraits of his favorite horses as well as a shoe from each of his winners dipped in gold and chained to a little gold plate giving the name of the horse and the event. Every hill, every pasture that Man o' War passed that day, and many that he could not see but that lay in a radius of ten or twelve miles around Lexington, were a part of the horse country that has become America's most famous nursery of thoroughbreds.

But Red was probably more interested in his dinner than he was in traditions. He and Golden Broom were restive from their journey and they welcomed the fine new stallion barn, the bundles of fresh hay and the opportunity to stretch their legs. It was a new life, a new routine, new friends, but Red was adaptable. He liked Buck, the groom with the slow movements and the gentle voice, and Harrie Scott, who managed him. The paddocks were large, and every day Buck exercised him. They cantered for a five or six mile stretch along the lanes still frost powdered but greening with the first promise of spring.

The grooming was not so strenuous as it had been for the

125

race track, not so much shining and combing and polishing, and there was less routine. Buck's chief job was to keep Man o' War from getting bored. When a horse is retired from the excitement and variety of life at the track he may fall into a state of lassitude or develop a temper if his manager does not contrive some substitute for the music of the bands and the exhilarating fervor of the crowds, so he plans as much variety as he can, riding on new roads, different lanes, varying the scenery and food, not the same old hay and oats every day. Sometimes Man o' War was fed carrots and he liked them. He was still an omnivorous eater and ate everything Buck gave him, then whinnied for more. There was never left in his feed tub an oat that his eager tongue could reach.

Red's first concern was to get acquainted with his mares, for spring had come to Kentucky and the breeding season was at hand. One of the English mares had died and Florence Webber and Miss Starlight were not ready, but a mare had been added to the harem, Sea Name, who belonged to James Maddox, a close friend of Mr. Riddle, and was given a courtesy service. Thirteen mares in all carried the foals that were to be Man o' War's first crop. It would be three years before the sports world would judge the value of these foals and determine whether or not Red would be as sensational a sire as he had been a racer. It would be a national disaster if he failed, a staggering blow to the breeding industry, but nobody could imagine that he would fail.

With the breeding season over, Man o' War was taken out to work for an hour or so every day. Miss Daingerfield did not intend that he should grow fat and lazy. Then came the winter, the short days when Red loafed and nickered for his dinner or warmed himself by a gallop along wintry roads. His new duties had not made him irritable and difficult to manage. Some stallions are so excitable that it is necessary to lead

126

them to their exercise, but Red was always willing to be saddled. In spite of his new dignities, when he was let loose in the pasture he was very much a colt. Mr. Jeffords came to see him often, and so did Mr. Riddle, who always had sugar in his pockets. But his closest friends were Miss Daingerfield, who almost every day looked him over to see that he was fit, Harrie Scott, and Buck, the comrade who talked to him in a slow, quiet drawl as he moved about the stall, cleaning the feed box, disinfecting, spreading fresh hay.

Again it was spring and one by one as their time approached the mares who had been carrying their babies for eleven months moved to the roomy foaling stalls. The hurrying of feet in the night, the yellow spots of flash lights moving along the lane, may have stirred in Red vague memories of the spring when he was a yearling at Nursery Stud. One after the other they were born, these first foals, seven colts and six fillies that might well have been worth fantastic sums if they had been offered on the market, for there were any number of horsemen who would have been willing to gamble an extravagant sum on Man o' War's first children. Every week or so Miss Daingerfield announced their arrival in the *Thoroughbred Record*. All of them were lively babies except one, Masquerade's brown filly, who died soon after it was born.

Curiously the grooms looked at the hairs on the muzzles of these new babies to see what color they would be when they had shed their baby fuzz, since these hairs never change their color and they indicate what the coat of the horse will be when it is grown. Nine of the twelve were chestnuts like their sire, and the rest were bays. Soon they were named, most of them with dramatic warlike names that have distinguished Man o' War's family. Star Fancy's colt was called Gun Boat; Shady's, First Mate; Understudy's, Flagship; Batanoa's, Homeric; Lady Comfey's, American Flag; Collette's little bay foal broke the sequence, it being named By Hisself because his father always ran alone.

Even the fillies bore names that suggested war. The Nurse's brown daughter was called, appropriately enough, Florence Nightingale; Thrasher's filly, Maid at Arms; Smoky Lamp's bay, Lightship; Santissima's daughter, Flotilla; and Bathing Girl's baby, Sea Plane. The courtesy foal that belonged to James Maddox was christened Friendship Two.

American Flag had Man o' War's white blaze on his face and looked most like his father. As he wobbled to the pasture and tried to imitate Lady Comfey nibbling grass, he was most like Big Red in his mannerisms and temperament, alert, bouncing with energy, good-tempered but inclined to want his own way. As he grew older the similarity became more pronounced. Miss Daingerfield always maintained that he was more like Man o' War than any of his get.

It had been a pleasant year for Red; he had become accustomed to his new duties, and he liked the freedom of the paddocks. Nor did he miss the adulation which had followed him from track to track. Admirers were beating a dusty road to Hinata Farm and every sunny afternoon crowds of tourists swarmed through the gates to see the famous horse. Even when it rained they came in slickers with dripping umbrellas —too many of them. Miss Daingerfield was afraid they were disturbing the stallion, but Man o' War was a celebrity, he belonged to the world, and the world was entitled to see him; one could not shut the gate in the faces of his admirers.

However, she believed that if he were farther away from Lexington he might lead a more quiet life, so she began to look around for a suitable stud farm for Mr. Riddle. The tract she decided upon was a beautiful piece of high, rolling land that was part of James Lee Haggin's Mount Brilliant farm.* It was two miles farther out the pike than Hinata, two miles farther, she hoped, from Man o' War's swarming admirers. So Mr. Riddle bought the land, and Miss Daingerfield designed the barns and paddocks. In May of 1922, while Red's first foals were still sucklings, he, the harem, and the babies were moved to their new home, Faraway Farm, where he was to remain for the rest of his life and where his future sons and daughters were to be born.

In the spring of 1923 when his first foals were yearlings, Man o' War's second crop was born. Of these thirteen the greatest were to be Crusader, Mars, Corvette, Edith Cavell, and Taps. This was perhaps his finest crop. Crusader was to be his most famous son until eleven years later War Admiral came along.

A year later, while American Flag and his brothers and sisters were being trained to the starting post, Red's third group of children were keeping the staff of Faraway Farm on twenty-four hour duty. In this crop were fourteen fillies who were to make Man o' War one of the leading brood mare sires of all time. One of them, War Feathers, a chestnut daughter of Tuscan Red, brought the phenomenal price of $50,500 when she was sold as a yearling a year later. She was one of the few (only 45 in all) of Man o' War's children who was ever sold away from Mr. Riddle's stud. She was a colossal failure as a racer, but produced three stakes winners in later years. Scapa Flow, Broadside, Son o' Battle, War Eagle, Frillette, and Yaddo, all stakes winners, were among this group as well as seven minor winners.

As the racing season of 1924 opened, Mr. Riddle and Mr. Jeffords had eight of Man o' War's first children in training

* Not to be confused with James Ben Ali Haggan who was perhaps the largest breeder of thoroughbreds and who operated farms at Lexington, Ky. and Sacramento, Cal. around 1900.

and ready to try their mettle. Walter Jeffords started first with Lightship on July 4th at Aqueduct. The pretty chestnut filly met three powerful opponents, Harry Payne Whitney's filly Maud Muller, who was later to become the mother of The Darb; Mother Goose, who later that season won the Futurity, and Swinging, who was to go down in history as the dam of Equipoise. Lightship showed early speed, but she could not keep up the pace, and came in last. It was a great day for Jim Rowe, a partial solace for the beatings he had taken from Man o' War.

The first winner by Man o' War was Mr. Riddle's colt, American Flag, who won his maiden race in August at Saratoga. Race fans who remembered Man o' War as a two-year-old on that same track thought they were seeing the ghost of Big Red, the same white blaze and fiery coat, the same great leaps that ate up the ground. American Flag was decidedly the best of the crop although he had been entered late in the season and was not to make his best record until he was a three-year-old.

The others did not do so badly, but none of them sparkled as juveniles. Already they were setting a pattern that was to become characteristic of Man o' War's get: they were developing into horses for distance at any weight, horses of great heart in their maturity, not precocious youngsters already burned out soon after they left the nursery.

When the two-year-olds returned to the track the next spring as three-year-olds, they established Man o' War as without doubt one of the leading American sires. American Flag won the Bayside Handicap and three of the races that were associated with his father. He won the Withers, the Belmont, and the Dwyer in which Big Red had run the deathless match with John P. Grier. The fans were transferring to him

130

LEADING AT BELMONT ON SEPTEMBER 11, 1920, WHEN HE SET A WORLD RECORD

DEFEATING SIR BARTON IN THE $80,000 MATCH RACE IN WINDSOR, CANADA

SAMUEL D. RIDDLE WITH HIS MOST FAMOUS HORSE AT FARAWAY FARM

BEING GIVEN HIS MORNING EXCERSISE AS A 22-YEAR-OLD

the almost hysterical adulation that they had felt for Man o' War.

Florence Nightingale also did well this year, winning the Coaching Club American Oaks, our nearest approach to the renowned English Epsom Oaks and the toughest test for three-year-old fillies in the United States. On the whole this first crop made a very creditable showing. Looking ahead a little to the end of their racing careers when Mr. Riddle and Mr. Jeffords would count up their winnings: Florence Nightingale won five races and took home $18,650; By Hisself won five and made $21,875; Flagship pranced into the winner's circle ten times for $12,741; First Mate won seven starts and $7,065, and even Lightship, who was defeated so cruelly in her first race, won three and $6,250. The other five were all stakes winners.

But Mr. Riddle had very little time to cast up accounts, for while American Flag was repeating his father's triumphs, a second crop, now two-year-olds, was making records. In Crusader he saw that he had a sensational horse. The colt was the son of Star Fancy, a daughter of the great brood mare sire Star Shoot. Mars, another one of this crop who looked like a winner, was out of another daughter of Star Shoot. This was the most successful of the strains combined in Man o' War's children. A high-class filly, Edith Cavell, also looked particularly good.

The activities of the Riddle stable were expanding so rapidly that he and Walter Jeffords devoted most of their time to it. Meanwhile Miss Daingerfield supervised the stud at Faraway Farm. There Man o' War was king. Now that there was no question about his success as a sire, the establishment at Faraway Farm settled into the routine that it was to maintain for the rest of his life. Stallions came and stayed or died, most of them Man o' War's own sons, but always the farm revolved about Big Red. Not one of them attracted the curiosity and admiration of the old campaigner. The sight-seers glanced at the others, passing their stalls, but it was before Man o' War's stall that they clustered. He was the one they had come to see.

Meanwhile, when he was assured of the success of Man o' War's first get, Mr. Riddle advertised the horse for stud. He did not name the price, but he raised it from $2,500 to $5,000 and offered only a limited number of services to out-side mares. This was a large fee, but for Man o' War it was not considered too high.

Chapter XVI

SPRING FOLLOWED SPRING with new stallion duties for Man o' War and new foals to grow plump on the blue grass before they journeyed to the yearling sales or to Glen Riddle to train for the races. As Red took on weight and dignity as a sire, in Nursery Stud not far away an era in racing had come to an end—a brilliant era of which he was the final and most dazzling product. Major Belmont had died and in the summer of 1925 Man o' War's sire and dam were put on the auction block.

Many a horse lover remembers that sunny afternoon when Fair Play was led out by weeping stable boys. He was twenty years old, but his golden coat was unfaded and he stood erect with the old contemptuous grace. Joseph E. Widener bought him for $100,000, and took him and Mahubah to Elmendorf to spend their last days in the pastures of Elk Horn Creek. Fair Play lived for four more years—they are a long-lived breed, the get of the Godolphin—and was buried in the horse cemetery at Elmendorf under the life size statue of him by Laura Gardiner Fraser. Through the years he lies in good company, close to Mahubah and Quelle est Belle, Quelle Chance, Rose Pompom, and Stage Craft.

133

But Man o' War was not disturbed by wistful memories. It was a good life at Faraway Farm, no monotony, no set routine. After the breeding season he was worked hard to keep him from putting on weight and in the spring he was worked just as hard to take off the winter's fat. Every day he cantered for five or six miles and downed his quota of nine quarts of oats, his fresh hay, and the lumps of sugar that Mr. Riddle gave him. There was no pampering, no clipping, no steam heat, just a natural healthy life.

Ordinarily Red was a good-natured horse and did not object to being handled, but during the breeding season he became temperamental and led his grooms a hectic dance. One of his tricks was to come out of his stall rearing on his hind legs and flailing the air with his forefeet. It was a dangerous trick, he might well have hurt himself and was almost sure to hurt his grooms, so Harrie Scott, the foreman, told Mr. Riddle that he would cure Red of it if the owner was willing to take the risk. Mr. Riddle agreed, and the next time Red pranced out on his hind legs, Scott pulled him over backward. Red fell with a thud that shook the barn. Then he scrambled to his feet, shook himself, snorted a startled protest, and looked reproachfully at Scott. Whatever his indignant thoughts may have been, he decided that he did not like that thud and he never tried his circus act again.

As the years sauntered by, Red's older sons came back to occupy the other stalls in the stallion barn; first, American Flag, who was so handsome with his shining red coat and the white blaze on his face that visitors often took him for his father; next came Crusader, followed by others of lesser distinction, and later, many years later, the stalls were occupied by War Admiral and War Relic.

Red ignored his sons when they came home with laurels, but he liked the foals. One of the happiest of the many thousands of photographs taken of Red shows him in the pasture frolicking with a crop of his yearlings. He looks as though he just had told them a hilarious reminiscence of his racing days, maybe the tale about the horse at Saratoga who went into fits of terror when the band struck up to lead them to the post until his master engaged a hurdy gurdy to serenade him every morning. Or Red may have been remembering the appetite of the onion-eating horse who once occupied a stall next to his. The racer had a passion for onions and would stand with his head out of his stall door crunching the onions greedily with tears running down his muzzle. Or again Red may have been warning his children not to display their tempers like the mad steeplechaser at Belmont, who used to fly into such rages that he threw himself on his knees in the paddock and tore at the grass with his teeth. Whatever Red was telling them they thought it very funny, for the photographer caught them romping hilariously around their "old man."

For ten years Miss Daingerfield managed Man o' War, the ten years in which he made his greatest record as a sire. Then she retired and turned the management over to Harrie Scott. The foals that came later did little to enhance Red's reputation, with the exception of War Admiral whom many fans rate his greatest son. This brown colt, born to the Sweep mare Brushup, was as unlike his father as a horse could be. Instead of being large-boned and a flashy chestnut, he was sleek, brown, moderate-sized and compactly built, the kind of horse that Colonel Bradley preferred above all others. In fact, the Colonel had been one of the detractors of the Fair Play line until he saw War Admiral, and then he liked the horse so well that he changed his mind. Like most of Man o' War's sons, War Admiral was slow in developing; he did nothing spectacular in his junior year, but as a three-year-old he won the triple crown and brought new glory to the Riddle stable.

When he retired to stud he inherited the honor stall next to that of Man o' War.

Big Red was seventeen in 1934 when he sired War Admiral; he had been in stud for fourteen years, far longer than most stallions, but he showed no signs of age, and a stallion is fertile as long as he is healthy. Three years later a ripple in his tranquil life was his mating with C. V. Whitney's great mare Top Flight. She had been the leading two-year-old winner of 1931 and had come home with $219,000, a record that was high for two decades.

The sports writers advertised this as "the mating of the ages." One newspaper held a contest to pick the best name for the foal, and finally awarded the prize to the reader who suggested "Sky Raider." A year later the colt was born, a fine, healthy youngster. In the spring of 1940 he got to the races and the fans expected a miracle. Sky Raider started well, he won his first two races, and then he came down with a chronic misery of the feet and was retired to stud, blushing furiously. He might have been a great horse, but no one would ever know. It was a sorry anticlimax.

But life at Faraway Farm was not too much ruffled by the ups and downs of Man o' War's children. The event that affected Big Red personally was not the winnings of War Admiral or the failure of Sky Raider but the coming of Will Harbut to the stallion barn. When Miss Daingerfield retired to Haylands she took with her Buck, the groom of the famous Keene stallions, and Harbut took his place. He was a plump, quiet, uneducated groom with a toothy smile, a way with horses, and an unsuspected histrionic talent that was to make him through the years almost as famous as Man o' War himself. It was Will who opened the gates to visitors at nine o'clock and closed them at four. Where his charge was concerned he was adamant—to him four o'clock meant four

136

o'clock and not a minute after. He closed the gates and kept them closed even in the face of the wife of the Secretary of the Treasury, who explained hopefully that she had missed a train and anyway she was only five minutes late.

With the more general use of automobiles the crowds of visitors increased. No one ever will know how many they were. They filled great guest book after guest book, but even if the signatures in these were counted they would mean nothing, for many of his guests forgot to register. Red probably had the world's most famous autograph books. Among the signatures are those of princes and ambassadors sandwiched between thousands of nobodies. Every day, rain or wind or snow, they came out, chiefly in the spring and summer; a continual stream of them, alone or in parties or specially invited guests of Mr. Riddle.

Will Harbut was guide and entrepreneur and he had a strong sense of drama. Always he worked toward a climax. It was impossible to go to Faraway Farm and see only Man o' War. First Will conducted the visitors to the other three stallion stalls. The occupants changed through the years, Golden Broom, American Flag, Crusader, Mars, Boatswain, War Admiral, and War Relic—Man o' War outlived most of his children. Harbut would point them out one by one and chant their records, building up to the high climax, the giant flame-colored horse in the fourth stall. Before it Harbut would straighten himself like a courtier about to enter the royal presence. His knotty hand flicked bits of straw from his clothes, then it swung wide the gate.

"And here he is," he would say, "Man o' War (he always pronounced it 'Mannie Wah') himself."

Man o' War would walk majestically to the door, nuzzle the shoulder of his friend, and look over the throng with his deep, intelligent eyes. His pose was regal and his glance a trifle bored; he had heard Will's spiel so many hundred times. Once in a great while he stepped out of his role and jabbed at Will playfully with his nose. Will would pretend not to notice this lapse from majesty.

"This is Mannie Wah." Will savoured the words as they rolled off his tongue. "Stand still, Red. No, M'am, I'm sorry, but I can't give you no hairs out of his tail." Then he would plunge into his spiel, varying it according to his audience. He was a shrewd judge of people, and if he saw that Red's visitors were just curious sightseers to whom a mile in 1:36 meant nothing more than a figure in arithmetic he would skimp his talk, but when he felt that his audience was composed of true horse lovers he gave them his longer treatment. It went something like this, although each listener reported his own version.

"He was folded right over there at Major Belmont's farm and Mr. Riddle bought him for five thousand dollars. Few years ago a man offered Mr. Riddle a million dollars for him and Mr. Riddle say 'No.' Say any man could have a million dollars, but only one man could have Mannie Wah.

"He ran twenty-one races and he win 'em all but one, an dat time they had him turned sideways at the start and he couldn't quite catch the one that beat him. But he whipped him good every other time they met. Look at the way he stands. He knows who he is all right."

Then followed an account of Red's triumphs, varied according to the audience, winding up with: "He broke down all the records and he broke down all the horses and there was nothing for Mr. Riddle to do but retire him."

Will had Man o' War's stud record down pat also, touched up only a little here and there for the sake of drama. Of his accomplishments as a sire, his son War Admiral was in Will's eyes the best.

"He won most all the races his daddy won. In the Preakness he went wide and let Pompoon run up to him, den he looked over Pompoon and he said, 'Pompoon, my daddy broke John P. Grier's heart—Come *on!*

"1938 was a great year for Mannie Wah. His son Battleship won de Gran' National in England and his son Blockade was de best timber hoss—he won de hunt cup up in Maryland.

"Yes, sah, Mannie Wah broke all the records and he broke down all the horses. He's got everything a horse ought to have and he's got it where a hoss ought to have it. He is de mostest hoss!"

Yes, Red was the "mostest hoss." Will Harbut's phrase remains the most perfect tribute to his sovereignty. When the old groom rolled it from his tongue and looked at Red with loving, reverent eyes, the visitors stood entranced.

As time passed and the affection between Harbut and Man o' War deepened, he became as great an attraction at Faraway Farm as Man o' War himself. People came just to listen to him. When Will really gave them his lengthy treatment they went away bemused. Once Lord Halifax, then British Ambassador, listened to him spellbound for twenty minutes. Will had been bribed to outdo himself and he found it easy before such an appreciative audience. After he had finished, Lord Halifax exclaimed, "It was worth coming halfway around the world to hear that." Even discounting the diplomatic language, it was clear the Ambassador was impressed.

In all these years Red never let his friend Will Harbut down by being too tired or ill to pose for his admirers, except once in 1936 when he went off his feed for a little while and the gates of Faraway Farm were closed while the veterinarian fixed Red's teeth. Harbut fussed over the horse as though he were having a major operation and did not wipe the cloud from his face until Red was champing his oats again and pursuing each last grain as though his tongue were a vacuum cleaner.

On Red's twenty-first birthday he was a hale and hearty middle-aged gentleman comparable to a human of sixty-five. To celebrate the occasion Mr. Riddle gave a birthday party. Most of the sports world was there, Clem McCarthy broadcast the event over a coast-to-coast network, and distinguished guests sipped Mr. Riddle's champagne while they recalled the exploits of Man o' War. Kentucky's governor, "Happy" Chandler, commented that at last Man o' War was old enough to vote. No one, man or horse, interested the governor, he said, until they reached that interesting age.

The boards of managers of the race tracks on which he had shattered so many records, Belmont and Arlington and Pimlico, sent birthday cakes of grain and carrots. Red was given a bite and a sniff of the champagne in which they were toasting him, but otherwise the party meant nothing to him. As Joe Palmer, then managing editor of *The Blood Horse,* remarked, Red probably would have preferred to invite a few horses.

They were a heart-warming sight, Mr. Riddle, the gracious old sportsman, an octogenerian then, drinking champagne to the proud old stallion who had conferred on him the assurance of immortality. Everyone who toasted Big Red knew that as long as Man o' War's name was green in the history of American racing, so long would posterity remember the man who took a chance with him as a yearling and developed him into the greatest race horse of this or any other day. As he stood in the verandah looking over his wine glass to the hillside where Man o' War's grandchildren played, he told his friends that owning Man o' War was the greatest thrill of his life.

After the party Mr. Riddle did not come as often to Far-away Farm. He was old and tired and the journey took too much energy. Nor did Red ever leave these Kentucky acres. Once when Mrs. Riddle was very ill at Glen Riddle, her husband asked her if she would like to see Man o' War once more, but she shook her head. The horse was old too, she said, and the journey might not be good for him. So Red never again nuzzled the gentle hand that gave him sugar or heard the gay voice that used to tell him what a handsome fellow he was. Red too was an octogenarian counting in human terms. He had outlived most of his children and almost all of his contemporaries. Major Treat was gone. Farm managers came and went; only Will Harbut remained, and he was rheumatic in the knees. Mr. Riddle was so confident that Big Red would outlive him that he set up a trust fund for the sturdy old fellow.

In these later years the character of Red's visitors changed; there were not so many who told Will Harbut how they made a tidy sum the day Red won the Preakness or how they heeded Jim Rowe's boast and lost on the Travers. Now many of the visitors were youngsters who had been crawling about the floor in rompers when Red's pounding hoofs cut the tracks. To them Red was a legend, a monument, a part of American history. This was especially true during the second World War when thousands of soldiers in uniform came out to Faraway from the nearby camps. Not one of them had lived long enough to watch him race, but they wanted to see the "greatest horse that ever lived."

And they were not disappointed in Red. He came to the stall door as he always had, statuesque, magnificent, his coat a little duller perhaps than it had been twenty years ago and his mane and tail a bit faded. His sharp ears pricked when he heard their voices, but he did not see them, his eyes were fixed at something far beyond as though he were lost in memory—or expectation.

Will Harbut went into his spiel, but he was tired now, and did not dwell quite so long on Man o' War's record or the accomplishments of his children. But his old eyes still gleamed when he reached the peroration, "He's got everything a hoss ought to have and he's got it where a hoss ought to have it. He is de mostest hoss!"

Chapter XVII

As MAN O' WAR lived for four years after his last foals were born, his record was singularly complete. His sons and daughters all had gone out to try their fortunes, and their winnings had been chalked up in racing history. His first five crops were his best and, contrary to tradition, his second was better than his first; breeders usually like to send their mares to a stallion during his first season. In almost a quarter of a century at stud Man o' War sired 379 foals who lived to be named, and of these fifteen won high distinction and sixty-one were stakes winners.

Of the first crop the most promising was American Flag, the bright chestnut who was the "spitting image" of his father. After winning the Bayside Handicap, American Flag followed in his father's footsteps by winning the Withers and the Dwyer; then, just as the racing fans were beginning to accept him as the second Man o' War, accidents began to plague him. He managed to get through his second year with a banged-up knee and spreading forefoot, and before he retired in the middle of his fourth year, hopelessly crippled for racing, he gave one last dramatic exhibition of courage by running second in the Suburban to Man o' War's younger

143

son, Crusader. He was retired to Kentucky, where he inherited
the stall in the Riddle stallion barn next to Man o' War. When
the two of them stuck their heads out of the stall doors, one
could scarcely tell them apart. In the paddocks where they
raced together Big Red seemed as young and high spirited
as his son.

Until his death in 1942 American Flag was the second
attraction at Faraway Farm. As guests were led in front of the
stalls they came to him first and for a minute they thought
they were in the presence of Man o' War. Like his father,
American Flag stood high on the sire list. His greatest son
was hard-working Gusto and his outstanding daughter the
fine mare, Nellie Flag.

It was a long time between the day that Man o' War saw
his great son of the second crop, Crusader, shipped to Glen
Riddle to learn his racing lessons, and the day that he came
back to Faraway Farm covered with glory. Crusader also was
a chestnut, out of a daughter of Star Shoot, the sire of Sir
Barton and the greatest brood mare sire of his day. Crusader
was not outstanding as a two-year-old, so no one paid much
heed to him as he entered his third season; the drums were
beating for the brilliant Pompey, Display, and Mars, another
son of Man o' War from another daughter of Star Shoot. But
Crusader soon sprang into the limelight when he ran second
in the Withers, took the Suburban from American Flag, won
the Belmont, the Dwyer, and the Jockey Club Gold Cup.

On the same afternoon that Crusader won the Gold Cup,
Scapa Flow, a two-year-old son of Man o' War and Florence
Webber, won the Futurity for Walter Jeffords. It was a great
moment for Mr. Riddle. To see two of Man o' War's children
win on the same day, each a potential champion, was a thrill
to warm the heart of any breeder. Mr. Riddle always believed
that Scapa Flow would have been the greatest of Man o' War's

sons, but the horse was dogged with misfortune. He suffered a severe injury, was never able to accomplish anything at three, and had to be destroyed the year after.

Meanwhile, Crusader piled up his winnings, the Havre de Grace Handicap, the Maryland Handicap, the first running of the Riggs Memorial. At four he won the Suburban Handicap a second time, a feat never duplicated before or since. He was also to "double" the Brooklyn Handicap, but at the start was kicked so severely by Peanuts that he could barely finish the course. Although he did come back and win three out of five starts later in the autumn, the kick had finished him. He retired with a purse of $203,361, no mean sum in those days when a hundred-thousand-dollar horse was exceptional.

Crusader also returned to Faraway Farm and inherited the third stall next to his father and American Flag. At stud he gave his father no such competition as he had as a racer. Many an expert has made a sound case for Crusader against not only the record of Big Red but of every other American three-year-old. Most of them agree that he is in the company of his father, Sysonby, Sir Barton, Blue Larkspur, Gallant Fox, Twenty Grand, War Admiral, Whirlaway, and Citation.

Mars, the second son of the crop, was, like Crusader, from a Star Shoot mare. He was a small horse who won his races the hard way and never learned to get off fast enough to avoid his larger opponents. Despite these handicaps he won $128,-786, but when he came home to Man o' War and Faraway he was an abysmal failure as a sire, partly, no doubt, because the other four stallions were given the choice of mares. The three fillies, Corvette, Edith Cavell, and Taps, all of this same crop, brought home handsome purses. Edith Cavell even had the temerity to take the Pimlico cup from Crusader.

The star of the third crop was tragic Scapa Flow, along with five stakes winners and fourteen fillies that were to make

Man o' War one of the leading brood mare sires of all time. The fourth crop starred Bateau, a filly who won the Suburban Handicap, making the third time the get of Man o' War had won it in four years. In the fifth group came Clyde van Dusen, the first of Man o' War's get to win the Kentucky Derby.

These were the great years. During them Man o' War produced four "hundred-thousand-dollar" horses, a remarkable achievement when one considers that in 1928, when Clyde van Dusen brought home $122,452, only sixty hundred-thousand dollar horses were recorded in the American turf.

After 1926 Man o' War's record began to fall off. During the next five, his get (exactly the same number of named foals) included exactly half as many stakes winners and after that the number fell even lower. But among the later foals two or three stand out. Battleship, born in 1927, was perhaps the most versatile of Red's sons. The horse, a courageous and comparatively tiny chestnut, won high honors for his owner, Mrs. Marion du Pont Scott. First he was a stakes winner on the flat, winning among other races the Grand National at Belmont, and then he was entered in the Eastern Hunt Club meetings, where he made a brilliant record and at the same time became an outstanding steeplechaser on the big tracks. When he was nine years old he was sent to England and two years later won the most coveted of all steeplechase races, the Grand National at Aintree.

Another son of Man o' War, Holystone, one of the handsomest of the lot, was unlucky on the track—he won only one race—but he became outstanding as a show horse. Of the racers, War Hero and Boatswain were good, but Boatswain started in only six races.

1934 was Man o' War's comeback year, the birth year of War Admiral, the excellent filly Wand, and three other stakes winners. War Admiral, the brown colt born to the Sweep mare, Brushup, was not typical of Man o' War's sons, not a large-boned, bright and shining chestnut but medium-sized, beautiful, smooth and dark. Colonel Bradley fell in love with the horse and tried to buy him for he considered War Admiral his ideal of a race horse, but when Mr. Riddle declined to sell, the Colonel booked half a dozen of his best mares to War Admiral for the first stud season.

But before he was to retire to Faraway Farm, War Admiral had his record to win, a record that was to rank him with Crusader as the best of Man o' War's sons. You can choose Crusader or you can take War Admiral, no matter which one, and you can produce proof to support your claim. Like most of the sons of Man o' War, War Admiral did not shine in his juvenile year, bringing back a purse of only $14,800 as against $82,260 won by Pompoon, the champion two-year-old of the year. But as a three-year-old he was a different horse. After he romped to a six-length win in the Chesapeake, Mr. Riddle decided to enter him in the Kentucky Derby, which he won easily from the favorite, Pompoon. He triumphed in the Preakness and then a week later he won the triple crown at Belmont, being the fourth to win it, following Sir Barton, Gallant Fox, and Omaha. But when he returned to the winner's circle at Belmont he left a trail of blood all the way from the starting gate. He had run the race with a deep and painful ankle cut.

During the rest of his third year and his fourth, War Admiral won a succession of victories: the Pimlico Special, the Widener Handicap, the Wilson Mile at Saratoga, the Saratoga Handicap, the Whitney Stakes, the Jockey Club Gold Cup. By this time there was a clamor for him to meet Seabiscuit, a grandson of Man o' War through Hard Tack, who had been making sensational history. A match race was arranged at Pimlico with a $15,000 purse for the winner. This match also was going to be one of the "races of the ages."

The Pimlico track was jammed to capacity that November afternoon. War Admiral was a 1-4 choice with Seabiscuit getting strong support at 11-5. The dopesters were sure that Charley Kurtsinger, who was War Admiral's regular jockey, would set a blistering pace, with Georgie Woolf, a famous hot spot rider, on Seabiscuit, "roaring through the stretch." Seabiscuit was a famous last quarter runner.

When the two took off on a walk-up start, Seabiscuit went immediately to the front. The crowd was puzzled, they had not expected Woolf to try to set the pace. Nor had he, but War Admiral just didn't want to run that day. Seabiscuit, running easily, increased his lead to four lengths, but War Admiral didn't care, and refused to put up any competition. Seabiscuit's time was 1:56⅗, a record for the track and equalled only by Twilight Tear in 1944. With War Admiral's acquiescence he became the greatest money winner up to that time. And, like his grandfather, he had the personality that should, but so often does not, accompany greatness. His memory remained so bright with racing fans that in 1941 he was honored by a bronze statue in Santa Anita Park. He came out of retirement to attend and his admirers, who had never forgotten him, flocked to do him honor.

War Admiral was not so great a money winner as Seabiscuit, but he won two sparkling victories before he finally went out of training. He had won twenty-one starts out of twenty-six and failed to make the winner's circle only twice in twenty starts as a mature horse.

Back at Faraway Farm, War Admiral took his stall in the line of champions, fourth from the "old man." As a sire he was outstanding, rivalling the record of his father's earlier years. Among his most brilliant children were War Jeep, War Date, Wee Admiral, Bric-a-brac, the great mare Busher, her brother, Mr. Busher, Blue Peter, and the large, rangy mare, Bee Mac, who did much to bring back the popularity of the Fair Play line. War Admiral was the first of Man o' War's sons to be offered at stud with a wide open book and consequently had the advantage of servicing the best mares of many successful breeders. In 1945, four years after he retired to stud, he led the list of American sires.

Man o' War was sixteen when he sired War Admiral. He had been in stud for thirteen years, longer by far than most stallions, but he was in excellent condition, and one must look for some other reason for the fact that of the last nine crops of foals he produced nothing of distinction except War Relic. Most authorities agree that the explanation lies in the mediocre quality of the mares with which Faraway Farm was restocked. As he serviced few outside mares he was restricted to these indifferent ones. Even when a stud boasts mares of highest quality, one farm cannot furnish enough first-class ones for a stallion. The last seven years of Man o' War's life he was bred to no more than a dozen mares which had previously distinguished themselves either on the track or by their foals by other sires. Most of the leading stallions of Red's time were bred to more distinguished mares in one season than Man o' War covered in a decade.

Man o' War was a great sire in spite of handicaps. The record of a horse's offspring, according to Mr. J. A. Estes of *The Blood Horse*, "is a record not only of his genetic worth but of a thousand other scattered and unmeasurable influences. In the first place the dam of each foal will have as much influence genetically as the sire, and will have an added influence through her contributions to its nutrition and environment. Beyond that, soil, feeding, training, the conditions made by racing secretaries, the natural hazards of accident and mortality and all other things must be accounted for—or rather unaccounted for. In some of these Man o' War was not especially favored. His later years were all but wasted through careful selection of undistinguished mates for him."

In the yearling sales Man o' War did not make an impressive showing. His first yearling to be offered at auction was Siren, a filly of the second crop for whom Harry R. Sinclair paid $8,000. That was in 1925 before any of Man o' War's get had reached the race tracks. The next year, four days after American Flag had won his maiden race at Saratoga, Admiral Cary T. Grayson, a popular racing fan, sold a filly of Man o' War for $50,000. Tuscan Red, the dam, was not distinguished either as to performance or pedigree, but the filly was such a magnificent looking creature and the prestige of her father was so great that she topped all prices for American auction sales of yearlings. Two others brought $16,000 and $27,225 respectively, and during the next four years five yearlings who reached the auctions brought an average of $31,562.50, but only one of them earned the purchase price.

After that Man o' War's yearlings lost their popularity and the next seven, none of them out of distinguished dams, averaged slightly over $21,000 each. In 1936 Mr. Riddle sold his yearling crop at Saratoga, seventeen of them. One brought $18,000 and another $9,000, but only one of the seventeen won above $5,000. All in all, the forty-five yearlings by Man o' War that reached the auction sales averaged about $9,000 and earned about $4,500.

These figures are an excellent example of how deceptive statistics can be. Looking at them one would be inclined to write Man o' War off as a comparative failure, when actually he was an outstanding success. Although he headed the sire list only once, in 1926, he was unlucky in the rules of the racing secretaries, who rate the sire list quantitatively according to the largest representation instead of the highest averages. Man o' War was never a big producer, he was never bred to more than twenty-five mares a season, and yet, in spite of his small number of offspring, by 1945 his get had earned more money than those of any other sire, living or dead.

In his stud career as in his racing history, Man o' War was a breaker of precedents. The breeding pundits never could predict with any degree of accuracy the value of his get. The old and trusted rule is that you can get good racers only if you breed to a good sire mares of fine quality. Yet daughters of Man o' War who have been utterly worthless on the race track have been fine producers at stud. Indeed, there seems to be no rhyme nor reason to them. Stakes winners, winners, non-winners, and mares who have never raced at all have produced roughly an equal proportion of stakes winners. None of Man o' War's best daughters had many foals, some of them none, most of them one or two, and yet his stakes winning daughters have produced thirteen per cent stakes winners, which, as all students of racing percentages know, is a high percentage. One of his best daughters, Valkyr, although she herself is not a stakes winner, is the mother of four who are. As Andy Joiner, the veteran trainer, exclaimed, shrugging his expressive shoulders, "Man o' War's mares are a law unto themselves."

So, although Man o' War lived to see his own personal record as a sire fairly well completed, his record in the broad sense is not finished, if, indeed it ever will be. In spite of the increasing number of outstanding stallions that are being imported from Europe, Big Red's name appears in ever larger numbers of our American pedigrees. As J. A. Estes says, "his was probably the most powerful single genetic influence of the century in thoroughbred breeding."

Chapter XVIII

THE YEARS CLOSED in on Man o' War, but he scorned them. At twenty-four and twenty-five, almost an octogenarian by human standards, he still wanted to run when he saw the other stallions streaking across the pastures. While his blazing speed was gone, his hoofs still chopped out great chunks of sod that spattered behind him as he raced the youngsters. But the strain was too much for his heart. When the others were let out, Will Harbut shut Red in his stall and reasoned with him, urging him to remember that he was no colt and had no business "running with them young hosses."

In 1943 when he was twenty-six years old, Red had a heart attack and was retired from stud. Faraway Farm was living on gilded memories, for there was no other to take Red's place. One by one his sons had died, American Flag and Crusader. Only War Admiral and War Relic remained in the stall beside him. Man o' War's vitality was so superb that he seemed indestructible. He had outlived all his contemporaries, Sir Barton, Exterminator, John P. Grier, Upset, Paul Jones, and Wildair. He was the oldest thoroughbred on record.

However, time was short now and not even Red could live forever, so Mr. Riddle commissioned the eminent animal sculptor, Herbert Haseltine, to do a heroic statue of Man o' War to stand as a monument above his grave. The grave itself was to be in a memorial plot in Red's old paddock, a little island surrounded by a moat in the center of which was to be placed the bronze statue of the champion. Mr. Haseltine went to Lexington, and Red posed for the statue. Although he could no longer cut the breeze with his old speed, when he stood in repose he did not show his years. His superb frame had not drooped and telescoped from weakness, the slight dip in the back had deepened a trifle; his muscles had not grown flabby for they still swept powerfully beneath the coat that was a little lighter than it used to be—you could scarcely tell whether it was red or yellow. He still had the high head, the imperial air, the look of mastery.

The sculptor completed the model, which was to be enlarged and cast, and it had not been finished when Man o' War had a sharp attack of colic. This was his fourth, the other three he had beaten off, but now his gallant old heart was tired, and he missed Will Harbut, who himself had been stricken with a heart attack in the spring of 1947. Will no longer was able to come to the stable and adorn the horse's history with his brilliant and reverent imagination; but he had no rival, no other groom attempted to tell the saga of "de mostest hoss."

That spring Mr. Riddle had closed the gates of Faraway Farm to visitors; the stream of admirers who had been coming to view Red daily for a quarter of a century were beginning to tire the aged prince.

In the twenty-six years that he had been on view at Faraway more than a half million people had signed his guest book; and these were only a fraction, for most of them were so enthralled by Will Harbut's story that they forgot to sign. They had come and they had gone, stenographers and clerks, delegations of South American army officers, European celeb-

153

rities. For distinguished visitors Will Harbut had led Man o' War out of his stall, but now the horse stayed alone in his big stable or sunned himself quietly in his paddock.

On October third Will Harbut died. A month later Red suffered a fifth attack of colic and this time he could not fight it off. Always he had fought pain as if it was something live and hostile that he could stamp out of his way, but this time he could only lie on the floor of the stall and thrash in suffering. The veterinarian eased his last days with sedatives—it was all he could do for Red. A few minutes after noon on Saturday, November 1, 1947 he died. After the embalmer had prepared his body—for it would take three days to construct the grave—he was laid in a huge oak box that stood in state in the hallway of the stable where so many guests had paid him homage.

On the following Tuesday afternoon a crane swung Man o' War's coffin into the grave that had been dug at the foot of the concrete base for the statue. It was a crisp and chilly afternoon, the staff of Faraway Farm and a few friends stood about the monument heaped with flowers, the great granite slab with Man o' War's name on it, and held a quiet ceremony, one of the most impressive services that ever had honored the memory of a horse.

Man o' War was dead, but the fact that his body lay under a granite slab in a Kentucky pasture made little difference. He already had become a legend, a part of the folk history of great Americans. Millions of people remembered him, some of them had patted his neck at Faraway Farm or could tell you about the wen on his shoulder, others had seen him spurting like a flame down the stretch at Belmont or Saratoga, and still others had only read about his flashing speed and his red gold coat, but to every one of us he was the great Red whose like we shall never see again.

AS A 21-YEAR-OLD WITH HIS FAMOUS GROOM, WILL HARBUT

STATUE OF MAN O' WAR OVER HIS GRAVE AT LEXINGTON, KENTUCKY

Nor have we. In the last quarter century many brilliant horses have lowered records and made track history, but not one of them has touched the imagination as did Man o' War. Not only in the minds of racing fans and the generality of us does Red still reign supreme, but also among such hard-headed realists as the sports writers and broadcasters. In the Associated Press Mid-Century poll to determine the greatest thoroughbred since 1900 they cast 305 votes for Man o' War out of a total of 388. Man o' War finished far ahead of his closest rival, Citation, who received thirty-eight votes. Only twelve horses were listed among the immortals. Whirlaway received fifteen votes, and Man o' War's grandson, Seabiscuit, twelve. Plucky old Exterminator won six votes, Dan Patch the pacer, five, and War Admiral, four. One each went to Equipoise, Assault, Protector, Roseben, and Gallant Fox.

Why should Man o' War win with such a broad margin over Citation, who won more than three times as much money as well as the triple crown and runaway victories in the Sysonby Mile, the Jockey Club Gold Cup, and the International Gold Cup, feats to give any horse immortality? And why should Stymie, then the greatest money winner in the world, fail to get a single vote? The answer lies in the intangible but none the less dynamic force of personality. Man o' War gave those who saw him an exaltation that lifted them out of the humdrum everyday and made them for that moment peers of gods and giants. Watching him, they felt that they were touching an elemental force and the vibration made their eyes shine brighter and their hearts beat faster. Some men call it one thing, some another, but, whatever they name it, the word will be a synonym for a touch of greatness.

The summers glide quietly over the Kentucky pastures, visitors still come to look at the great bronze statue of Man o' War, but their eyes are likely to wander to the woolly foals nibbling in the pastures. If every foal wore his pedigree tied around his neck, they would find a descendant of Man o' War on almost every blue grass hill, for the blood of Big Red flows in a large proportion of American thorough-breds. Perhaps one of these rusty colts with his head held high and his long legs bounding uncertainly across the sod will bring back the glory of the greatest horse America has ever seen.

≫≫≫≫≫≫≫≫≫ *APPENDIX* ≫≫≫≫≫≫≫≫≫

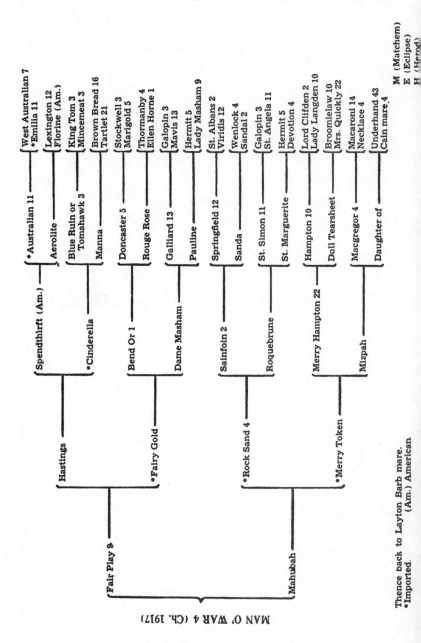

MAN O' WAR 4 (Ch. 1917)

M (Matchem)
E (Eclipse)
H (Herod)

Thence back to Layton Barb mare.
*Imported.   (Am.) American

MAN O' WAR'S FAMILY

THE SIRES

THE FULL STORY of Man o' War's family has never before been published in one concise document. The information has existed, but has been difficult to gather. Much of it comes from the browned and fragile pages of ancient English record books, some of them contradictory and inaccurate, and many of them incomplete. Thanks to the *Racing Calendar*, first published in 1727, and the *General Stud Book*, first printed in 1793, and to the present-day successors of these two ancient record books, it is possible to trace the ancestry of the modern racing horse back through more than twenty generations.

A horse's future is forecast, before his conception, on this ancestry; after he has passed on to history, he is judged by the influence of the blood he has left to his family tree. The study of Man o' War's ancestry, the factors which made him what he was, can neither be presented nor understood without emphasizing the primary fact that all thoroughbred horses descend from only three original males, and no more than sixty foundation mares. That they are intensely inbred, therefore, is obvious, and also fortunate; otherwise there could be no logical or clear-cut study of breeding, and no conclusions could be drawn for future experiment.

If Man o' War's pedigree were to be written out all the way back on his "tail-male" or paternal side to the Godolphin Arabian, and on his maternal side to the Layton Barb mare, it would contain the names of the same ancestors, not in hundreds but in thousands of steps on the ladders, although Man o' War was only the fifteenth generation removed from the Godolphin Arabian on the male side, and twenty-two generations away from the Layton Barb mare on the maternal.

In 1689, at the Battle of the Boyne in Ireland, a stallion was ridden by Captain Robert Byerley, of Goldborough Hall, York, Eng-

159

land, which escaped unhurt, returned home with his owner, and became known as the Byerley Turk. He is the first recorded sire of the entire thoroughbred world, an Adam of the kingdom of the horse.

The second father of the realm arrived in England direct from Arabia in 1706 and was known thereafter as the Darley Arabian. Both served well the small group of about forty Arabian and Turkish mares then living in England, and passed on to restful pastures before the Godolphin Arabian appeared.

(GODOLPHIN ARABIAN) Where the Godolphin was foaled no one knows. It may have been in Arabia, or Turkey, or some spot in the desert, or even in France—which is most probable, as it is there he makes his first recorded appearance in a tragic, brutal scene which opens his story with a true rags-to-riches flavor.

One spring day in Paris in 1728 a crowd gathered around a heavy wagon whose driver was lashing blows on a defiant horse hitched between the shafts. Despite the cruel abuse, the horse was not giving in even a little, but, with ears pinned back, eyes flashing hatred, was trying to grab the tormenter with his teeth and reduce the cart to kindling wood with his heels. A beautiful horse, sleekly brown, richly dappled, with two white stockings on the hind legs, he is regal in his wrath. Finally, when he slips to the pavement for more punishment from the brutal master, a visiting Englishman steps from the crowd and stops the inhuman scene. Then he purchases the battered, but still defiant, stallion from the heartless owner.

The Englishman's name is Mr. Coke. Only that—and although he was responsible for saving from oblivion this horse which would be known through all history as the Godolphin Arabian, history cannot guarantee which Mr. Coke he was. Almost certainly, though, he was a member of the eminent Cokes of Norfolk, and probably he was the same Coke who had bought, forty-three years before, a twenty-year-old Barb mare from the estate of Charles II for the sum of forty guineas. This mare is important to our history because when she arrived in England she foaled the colt called Dodsworth, who sired, by the Layton Barb mare, the founder of the maternal family of Man o' War. Thus, if deductions and sketchy records bring the true conclusion, Mr. Coke owned both the original father and mother of the two million "crosses" which would result in Man o' War.

After the rescued horse had been returned to England and regained his health under kind handling, Mr. Coke realized that he had no particular use for the handsome stallion. For Mr. Coke was a racing man, not a breeder, and, even if he had been the latter, he would have sent his mares to the fashionable sires of the moment.

So the still unheralded horse was turned over to Roger Williams, proprietor of St. James' Coffee House in London where turfmen gathered, and from there the horse went, possibly as a gift, to Lord Godolphin, who sent him to his stud farm at Gogmagog near Newmarket to become a "trial-horse" for the mighty stallion, Hobgoblin, a grandson of the Darley Arabian.

There the Parisian refugee might have lived out his years in complete obscurity had not the good race mare Roxanna been scorned by the haughty Hobgoblin and been mated with the trial-horse because there was nothing else to do at the moment if Roxanna were to foal the next spring. The result of this mating, a colt, was called Lath. Three years later he became the best race horse in England, and immediately the neglected, humiliated hero of the episode in Paris became the Godolphin Arabian, successor to Hobgoblin as sultan of the Gogmagog stud farm.

Before Lath became famous, Roxanna was again bred to the Godolphin, produced still another colt, and died within a few days. The last colt was called Cade, an old English slang word meaning a motherless animal raised as a pet; in Yorkshire dialect it designated a spoiled child. Cade would carry on the golden blood for the next generation.

Further checking into this brief story of the Godolphin Arabian gives evidence that he may have been a Barb rather than an Arab; that he may never have actually left the ownership of Mr. Coke; that he may have been farmed out to Lord Godolphin's stud; and that Roxanna may also have been Coke's property. Of prime importance, though, is that Roxanna and the Parisian unknown did meet and did produce Cade.

The Godolphin Arabian came upon the scene when the Byerley Turk and the Darley Arabian had finished their stud careers, and from the least advantageous start as a sire forged his way to the top of the list over the fashionable sons and grandsons of those two founding fathers. His blood has been the fountain of life to most of

161

the great horses of history; his name is crossed many times into each of the top families. Until his death in 1753, when he was given a public funeral in his thirtieth year, he forced his way to the list of immortals through character and merit.

American thoroughbred families trace back to the Godolphin since 1751 when the mare Selima, his daughter, was imported by Colonel Tasker to Maryland, where she became the first queen of the Colonial turf and later the most potent maternal influence in the American Stud Book. Two grandsons of the Godolphin, called Janus and Fearnought, came to America in 1757 and 1764, and were credited with producing the finest horses before Revolutionary days. Of the thirty-eight sires and twenty-one mares named by the Hon. Fairfax Harrison as being the cornerstones of the Virginia thorough-breds of today, eleven stallions and seven of the mares were direct descendants of the Godolphin.

(CADE) Cade, the dark bay son of the brown Godolphin Arabian, amounted to little as a race horse, plodding in the background while his full brother Lath became the fastest horse in England. Cade won the King's Plate at Newmarket in 1740, but otherwise his racing career deserved but casual mention. However, as has happened many times, when the two brothers retired to their stud careers it was Cade, not Lath, who wrote his name deep in the history of the thoroughbred. He was retired permanently to stud as the property of Thomas Meredith, one of the most extensive breeders in Yorkshire, the heart of the English breeding country. When, at eighteen, in 1752, he became the leading sire of England with winners of seventeen races, his fee was doubled to "10 guineas, plus a half-crown to the groom." The next year Cade again led the list of winners with twenty-six; and the following year was second with twenty to his paternal half-brother, Regulus, who scored with twenty-four.

Cade died in 1756 at the age of twenty-two, and the next year eight of his sons were advertised extensively for stud service in a rush to take over the popularity of their sire. The best was the brown-bay called Matchem, who was to become the only instrument through which the blood of the Godolphin would be carried on for the future. Cade was also the sire of many mares who proved invaluable in carrying on, and doubling back on, the glorious heritage.

Aside from Matchem, Cade produced one more son who should

162

be mentioned. He was called Warren's Sportsman, whose daughter, Sportsmistress, got the mighty horse with the strange name Pot-8-o's, the most influential son of Eclipse, whose direct descendants have won the English Derby more than a hundred times, with nearly seventy per cent of the winners tracing directly back to Pot-8-o's.

(MATCHEM) Matchem, a dark-bay horse with a barely noticeable star and the near-hind coronet white, had the length and height for true staying power. He, along with Herod and Eclipse, had been chosen by the fates to be the only three through which the blood of the original three sires of history would be carried on to the present.

This simple chart will show their relationship:

Godolphin Arab (1728) Byerley Turk (1689) Darley Arab (1706)
Matchem (1748)   Herod (1758)   Eclipse (1764)

While Herod was four generations removed from the Byerley Turk, and Eclipse the same distance on the chart from the Darley Arabian, Matchem was the grandson of the Godolphin and thus much closer to the foundation blood source.

Matchem, bred by John Holme of Carlisle, county of Cumberland, was a son of a mare known both as Changeling's Dam and the Sister to Miss Partner. He was sold at an early age to William Fenwick, a member of the fabulous family of Fenwick, whose name had been associated with royalty and racing for several centuries.

Matchem did not race until he was five, and retired in his tenth year. During his career he won eight contests, collected three other purses because no owner cared to run against him, and suffered only two defeats. Unlike the short-going horse of today, Matchem won his races in heats, or races, of four miles each, carrying up to 140 pounds. "Go the distance" really meant something in early racing history!

Then Matchem went to stud at ten to carry his marvelous potency into his thirty-second year, when he got a mare with foal only a few days before his death, which because of his fame is recorded even to the day of the week—Wednesday, February 21, 1781. During his stud career he had earned more than the equivalent of $85,000 in pounds sterling, a tremendous sum in those days, or even now except for a few outstanding sires.

Matchem's children, running on the English turf through twenty-three seasons, won 354 races and more than $750,000 in addition to

163

unrecorded "subscriptions," cups and plates of value unknown. His daughters, the finest family of brood mares of their age, are scattered everywhere through the pedigrees of the stars of racing heavens. On the male side, Matchem was the father of many great sons including Alfred, Chymist, Dux, Espersykes, Pantaloon, and many more. Best of all was Conductor, who would continue the tail-male parade.

Matchem, whose children were racing ten years before the get of Eclipse appeared, and seven years before Herod's family, suffers in cold figure comparison with these other two unless that time element is given its proper value. As in modern racing history, with purses eternally increasing, the value of a sire cannot be truly given without the realization of ballooning prizes for the same or less accomplishments.

Some of England's classics which still endure were first run in the twilight of Matchem's life while Eclipse and Herod were young in the stud. The St. Leger was started in 1776 when Matchem was twenty-eight; the Oaks in 1779, when he was thirty-one; the English Derby the next year when he was thirty-two. Despite this late start, Hollandaise, his daughter, won the second St. Leger; Teetotum, another daughter, got when he was twenty-eight, sped home first in the second Oaks, to show the extraordinary vigor of the aging Matchem.

To America through these years were migrating many members of the horse-loving Fenwicks of England. They scattered to Maryland and Virginia, Kentucky and the Carolinas. With them came other refugees from the family of Matchem. Edward Fenwick, founder of the John's Island Stud, on an island south of Charleston, South Carolina, and his son of the same name imported nine Godolphin family stallions to found their tribe of great horses in the southland. One called Matchless was the last son of the incomparable Matchem, and lived to the patriarchal age of thirty-four on John's Island. We shall meet their descendants later as the long trail of the Godolphin and Layton Barb essence finds its way to the heart of the long-legged foal of Mahubah who was known as Man o' War.

(CONDUCTOR) Conductor, the son of Matchem, was the first chestnut-colored horse in the tail-male line of Man o' War's family tree. Thus from the brown Godolphin Arabian, through the dark bay Cade, the bay Matchem, and the chestnut Conductor, we can com-

164

plete the color cycle with Trumpator, the son of Conductor, who was a pure black. There is no grey in the tail-male ladder of Man o' War, although there is some far back in Mahubah's line.

The records are more sketchy than usual on Conductor, who was foaled when his father Matchem was eighteen, in 1767 from an unnamed daughter of Snap. He was her first foal, and, strangely, although he was most prominent in both racing and breeding, there is no known picture existing of him today. The unnamed Snap mare, who must have been a chestnut, although there is no documentary evidence to prove it, was a most prolific and forceful fountain of good breeding. In twenty years she produced fifteen foals, eight by Matchem, all of them fine horses.

Conductor himself, owned by a Mr. Pratt through his racing career during which he was campaigned extensively and won ten races at distances from seven furlongs to more than four miles, went to stud as the prized stallion of the Earl of Clermont, a hard-drinking English horseman who was probably the model for the profligate Marquis of Steyne in Thackeray's classic *Vanity Fair*. Conductor stood at Chippenham for the Earl until death at twenty-three and sent out the winners of fifty-two races worth more than $100,000. His most successful matings were with the brown mare Brunette, the daughter of Squirrel. Their effort produced the black colt Trumpator, who would go down in history as the "King of the Blacks" although some experts have claimed that Trumpator's own son, Sorceror, deserves that designation more than his father.

(TRUMPATOR) Trumpator, who was to live for twenty-six years, remained always the property of the Earl of Clermont. He was the first black stallion of importance in the triumvirate families of Matchem, Eclipse, and Herod, and his color must have derived from the well-known affinity of chestnut for black, not from his ancestors. As mentioned before, his mother was a brown, the daughter of two bays. Trumpator raced at from two to five years of age, winning eleven and losing but four—all, incidentally, when he was three and all later avenged by beating those which had bested him. For twenty-one seasons he served faithfully and vigorously as a sire, being confined mostly to mares belonging to the Chippenham Stud of Lord Clermont. When he died on May 7, 1808, his offspring were credited with 207 wins worth about $325,000.

Trumpator was a smallish, compact black, recorded as being without a spot of white. His greatest son, who would carry on the Godolphin blood, was Sorceror, a gigantic—for the time—son from the daughter of Diomed named Young Giantess. Since then, all horses as well as all other scientifically bred animals have been increasing their average stature through selection, proper feeding, and medicinal advances.

To show how the Godolphin blood is already concentrating even in this fifth generation, Diomed's mother was Giantess, a daughter of Matchem, who was also Sorceror's great-grandsire on his paternal side. Further back in Giantess' pedigree she traced to an own sister to Roxanna, the Godolphin's "first wife," thereby lacing in another portion of the royal blood. Later Young Giantess produced the famous mare Eleanor, the first of her sex to win both the English Derby and the Oaks, and later to become the mother of Muley, whose sons, Leviathan and Margrave, had such a strong influence on the early American thoroughbred families.

(SORCEROR) Sir Thomas Charles Bunbury, who bred both Young Giantess and Sorceror, was the owner of Diomed, winner in 1780 of the first Derby. Diomed came to America when he was twenty-one years of age after leaving a trail of Derby winners, and proceeded to found a family which dominated the American turf for nearly a hundred years.

Besides Eleanor, a later son of Sorceror named Smolensko won both the Derby and the 2,000 Guineas for Sir Charles Bunbury, who had become the first dictator of the English turf.

Sir Charles, not with legal right but through his own forceful personality, inaugurated the racing of two-year-olds and partially discontinued the punishing system of running races in heats. He even went so far as to warn the Prince of Wales, later George IV, that steps would be taken if the Prince's horse, Escape, did not cease and desist from showing so many "startling reversals of form," as it is still politely called in racing circles to explain the sudden awakening of dazzling speed in a horse which has been running consistently badly.

Sorceror was a statuesque black horse standing more than sixteen hands high, which was tremendous in his time. He won fourteen races, was second five times, third and fourth once in twenty-one starts; sired the winners of more than $400,000 in 180 triumphs. Although his most famous racing son was Smolensko, Sorceror's sons and daughters spread the good blood in every country where the thoroughbred is known. Soothsayer won the St. Leger, sired Tiresias, a Derby winner, and Interpreter, winner of the 2,000 Guineas, and then departed to Russia to carry the blood to the country of the Czars. Through his daughter Gramarie, Sorceror sent his blood to two Derby winners; four French Derby winners; to the great French sire, Maintenon; to Germany and Austria in the renowned Gamiani and Taurus. And through the off-shoots the blood flowed down the ladder to return once more to Man o' War after being refined and sparked through a series of crosses.

(COMUS) Comus, the son of Sorceror, who occupies the next step down the tail-male ladder, was most appropriately named after the poem of the same name by Milton in which Comus was a sorcerer. Carrying on the poetic theme, he was bred by Sir John Shelley, a cousin of the immortal Percy Bysshe Shelley, only a few miles from the birthplace of the poet.

Once again, in the breeding of Comus we find a doubling back to the blood of Cade, son of the Godolphin Arabian. Comus' mother was Houghton Lass (dam also of Calchas, Caliban, Calypso, and Circe), a daughter of Sir Peter Teazle, who was in turn a son of Highflyer, the unbeaten son of Herod. From there he traced back to King Fergus, a son of Eclipse, and to Young Marske, a paternal half-brother of Eclipse, as well as to the daughter of Cade. The black color of Trumpator and Sorceror disappeared in this generation with Comus being a chestnut heavily flecked with black and white spots—a most unusual combination. He raced at three and four, winning eight starts and running an excellent third in the Derby of his year. Then Comus' eyes went bad, becoming completely white, probably from cataracts, and Sir John Shelley, fearing he might transmit this trait to his offspring, sold him to Mr. Christopher Wilson, later known as the "Father of the Turf." Later Comus was taken over by Sir Tatton Sykes and transferred to the Sledmore Stud, still one of the best known in all England.

Comus started his stud career sensationally in his sixth year of life. Bred to seventeen mares the first season, he was the father of seventeen when the next spring came around. Three of these (The

Marshall, Ranter, and Reveller) gave early polish to his record by running one-two-three in the St. Leger of 1818. Four years later he almost did it again when Violet, The Professor, and Corinthian ran two-three-four in the same race, beaten only by Theodore, the rankest possible outsider who started with odds of 200-1 against.

Like Matchem, his great-great-grandsire, Comus carried his potency late in life, for at twenty-six his union with an unnamed Cervantes mare produced a renowned grey called Grey Momus, of breathtaking beauty and heart-stopping speed. Among many other triumphs this brilliant horse won both the 2,000 Guineas and the Ascot Gold Cup in his third year, a feat not repeated in more than a century. Retired from racing, Grey Momus was sold to Germany.

Comus mares, as have those of all this grand family of the Godolphin Arabian, spread the good blood far and wide. His sons, with the exception of Reveller, Humphrey Clinker, and Grey Momus, who became obscure after his racing career, faded from history. Clinkerina, daughter of Sir Peter, and by Comus, the mother of Humphrey Clinker, was a remarkable brown mare who produced eighteen foals in nineteen years and "was shot January 26th, 1837, being barren and worn out," according to the *General Stud Book.*

Humphrey Clinker was her fourth and was the first of the Godolphin family to die at an early age (twelve) in a line which had already become remarkable for the longevity of each horse since the beginning. The Godolphin himself had lived to twenty-nine; Cade twenty-two; Matchem thirty-three; Conductor twenty-three; Trumpator twenty-six; Sorceror twenty-five; Comus would outlive his son by three years and pass on in his twenty-eighth.

(HUMPHREY CLINKER) Humphrey Clinker, a golden yellow bay, was a "roarer," which did not help him as a desirable stud, and there were moments in history when the glorious Godolphin blood might have died entirely except for the fortunate fact that before his untimely death Humphrey Clinker, with the help of a Cervantes mare—again unnamed, but not the mother of Grey Momus—produced the horse called Melbourne. Had Humphrey Clinker done nothing else, as some historians have claimed, this one act made him immortal.

Before leaving Humphrey's dam, the good Clinkerina, one must record that she, among her eighteen children, had one called Beaudesert, who in turn sired Belle Rose. This is important to America, for it was Belle Rose, imported by James R. Keene, who founded the family which contained Sweep, one of America's greatest sires; Pennant, the sire of Equipoise; John P. Grier, who gave Man o' War his toughest race; and Iron Mask, champion sprinter, to name a few. Equipoise in turn was grandsire to the nearly indestructible Stymie, who led the money-winning list at $918,485, when he retired in 1949.

Despite his wind handicap, Humphrey Clinker won ten races, showing remarkable gameness and a majestic physique. He was sent to stud in 1828 at the end of his fifth year by his owner, Lord Fitzwilliam, and when his notorious affliction prevented him from "making a living" there, he went on to Ireland to improve the stock of farmers' horses. The blood of the Godolphin had reached its most perilous moment in history.

Before his journey to exile, Humphrey Clinker had sired but eight, none of whom ever scratched many serious records into history except in the birth and death notices. The next three years in Ireland resulted in but twenty nondescript foals, and then, for obscure reasons, Humphrey Clinker was returned to England and was sent to Mr. William Allen of Malton, Yorkshire, where he passed the last two years of his life in almost complete solitude. Only one foal bred before his exile ever amounted to anything, and that was Rockingham, who won the St. Leger in 1833. It is possible that this triumph caused the return of Humphrey Clinker from his exile in Erin. The next year Bran, an Irish product of Humphrey's, ran second in the same race, but, as this was the spring of Humphrey's tragic death, that did him little good.

The one which counted more than any other horse born within that decade developed under such extraordinary circumstances that his story alone makes the search through the ancient records worthwhile. He was Melbourne, son of the despised Humphrey Clinker, from an unnamed Cervantes mare.

(MELBOURNE) The story of Melbourne mocks all the grand theories of breeding plans by mere humans, and indicates that when men cannot handle the golden treasure which stands in their stable

or pasture a wiser power will step in to take charge, make a few adjustments, and set things right.

In Yorkshire in 1833 there was a nine-year-old mare, never raced, never mated, never even named, although a daughter of the fine stallion Cervantes. She belonged, along with two more of equal nonentity, to a family named Robinson, who lived in Carnaby, twenty miles cross-country from Malton. This Robinson family had been around the fringes of the horse world for a few generations; one of its members, Jem Robinson, had been a jockey of considerable merit. In the present-day language of the tracks, they would be called "gyps" or "gypsies," struggling along with a horse or two, never sure where their next meal or bale of hay was going to be found, bought or "borrowed."

Why is not known, nor important now, but the Robinsons sent their three mares to Humphrey Clinker. All conceived, foaled live colts which were nursing when the unhappy Humphrey went on to greener heavenly pastures, where, it is hoped, he has not been scorned as he was on earth. That same spring, Rockingham, Humphrey's son, made a name for himself in the St. Leger, and the three little colts at Robinson's farm became marketable merchandise. Two of them were beautiful little bays; the brown by the side of the Cervantes mare was practically a monstrosity. So thought the Honorable Sidney Herbert when he came to the Robinson farm looking for stock. After routine haggling, Sir Herbert paid $1,000 each for the bays, but turned down the brown with some unkind remarks about knuckle-knees, a head three times too large for a body, and the thoughtful suggestion that "the beast should be shot."

When the Hon. Sidney Herbert made disparaging remarks about the colt, young Charles Robinson, who loved the queer-looking, misshapen colt, made disparaging remarks about the Hon. Sidney. This outburst brought an offer of a small amount of money from the wealthy patron, but now young Charles angrily told Sir Sidney that he, Charles, would raise the colt, train him, and moreover would win many cup races. The Hon. Sidney laughed indulgently and departed with the two young bays.

In that same year, William Lamb 2nd, Viscount Melbourne, became Prime Minister of England, and what was more natural for

Charles Robinson than to name his homely pet after the great states-
man? The Viscount himself probably had no choice in the matter,
otherwise Humphrey Clinker's grotesque son might have come down
through history with another name.

Melbourne, the horse, went, as might be expected, to the top the
hard way. The young Charles Robinson was probably no Ben Jones
as a trainer, and, although Charles got some help from the great
retired rider, Job Marson, Melbourne was still in the rags period
during the first years of his career. He started racing at three on the
carnival circuit and worked his way up the scale until he retired at
six with nine races won and $6,225 in the pocket of Charles Robinson.

In the meantime, Melbourne's two half-brothers, who had gone
away to race in style for the Hon. Sidney Herbert, had amounted to
practically nothing. Still the dramatic story went on for Melbourne
at the end of his racing career. Although listed by the turfmen as one
of the finest flowers of British racing horsedom, Melbourne was
literally peddled from door to door as a stud with no takers.

Finally, when he was eight, Melbourne was mated to a mare—unnamed of course, who belonged to a strange character called "Stables." Brother Stables—he rated no "Mr." in the snobbish racing
circles and "Stables" was, perchance, a nickname—had his own
ideas about the mating of horses. It was his theory that no good
colt or filly could be produced by any stallion and mare unless their
marriage was a love match. So the nameless daughter of Margrave,
winner of the 1832 St. Leger, was introduced to Melbourne, allowed
to make up her mind at her leisure, and when love had surely blos-
somed the marriage was consummated.

Several months later, Stables was forced to sell Melbourne's bride
for $90 to a friend, Bill Scott, a jockey who knew his horses—and
his bottles. The colt that was born to the unnamed Margrave mare
was purchased by Bill for $500 "payable after he had won his first
race." Bill Scott was no fool.

Time went by, and only the fact that Bill Scott knew his bottles too
well prevented this son of Melbourne from being the first colt in
history to win England's triple crown. As Sir Tatton Sykes and ridden by Bill Scott, he won easily the 2,000 Guineas; in the fall he

won the St. Leger. In between, he went, with twenty-six more, to the post for the Derby, and when Bill Scott, apparently loaded to the gills with more than hope and ambition, got into an argument with the starter, the rest of the field departed with Sir Tatton Sykes a bad last leaving the barrier. He was beaten for first place by a short neck.

Melbourne was busy after that. All the wise horsemen, who "knew it all the time" flocked their mares to the court of Humphrey Clinker's lonesome son. He did not fail them, and, as the years went by, Melbourne children scored heavily in the racing world. His fee, which had been considered too high at five guineas, was now forty guineas, and he was making more than $10,000 per year for Charles Robinson, who never tired of telling the tale of the squabble with the Hon. Sidney Herbert, and how Melbourne had showed them. The Hon. Sidney never made any recorded and printable comment about his failure to see the diamond in the rough exterior of the big-headed colt.

Melbourne's marvelous prepotency, which he bequeathed to all who followed in his family tree, may be explained by the fact that although Melbourne himself was only eight generations removed from the Godolphin Arabian in the tail-male line, he was blessed with no less than fifty-one crosses of the Godolphin's blood, twenty-three through his sire and twenty-eight through his dam. Only Harkaway, who was directly in the Eclipse line, had more Godolphin crosses, but Melbourne still had the advantage because he was a direct descendant.

Before Melbourne died in his twenty-fifth year, he had sired not only Sir Tatton Sykes, who should have won the triple crown but for over-indulgence on the part of his rider, but also the great West Australian who did win the triple in 1853. It was this "good hard yellow-bay" horse, as he was called, who would carry on the Godolphin line.

The reason for Melbourne's death was truly in keeping with the rest of his bizarre career. He fell from the mare Escalade, injured himself severely, declined, and died. He had played his part well with little thanks to the wisdom of men, and the germ that was to be Man o' War was winging on its way in the good blood of West Australian.

172

Man O' War's Family

(*WEST AUSTRALIAN*) West Australian, affectionately known as "the West," not only won the triple crown for the first time in English history, but went on to take the Ascot Gold Cup, and to retire at five with ten races won and a second in his only other start (this at two years of age) with total purses of $70,675, the largest to that time.

The breeder and first owner of "the West" was a Mr. John Bowes. He, with his trainer, John Scott, who was close to the top-rung of all British trainers, mated the Touchstone mare Mowerina to Melbourne to produce West Australian. They trained and raced him until before his Ascot Cup victory when he was sold for 5,000 guineas to Baron Lodesborough.

It was in the Baron's stud that "the West" served until the Baron died in 1860, and the horse was then sold at auction to Duc de Morny, natural brother of Emperor Napoleon 2nd of France. This departure of the beloved stallion for a foreign shore caused loud outcries in the public press, and the later realization in English turf circles that the current popularity of breeding to the get of Eclipse had made sound horsemen forget the possibilities in staying with the magnificent fire of Matchem and his children's children.

With the sale of West Australian to France, the direct line of the Godolphin was departing from England apparently forever (at any rate, by 1950 it has not returned). Before he left, he had been mated to the mare Emilia, and a chestnut colt was the result. The mare Emilia, with the suckling chestnut at her side, was exported to America and the name of Millington was claimed for the colt. He would later be called Australian, the great-great-grandfather of Man o' War.

(*AUSTRALIAN*) Millington, or Australian, came to America just in time to have his racing career become a casualty of the Civil War, for he was shuttled back and forth from Kentucky to Illinois. Within a year of arrival of the tiny Millington, the great English stallion the American Eclipse was brought over by Richard Ten Broeck, backed by Keene Richards' money; also the colt Bonnie Scotland came to New York.

This Eclipse, great-grandson of the original of the same name by way of Touchstone and Orlando, brought the Eclipse blood to

America, to flash through Alram to Himyar and to his son Domino, one of the greatest sires America has known. Through Domino the fire and courage pass on to Commando, his son Colin, his son On Watch. Another line speeds through Pennant to Equipoise and to his grandson, Stymie.

Bonnie Scotland, the other of the triumvirate, is the fountain for the family of Ben Brush, who begat Broomstick, who begat Whisk Broom 2nd, who begat John P. Grier, who begat Boojum. The great distance horse Diavolo was another son of Whisk Broom 2nd.

And then there was Millington, who was bringing the key blood of the family which would produce Man o' War.

Thus these three, who would dominate the American racing world for the next century, were the fourth triumvirate of great founders of thoroughbred families. First had been the Godolphin Arabian, the Byerley Turk and the Darley Arabian; second, Matchem, Herod, and Eclipse; third, Melbourne, Touchstone, and Stockwell; and now Australian, Bonnie Scotland, and Eclipse, all imported within two years to America. While Australian carried the tail-male blood-line from the Godolphin, Eclipse also went back to Trumpator, and thus any crossing of Australian with Eclipse—as has happened countless times—was actually inbreeding to Trumpator, concentrating that blood more than ever.

Australian started his racing career for his importer, Mr. A. Keene Richards, a wealthy Kentucky sportsman, as Millington, a three-year-old, in the spring of 1861. When the intensification of the war caused Richards to go to New Orleans, Mr. R. A. Alexander of Woodford County, who owned the great stallions Lexington and Planet and desired to own a fine imported English horse, made a deal for the colt. A. Keene Richards, a man who perhaps did more than any other for the thoroughbred in early America, thus passes from the scene of Man o' War's story.

Although Millington's name was changed to Australian as soon as he became the property of Alexander, he finished his racing career under his original name. Despite the fact that northern racing was at a standstill, with only one day of the turf being held in 1862 above the Mason-Dixon line, and with Southern racing being a rag-tag, fly-by-night operation, Australian managed to run nine races, winning three, placing second in two, and third in three, for total purses of $11,380, by far the highest nationally.

Australian was bred to a few mares in 1863, but in the next year fled to Illinois in time to miss a plundering of Alexander's farm by Confederate guerrillas who killed and appropriated many fine horses. After the war, Australian, Lexington, and Planet returned to the Woodford Stud to renew their activities, and in 1867 Australian sent eight to the barriers to win thirteen races and $9,065, making him sixth on the list of money-winning sires for that year.

For fourteen consecutive years, Australian and Lexington battled along for the honor of "leading sire," with Australian running second four times to Lexington, then second twice to Leamington. In fairness to Australian it must be pointed out that Lexington was given the choice mares at Woodford Stud until his death in 1875, the balance being shared by Planet and Australian. And equally in fairness it must be noted that Australian received partial restitution in having the opportunity to apply his royal blood on the splendid mares sired by his stablemate, Lexington.

Australian, like Matchem before him, fashioned sons and daughters who rose slowly to their greatness in their maturity, not as speedy youngsters fading fast into obscurity. They were horses for distance under weight.

(SPENDTHRIFT) Spendthrift, Australian's most famous son, and the great-grandfather of Man o' War, was a pure chestnut following a dark chestnut father who was a throw-back in his color, five of his immediate ancestors being bays, the other, Melbourne, his grandfather, a brown.

Aerolite, daughter of Lexington and mother of Spendthrift, was born in 1861, went to the breeding farm unraced at four because of the Civil War. That she might have been a fine race mare is indicated by the record of her full sister, Idlewild, three years older, and one of the greatest race mares of the time.

Spendthrift was sold as a yearling to Daniel Swigert, later honored as one of the greatest breeders of all history. Swigert was a relative of R. A. Alexander, the founder of Woodburn Stud, and had once been superintendent of that farm. Eventually he took over the Preakness Stud in Lexington, renamed it "Elmendorf" and made it famous.

Spendthrift did not start until the fall as a two-year-old. Then, within four weeks, he won five races in Kentucky and Tennessee in such smashing style that he had a national reputation when he was put away for the winter.

In the east that same year, Pierre Lorillard had developed such a strong trio of youngsters—Harold, Monitor, and Idler—that there were many outcries he "would ruin racing," for no one could run against his colts. There was even a campaign amongst unhappy rivals of Lorillard to find a horse to beat him. Finally, James R. Keene was persuaded to offer $15,000 and "contingencies" for Spendthrift.

Dan Swigert accepted the offer, and Spendthrift came east to take on, single-handed, the Lorillard line-up. Spendthrift caught the fancy of eastern fans immediately, and by early spring was carrying so much money in the winter books—much more widely played in those days both on single races and parlays—that the bookies could either win a fortune or go completely bankrupt, depending on the invader from Kentucky.

From this tremendous pre-season wagering on Spendthrift an incident developed which resulted in the ruling being enacted requiring an owner to make a declaration of which of his horses intends to try to win if he has more than one entry. The incident occurred in the Withers Stakes in which Spendthrift was entered with a stable-mate, Dan Sparling. Although Spendthrift could have won with ease, he was pulled almost to a stop to permit Dan Sparling to come home, thereby collecting a fortune in winter book bets for James R. Keene. The public, which had bet Spendthrift in the winter book both straight and in combination, was ready to lynch Keene, who cared not at all, being a cold, self-sufficient soul.

Harold, the eastern flash of Lorillard, by now a Preakness winner, had been left at the post in the Withers and had not threatened either Dan Sparling or Spendthrift. In the Belmont which followed, Spendthrift and Harold raced from the start as a team until Harold faded to dead last while Spendthrift won by an easy five lengths.

They met still again in the Lorillard, and this time it was Spendthrift who was left at the post with Harold away flying, after landing a vicious kick on Spendthrift's shoulder just as the barrier opened.

Man O' War's Family

There seemed to be no chance for the gallant chestnut, but after a steady pursuit, he caught Harold under a cruel whipping finish to win, lowering the American record for the mile and three furlongs to 2:25¾, and proving to the world that Melbourne's great-grandson was every inch a champion.

That kick from Harold, along with the punishing journey he had made, took something out of Spendthrift. He went to Saratoga to lose to the flashy Falsetto, who had the wizard Ike Murphy aboard in the Travers; Harold was third. Two weeks later, although Spendthrift was crying for a rest, the three met again, and, with Harold setting a blistering pace, Spendthrift was again beaten by Falsetto.

Spendthrift returned to Long Island, won the Champion Stakes, then lost to Monitor in the Jerome Stakes. His feet were giving him trouble; his shoulder bruise from the kick of Harold was still painful. He should not have raced, but, calling on all his magnificent courage, he lost by a neck in a blistering mile and three-quarter grind. He was sent home for the winter, the high winner of the year with $23,425.

Had Spendthrift been retired then, as he probably should have been, his record would have come down in history untarnished. But Mr. Keene, searching for new worlds to conquer, decided he would venture to England with part of his stable, and Spendthrift was sent over on what was to prove a disastrous trip. He caught influenza, recovered with his breathing seriously impaired, but was sent into training anyway. He went up against thirty-two other horses in the Cambridgeshire, although not at all ready for such a test. It was his first start in more than a year after serious illness, and one of the most foolhardy maneuvers ever made with a top-ranking horse. He finished far back. Spendthrift returned to America in the spring of 1881, and once more the indomitable Mr. Keene sent him into training for further humiliation. He was beaten twice, then retired two years after common sense demanded it. His true record should have listed nine wins and four seconds, with defeats only to Falsetto and Monitor, two magnificent racers.

Spendthrift, although never bred extensively outside the farm of James R. Keene, was a remarkable sire. His son Kingston, foaled in 1884 from Kapanga, a daughter of Victorious, raced for nine years, winning eighty-nine races. Bankrupt, another gelded son, foaled in 1883 by the Favonius mare called Authoress, campaigned for twelve years winning eighty-six. These records still stand more than half a century later.

Spendthrift passed through two more ownerships before his death at Spendthrift Stud in Lexington, named in his honor by Overton H. Chenault who owned him last. There he died in October of 1900, his get having won more than a thousand races and not quite a million dollars.

He had been a badly handled horse, and was apparently an evil-tempered horse almost impossible to tame. In his behalf, it can be said that he had much to be evil-tempered about in the later part of his racing career. His greatest gift to posterity was the slam-bang, knock-your-head-off colt called Hastings, born in 1893 to Cinderella. He would continue the line to his son Fair Play, the sire of Man o' War.

(HASTINGS) Hastings, a striking brown-bay colt with a white star in his forehead, was a mean, exasperating, and brilliant neurotic, so fiery with the desire for action and competition that he was almost unmanageable.

Hastings was bred by Dr. J. D. Neet, owner of a small group of mares in Versailles, Kentucky. Cinderella, his mother, was an English import, a daughter of either Blue Ruin or Tomahawk, "with Tomahawk preferred," whatever that may mean.

Cinderella herself merits attention. Besides the fiery Hastings, she also foaled Ferrier, by Falsetto, one of the only two horses to beat Spendthrift. Ferrier, one of the true indestructibles, raced continually from two to nine, starting in 148 races to win fifty-five times. Cinderella also suckled Plaudit, winner of the Nursery and Champagne Stakes at two, the Kentucky and Oakley Derbies at three, and founder of a family of his own which developed the line to Spur, Sting, Questionnaire, Hash, and Third Degree. Another of her sons, this one by Top Gallant, was Migraine, a track-scorching horse, later the sire of Star Fancy, who, when mated to Man o' War, would produce Crusader, one of his finest sons. Before Cinderella was through, her daughter Slippers, by Meddler, was born, and Slippers would be the dam of such as Buskin, the Preakness and Metropolitan winner; Polly Flinders, mother of Prudery, Macaw, and Prudish. Prudery herself is one of the very few mares ever to produce two winners of the stature of Victorian and Whiskery.

Fertile and illustrious as she was, Cinderella must yield in this account to a still more vital contributor, the headstrong Hastings. There was a paradox, brilliant and villainous, a courageous competitor, yet often running amok. He was the drive, the explosion that would recognize no barriers. When that impetuous competitive fire was later diluted a bit in the heart of Man o' War it resulted in the nearly perfect horse.

Hastings was sold at auction in his yearling year for $2,800, one of the highest bids of the year, to David Gideon and John Daly of New York, who raced in partnership. He came out in June of 1895, won three races quickly and easily. Then Gideon and Daly decided to dump their stable at public auction because of depression times. They put up, amongst others, Hastings, Hazlet, and Requital, the three most promising two-year-olds in sight, delectable bait for the bidders with rich fall races still to come.

It was at this auction that Major August Belmont 2nd bought Hastings for the then tremendous price of $37,000. Belmont shipped Hastings to Saratoga, where he immediately caught "the cough," that mysterious and pesky ailment which still has not been solved by the veterinarians, and was unable to keep any of his engagements. He was returned in the autumn to Sheepshead, and, not completely well, ran fifth in the Futurity. That was all for his freshman year.

Requital, kept by Gideon when he lost Hastings, was the Futurity winner; he later defeated easily the western menace, Ben Brush, and was judged the star baby of the lot. Like so many before and since, Hastings was chided in the press an an expensive disappointment.

In the spring, Hastings returned to face three of the toughest competitors ever to greet any three-year-old in racing history. Requital was there under new ownership; Handspring and Ben Brush would help to make Hastings' every race a war from start to finish. He won a five furlong warm-up; lost by a nose to Handspring in the Withers; won the Toboggan easily against older horses; reversed his defeat by Handspring, beating the bad-footed colt by a nose in the Belmont, then at a mile and three furlongs. Hastings ran a "courtesy" second for his stablemate, Margrave, in the Tidal Stakes, then, apparently going stale, was fourth to Requital in the Realization.

As Hastings went into his fourth year, his cantankerous spirit made him ever more difficult to handle. Training annoyed him; saddle and bridle were enemies to battle each time they were put on; exercise boys were exhausted after fighting him through his conditioning routine.

There is no evidence that he was a sulker, but he did run six times second in twelve starts, winning only four in his last season of racing, but he gave weight in great amounts to every horse which beat him. That Hastings' money-winning record shows but $16,075, after winning ten races, many of them famous stakes, should not be taken as a proper yardstick, for it was a gloomy era of economic collapse during the racing days of Hastings. His Belmont win paid him but $3,025. Fifty-one years later the same race paid $78,900 to Phalanx. Hastings' other purses were in proportion.

At about the same time he acquired Hastings, Belmont bought also the handicap star Henry of Navarre, who won the Suburban Handicap for him, but broke down and was sent to stud to replace Rayon D'Or. The next year Hastings joined him, along with Margrave. As they lined up for their harem duties, Henry of Navarre was an odds-on favorite to be a tremendous success as a sire, with Hastings being almost overlooked by everyone except August Belmont. But in 1898 Henry of Navarre sent out a flock of children almost worthless, to be followed the next year by Hastings' first offerings including no less than seventeen winners, many of a sparkling brilliancy.

To prove conclusively that this was no accident, Hastings followed up so well in the following year that he became, at nine years of age, with only two crops on the tracks, the leading American sire. His children won that year $113,865 with sixty-three firsts to his credit. No other horse had ever led the list so young, and with nothing but two and three-year-olds running.

Also it should be pointed out that Hastings scored in this sensational fashion although he never did get the full opportunity to test his real capabilities as a sire. First he was getting the second choice of the mares after Henry of Navarre; later he would be mated to what was left after the choices had gone to the court of Rock Sand, the magnificent English triple-crown winner imported by Belmont rom England in 1906. Despite these handicaps, Hastings led all the est in 1901, again in 1908, was second in 1910, and third the next wo years. In 1915, when he was twenty-two, he sent out the most uvenile winners, fourteen with thirty-five triumphs.

He lived until June 17, 1917, in his twenty-fourth year, dying a ew weeks after the birth of his greatest grand-child in Mahubah's stall. He was fractious, mean, vicious, unlovable to the end, a despotic snarling demon of the turf whose spirit could never be broken. Decades after his death, horsemen, observing temper in his descendants, invariably say, "That's the Hastings in him." And they know it is better than the faint heart.

(FAIR PLAY) Some of Man o' War's regal spirit might fairly be ascribed to Fair Play, his father. John Hervey, for more than half a century one of the outstanding turf writers of the world, and such a student of the thoroughbred horse as is seldom found outside of the inner circle of horsemen, loved Fair Play, son of Hastings, more than all the rest—until Fair Play's own son, Man o' War, came along to split his affections between the two. A eulogistic description written by Hervey of Fair Play says this, in part, about him:

"There was always something of a leaping flame about the son of Hastings and Fairy Gold, the effect of his flashing golden coat, his eager, agile movement, his disdain of familiarity, his lofty head and fiery spirit, unquenched to the last.

"It was difficult to fault Fair Play individually. He was never a big horse in the modern sense, standing little, if any, above sixteen hands. . . . Hastings did not transmit to him his own brown coat color, his molten chestnut hue being generally referred to as a heritage from his dam. . . . His only white was a beautiful reach in his face that just missed being a blaze—it was, in fact, the large diamond shaped star of both Spendthrift and Hastings elongated a few inches toward the muzzle. . . .

"Everything about Fair Play was balanced and proportionate and harmonious. . . . It was the justness and poise of his physique which excited the admiration of the connoisseur; he could, as the saying goes, be 'picked to pieces' and yet remain intact. . . ."

181

This was Fair Play, foaled in 1905 to the Bend Or mare, Fairy Gold, and destined to become the sire of the "mostest horse."

Fairy Gold, foaled in England in 1896, by Bend Or and the mare Maid of Masham, was purchased by Major Belmont in 1903 for $18,000. She has been named by many experts of the turf world as the most valuable mare imported since the Civil War. An examination of her pedigree shows further concentration of the blood of the Godolphin line which met and blended again within itself when she was mated to Hastings.

Fairy Gold produced two foals in England before the journey to Belmont's Nursery Stud. Of the nine living foals Fairy Gold had at Nursery Stud, four were by Hastings, two by Rock Sand, one each by Octagon, Vulcain, and Ferole.

Fairy Gold's two finest were Friar Rock, with the collaboration of Rock Sand, and Fair Play. Friar Rock at three won the Suburban and Brooklyn Handicaps, the Belmont Stakes, and the Saratoga Cup, a feat never before accomplished by one of his age. He was sold for $50,000, again for $100,000, and died too soon at fifteen, having sired the winners of eighty-two races and $125,987 in his last season. His celebrated unlucky son, Inchcape, died almost immediately after being purchased for $150,000.

Had it not been for a horse called Colin and an ill-advised invasion of England in his four-year-old season, Fair Play would have been immortalized as one of the great runners of all time. In his racing as a two-year-old, Fair Play won $16,045 from three victories, three seconds, two thirds in ten starts. Three of his defeats were by Colin, the unbeaten, who went back to winter quarters already awarded the title of the greatest horse of the era, better than his sire Commando, better than his grandsire Domino, better than El Rio Rey and Tremont, unbeaten two-year-olds of twenty years before.

Andy Joyner, trainer for Major Belmont, brought Fair Play out the next spring in sound condition, and knowing that Colin, although possessed of blistering speed and a heart which would never let him quit, was not perfect in his legs. He planned to chase Colin, if necessary, until Commando's fine son would fold up under the strain.

Colin and Fair Play tangled first in the Withers Mile that spring and it was the familiar story again, with Fair Play making a sensational charge in the stretch, driving Colin to the whip, and missing as that grand star came on to hold part of his early lead. It was getting a little tiresome for Fair Play to watch the flying rump of Colin whenever they got together.

The Belmont that followed the Withers by only a week was run under a cloudburst with rain so thick that details of the race must always remain obscure. No time was taken, nor is there any record of the relative positions of the four who started until they were less than a quarter mile from home. At that point Colin appeared in front, with Fair Play making his regular stretch drive, and this time catching Colin rapidly. Notter, the jockey on Colin, was whipping as never before as the mud-flecked golden Fair Play came charging up to catch Colin just as they passed the wire and to speed in front—too late by a matter of feet, as Dugan in Fair Play's saddle drove him mercilessly.

There were reports that Notter had misjudged the finish, started to pull up too soon, then gone furiously back to the drive when he recognized his error. This Notter always denied, and it is probable that Colin reached the point where even he had to slow down and then went on under punishment through courage and nerve alone. His fragile legs were about ready to give way for good, and only three weeks later did, when he won his last start and retired, a bad-legged horse who would never race again.

Fair Play, on the other hand, was back on the track only two days after the gruelling Belmont duel with Colin. Finally, after five seconds in five starts for the year, Fair Play was due, and ready, to win a few.

He won the Brooklyn Derby, the Coney Island Jockey Club Stakes, the Lawrence Realization, and a lesser handicap at Saratoga. In the fall he won at Gravesend and won both the Jerome and the Municipal Handicaps at Belmont.

In his final start of the year, or forever in the United States, one of those unpleasant incidents developed, never to be fully explained, leaving the aroma of doubt about the trueness of the race. It is most charitable to say that Lee, astride Fair Play, held him back too long, and lost by an open length to Master Robert. Major Belmont was reportedly livid with rage. Lee had no satisfactory explanation for his lack of enthusiasm, and even the coldly factual *Daily Racing Form* wrote: "The belief is general that Fair Play was not ridden to win today." An investigation was ordered, but, as in most such episodes, conclusive proof was lacking. Fair Play returned to the Nursery Stud. He was tired, disagreeable, fed up with racing, and deep in his turbulent heart apparently he had determined never to run his heart out again.

At this time, reform was sweeping the country. Exponents of purity and virtue were making life difficult for the turfmen, and it was obvious that the situation would be worse before it got better. The "gypsy" stables were liquidating their stock; the wealthy owners were heading for England and France where racing, and its attendant gambling, were accepted as part of the pattern of sport.

There, too, as had his grandsire Australian, Fair Play was shipped in the fall of 1908. But his strong personality turned bitter and pettish. He refused to train except under punishment, and his entire British invasion was a fiasco. He ran in six races, his only respectable effort being a fourth in the Coronation Cup at Epsom Downs. By midsummer of 1909, Major Belmont accepted the obvious truth, took Fair Play out of training, and returned him to Nursery Stud to stand beside Hastings and Rock Sand for the improvement of the breed.

Into the books went his complete record: ten wins, eleven seconds, five thirds in thirty-two starts; $86,940 won; he could carry weight, go a distance, drive unceasingly without flinching. Better than all he had countless crosses of the blood of the Godolphin.

Although Major Belmont had paid $125,000 for the English triple-crown winner, Rock Sand, to share with Hastings the duties of siring the future greats of Nursery Stud, he was convinced at the time Fair Play was retired that this one would be the best of all. Proof of this can be found in an issue of the *Racing Form* of February, 1910 in which Belmont is quoted as saying:

"Fair Play is the best horse I have ever owned—I expect him to show by his get that he is the superior of his sire (Hastings), Rock Sand, Singleton, and all the other sires I have had."

Racing, however, had been driven into an almost hopeless trap by the moralists. In 1911, yearlings sold under the hammer of the auctioneer averaged but $230—four years before many had sold in the five-figure brackets. Colin as a two-year-old in 1907 had won $131,007; Worth, the 1911 leader of the same division, won but

$16,645; the next year Helios could take but $12,524 to lead the younger generation.

It was, therefore, the worst possible time for a young stallion to enter the stud with the possible exception of the period of the Civil War when Australian, the first of Man o' War's tail-male line to come to America, had arrived in Kentucky. In 1912 Major Belmont shipped Rock Sand to France and sold him to a French syndicate, stripping his own Nursery Stud list of stallions down to Hastings and his son, Fair Play. The best of the brood mares went to the Major's French farm which he had leased. The future looked dark for the name of Fair Play, but it was all part of the design of breeding as Major August Belmont had come to understand it. That Belmont had unceasing confidence in Fair Play is shown again in his sale of Tracery, Rock Sand's greatest son, to South America after Tracery had won the St. Leger and had served for six years with fine success in the English branch of the Belmont stables.

That Belmont was right all the way about Fair Play can be pointed by Fair Play's record of get which won more than five hundred races and nearly $3,000,000, a new high in all turf history, approached only by the great English sire St. Simon. Fair Play sired Display ($256,526); Mad Hatter ($194,525); Chance Shot ($142,277); Mad Play ($139,769); Chance Play ($137,946).

St. Simon's children were precocious, winning in their babyhood, but not faring so well in maturity. Directly opposite were those of Fair Play who went on to win and win in the older, truer tests of mature horses.

Fair Play's sons were great on the turf. His daughters saved their priceless value for the breeding farm. Few ran at all spectacularly, but they made up for it in establishing the strongest family in America. The Fair Play family, like all dynasties, depends on its sons, and in this department Fair Play was supreme. Fair Play had justified the faith of Major Belmont, and he well deserves the monument, sculptured in bronze, that stands above his final resting place at Elmendorf in Kentucky.

MAN O' WAR'S FAMILY

THE DAMS

B ECAUSE THE male horse has always been the fundamental bread-winner of any thoroughbred family, the pedigree of Mahubah will not be searched with so much attention as was the tail-male line of Fair Play. The importance of the female line rests somewhere between the rather cold-blooded belief dams the mare is useful only as a vessel to incubate the young foal, and the extremists on the other side who subscribe and over-subscribe to the Bruce Lowe theory that the maternal side is by far the more important in the study of blood-lines.

E. Bruce Lowe, an Australian, and obviously a statistical fanatic besides being a lover of the horse, completed an almost superhuman task when he tabulated all winners of three great English races—the Derby, the St. Leger, and the Oaks—then traced those winners back through their maternal lines to the original "tap-root" mares. Finding no more than forty-three such foundation mares at the end of his long journeys through the musty record books, he numbered these families, giving the honored position of "Number One" to the ancient lady with the most successful family, and carrying on down the list.

Bruce Lowe did not live to see his work in print, but soon after his death William Allison of the London *Sportsman* rewrote Lowe's notes, published them in a book called *Horse Breeding by the Number System,* and sat back in amazement as the breeders of the world went wild over his conclusions. It seemed for a time that the stallions had become secondary factors in the improvement of the breed routine, until the pendulum of better judgment quieted the storm. No matter where may lie the true perfect formula for breeding, the Bruce Lowe system is easily adaptable to any formula, thanks to its concise and clear-cut numbering of families. This eases the sometimes complicated twisting and turning of blood-lines.

(LAYTON BARB MARE) Man o' War belonged to the Number 4 family, which descended from the Layton Barb Mare. This lady's past was completely lost in obscurity and contradiction in early English records. She may have been born in England, or in Barbary, or anywhere else. She may have been bred, bought, traded, or even looted, by a man named Layton or Laton. Her name may have been "Violet," as she is sometimes referred to as "Mr. Layton's Violet Barb mare." Since that could hardly have been her color, it might well have been her name. There is some inkling that her sire might have been a grey Barbary stallion. Records disagree on her time of life. In one she is listed as giving birth to a filly "about 1715," but elsewhere is shown to be the great-great-grandmother of another foaled in 1710.

Her main interest here is that, by Dodsworth, a natural Barb brought from Barbary yet unborn, she produced the Dodsworth Mare from which the entire Number 4 family descends. This particular mare was once owned by King Charles and was sold after his death for forty guineas to the same Mr. Coke who rescued the Godolphin Arabian from the brute in Paris.

The daughter of the Dodsworth Mare destined to continue the Number 4 family was sired by a white Oriental horse belonging to Oliver Cromwell, who denounced racing "for the record" but was one of its most ardent followers in private. His white stallion, called Place's White Turk, was named for Roland Place, who was studmaster to Cromwell. The daughter, with little imagination, was named The White Turk Mare. She in turn mated with Brimmer to fashion the Brimmer Mare, and it is through this one that most of the Number 4 family funnels up to the Layton Barb tap-root. Her most influential daughter was Brown Farewell, sired by Makeless.

She, apparently a brown, was a marvelous lady on the production line, bringing sixteen youngsters into the world in twenty years. Through her we meet the tail-male line for the first time when her daughter by Croft's Partner became the dam of Matchem.

Brown Farewell produced many influential mares and horses, but the one pertinent to this history was an unnamed filly by Greyhound, sometimes referred to as "the sister to Guy," a horse which had become famous as a racer.

This Greyhound mare was mated twice to a grey Arabian with the descriptive but rather unappetizing name of Bloody Buttocks, so called because of a red splotch on his hip. Her first foal was a filly called Bay Bloody Buttocks. The ancient records could hardly be more confusing than they are on Bay Bloody Buttocks. She too was a veritable factory for foals, and produced no less than fourteen, all but one being sired by Croft's Partner. Of the thirteen full brothers and sisters, only one received a name and fortunately that one was Spinster, chosen by fate to carry on the Number 4 family.

(SPINSTER) Spinster, third foal of her busy mother, was the first chestnut in the maternal line of Man o' War who can be spotted surely as such. She was also called the Widdrington Mare, the name of the man who raced her through those gruelling marathons which were run in four-mile heats. In one of these contests she ran four times at four miles, with a second, a fourth, and two firsts to her credit. And she carried twelve stone—168 pounds. After two hundred years of "improving the breed," a mile-and-a-half run but once under 135 pounds is considered "going a distance."

Spinster was sold to the aristocratic Planton Stud before her last race, where she became an outstanding matron, foaling at least ten and probably more. One of these was by the Godolphin Arabian and was born in 1753, the year the grand old patriarch died.

Spinster's first, a grey filly also called Spinster, carries our line down the next step on the pedigree ladder. The young filly was sold to a family named Leeds, horse people for generations, raced three times for one win, one second, one unplaced. She went to the farm then and produced eight fillies and four colts, only four of which were identified by name. And of the nameless fillies, that which would have been chosen as least likely to succeed was the one to carry on the family line to Mahubah.

She was known as the Janus Mare because her sire was Janus, and with the help of a horse called Skim she foaled a filly known as the Skim Mare. Janus, a son of the Godolphin Arabian, did not race, but was the sire of many mares who became the taproots of many American families.

The Skim Mare herself has a doubtful pedigree, as there is no guarantee which Skim is the sire for there were two, one owned by a man named Vernon, the other by a man named Portsmore. Still more trouble comes from a later historian who credits her to another mare known as Young Country Wench. It seems best to skip down the ladder to the next bracket, where stands Expectation.

(EXPECTATION) This grey filly was born when the Skim Mare was twenty-one years of age, and she seems to have produced none of the nine credited to her until she was twelve. The rest of her life remains in obscurity as vague as her parentage.

Expectation stands half-way down the ladder from the Layton Barb mare to Mahubah. She marks the point in the pedigree where inaccuracy disappears. Although her mother may have had either one of two sires, and a choice of two dams, the line from Expectation to the present day can be traced and documented as surely as a mathematical formula. Expectation brings to the maternal side of Man o' War's family the first injection of the blood of Herod, one of the great progenitors of history.

Herod was foaled in 1758. He won six phenomenal races, was second three times, and unplaced once, before he retired to stud where he became a sensational success. Herod's sons and daughters ran for nineteen years, won 497 races and approximately a million dollars, an almost incredible sum when we pause to consider that few races paid the winner so much as $10,000 or anywhere near it. In all countries where the thoroughbred is revered, there are thousands today which can boast of ancestry to Herod. It is regal blood, still blazing with courage and speed.

Expectation, the daughter of Herod, raced with little success, being one of those destined to shine in the nursery rather than on the turf. She delivered thirteen foals, six of them fillies. The last of these, born when Expectation was twenty-three and in the final year of her life, was the only one which ever produced a foal of her own. This, sired by Beningbrough, was the chestnut filly called Anticipation.

Beningbrough completed the magic mixture by bringing the exalted blood of Eclipse, along with some of Matchem's, to the maternal line which descends to Mahubah.

He was a son of King Fergus, one of the finest sons of Eclipse. His maternal grandmother was Pyrrha, a daughter of Matchem. Thus Beningbrough was probably the first horse to carry the blood of all three of the magnificent trio. He was described as a "horse of very great stamp and the living image of Herod himself." No greater praise was possible in his lifetime.

At three he won the St. Leger and the Doncaster Cup on successive days; at four he won the four-mile Doncaster Stakes, and a two-mile heat race the following day. He was as sensational at stud as he was on the track, and when he died, at twenty-four, a mulberry tree was planted in honor on his grave.

(ANTICIPATION) Like many youngsters born to aged mares, the filly, Anticipation, was worthless as a racer. She was sold to a man identified as "G. Cook, of Yorkshire," who apparently kept a mare or two on the side, bred them haphazardly, and sold the young stock for whatever he could get.

Anticipation proved an excellent investment as an "incubator," producing sixteen foals by thirteen different stallions, which might still be a record in fickleness if anyone cares to check into this sidelight of breeding idiosyncrasies. In this mass of progeny we find the filly elected to carry on the line at the top of the list—her first, a direct reverse of her dam who waited until her last to produce the important one.

(MANIAC) This chestnut filly named Maniac was sired by Shuttle, a son of Young Marske, and therefore was a grandson of Marske, who sired Eclipse. Since Beningbrough was Maniac's maternal grandsire, and was also a grandson of Marske, the blood which produced Eclipse was concentrating in Maniac.

Maniac was sold by Mr. Cook to a Mr. W. Ellis, another part-time horse breeder who thereby purchased a jewel. Coming down on her maternal side from mares of great fecundity—her grand-dam, Expectation, had thirteen living foals; her dam, Anticipation, had sixteen—Maniac outdid them both with the phenomenal record of nineteen living youngsters in nineteen consecutive years. This record, completed in 1829, still stands. Many mares have produced nineteen, but no other in nineteen seasons. Shuttle, her sire, must take part of the credit, for he had two other daughters who produced twenty each, and still another who had eighteen.

One more record did Maniac break. In 1815, she, a chestnut, by the chestnut horse Stripling, produced a bay filly, supposedly an impossibility but obviously not in the case of this maternal magician of the nursery.

Seven of Maniac's produce were winners, the rest were in the money many times. Through her ten daughters Maniac sent her splendid strong blood flowing down the pedigree steps of thousands of thoroughbreds.

The fourth, fifth, sixth, and seventh foals of Maniac were sired by Stripling, and the third of these was named Harriet.

(HARRIET) Stripling's sire was Phenomenon, a son of Herod, and his mother, called Laura, was a daughter of Eclipse. Harriet, like both her mother and father, was a chestnut, never raced, and started her career as a matron in the third year of her life.

However, unlike Maniac, Anticipation, and Expectation, who produced almost enough descendants to restock the horse world, Harriet either was a poor matron or had unusually bad luck with her children. She produced fifteen within twenty-two years; five died as infants; four more disappeared from the records; and of the four who eventually got to the races only one, the colt Primendorf, could win.

The jinx of Harriet hung on to her daughters, too. There were ten of them, but only three ever produced foals, and once again, as when it was saved when Expectation was born to the Skim Mare in her twenty-third year, the line faced extinction.

(ST. NICHOLAS MARE) The one to come through this time was called only the St. Nicholas Mare after her father. He carried the blood of Eclipse, Herod, and Matchem. St. Nicholas was sent to Germany after a few seasons in the English stud, and it was there that he earned most of his fame. One of his English sons called Yorkshire came to America, and his daughters were prolific in early thoroughbred history.

The St. Nicholas Mare was practically a complete blank; she had but three foals, of which one disappeared and one was a gelding.

The other—the all-important other—was the black daughter of Cain named The Slayer's Daughter. She would carry on.

(THE SLAYER'S DAUGHTER) Cain was a son of Paulowitz of the Herod line from a mare of the Matchem family. He was a win-

ner on the course and a powerful sire, and his most famous son was Ion, from whom, in three generations came the great Hermit, destined to be the outstanding stallion of his era.

The Slayer's Daughter went to the races at three, and in her first start won the Manchester Cup, a race then run at a distance of more than two miles in contrast to the ten furlongs of today. In winning she carried the almost incredible light weight of five stone (70 pounds), and one must wonder if her jockey "C. Edwards" was a midget.

She raced eight times in two years, winning but once more after the maiden effort, and then went to the nursery to give birth to fifteen consecutive foals in as many years.

The Slayer's Daughter was bred in a haphazard manner, leaving little in the way of class for posterity. Only two of her daughters were themselves mothers. One produced almost nothing; the other was to be known as The Underhand Mare, great-grandmother of Mahubah.

It might seem that the daughters of the Number 4 family of the Layton Barb Mare had developed a strange script which became a family formula to be replayed every few generations. For the daughter who stands on the next step of Man o' War's maternal pedigree— a bay called The Underhand Mare—was the last foal of The Slayer's Daughter, produced in her twentieth year only a few weeks before she died.

(UNDERHAND MARE) Underhand, the father, was a bay son of The Cure who traced back to Shuttle on his paternal side and to St. Nicholas through his dam. Thus the mating of Underhand and The Slayer's Daughter was a "double double-cross" of their own blood. In other words, they were very close cousins. Underhand must have experienced an interesting "childhood." As a yearling he was turned out to be pursued by greyhounds to sharpen his speed. Underhand, described as very small, was a fair racer and sound sire. He was little in demand in the latter capacity, probably because of his size, and his greatest claim to fame is as the father of The Underhand Mare.

This lady was one of the greatest. She produced ten winners who scored in one hundred races, and five more foals in her twenty-two years in the nursery, where she went at three, never raced. These ten winners were all by different sires, none of which were the class of the time. Had she been bred to worthy horses, the orphaned daughter of The Slayer's Daughter might have etched the greatest record as a matron of all time. Apparently she had the ingredients despite the mediocrity of her mates. Of her three fillies which became brood mares, this story is interested in Mizpah, by MacGregor. She is the maternal grandmother of Mahubah, only three removes from Man o' War.

(MIZPAH) MacGregor was a "Herod" deeply inbred to the old champion. To complicate "cousinships" further, MacGregor traces back to Maniac, who becomes thereby the fifth dam of both Mizpah and her father, MacGregor.

Mizpah was raced through five seasons with little real success, changed owners many times, and was finally purchased for $750 and sent to the breeding farm. A bay herself, she alternated with chestnut and bay foals and had but five which survived. She died in her fourteenth year a few days after her last foal was born dead.

It was the brown filly called Merry Token, a daughter of Merry Hampton who is important. She was to be the mother of Mahubah.

(MERRY TOKEN) Her sire, Merry Hampton, injected a new and exceptionally potent stream of blood into the cauldron which would fashion Man o' War.

Hampton, the sire of Merry Hampton, founded one of the dominant male lines of racing history. His blood was prepotent with the heritage of both the immortal Eclipse and Touchstone. He was not the best racer of his day, and his glory stems from the power of his record as a sire, particularly through his daughters.

Merry Hampton won the 1887 English Derby in his first start, breaking the record which had stood for twenty-seven years. He ran fourth in the Grand Prix de Paris after a hoof injury failed to heal in time for proper training, and was second to Kilwarlin in the St. Leger, which, from the description of rough riding, must have been more a rodeo than a horse race. He started only once when four, running dead last and coming out of the race broken down in both forelegs. Thus his career ended with but one brilliant performance in his maiden effort. He was not much in demand at stud, which was an unfortunate circumstance for the breeders of England, for his children proved to be fine individuals.

Had he produced none but Merry Token, he was assured of immortality. For fate, and the good judgment of Major Belmont, would lead Merry Token to the Nursery Stud in Kentucky, where she would eventually mate with the mighty Rock Sand to produce the mother of Man o' War. Before she made that journey, she started eight times as a two-year-old, winning two firsts, a second, and a third. At three, she took two more firsts and two thirds in seven attempts.

She was sent to breeding in 1895 when she was four and spent six seasons at the farm of E. J. Keylock before she was purchased by William Allison, Belmont's English agent, in 1902. It was this same shrewd Mr. Allison who also bought Fairy Gold, the dam of Fair Play, for Major Belmont the year after he had selected Merry Token.

Merry Token was bought from Keylock for about $200 by H. Eugene Leigh, one of America's outstanding trainers of the time. She was resold through Allison before shipment.

Merry Token, like many of her maternal line, was a strong, prolific breeder. Following her six foals dropped in England, she had eight more at the Nursery Stud. Her colts and fillies were all sound racers and good producers in their own right, but it is Mahubah who made her famous.

(ROCK SAND) The richness of the maternal side of Man o' War's pedigree was gathered in the magnificent body of Rock Sand, father of Mahubah. He was an imported horse, a son of the English Derby winner of 1890, Sainfoin, who was a son of Springfield, highly concentrated in the blood of Eclipse.

Sainfoin, a chestnut, was bred to Roquebrunne, a brown daughter of St. Simon, the most highly prized stallion of his time. Their offspring was the rich seal-brown colt later named Rock Sand. From his birth he was a kindly, gentle, and intelligent horse, being without the usual nervous tension of a thoroughbred, but always ready to consider each new situation on its merits.

When he came to the races at two, he was looked upon as a youngster most likely to succeed because of his classic breeding, and he did not disappoint his backers, winning five of six starts and finishing third in the other.

He was an overwhelming winter-book favorite for the Derby of 1903, his superiority scaring out all but six colts—a situation somewhat similar to that caused by Citation in 1948. Rock Sand won two warm-up races, including the 2,000 Guineas in which Glotsam, his former conqueror, ran second and Rabelais third. Rabelais, a son of St. Simon, was later to become a leading sire in France.

Rock Sand romped home in the Derby, winning as an odds-on favorite should, with Danny Maher, famous American jockey, in the saddle. He followed this with another victory in the St. James Palace Stakes, and then was shipped to Sandown for the $50,000 Eclipse Stakes for horses of all ages.

There, like so many good three-year-olds before and since, he found that the champion youth often loses to the champion who is mature.

Ard Patrick, his four-year-old "first cousin," had been aimed for the event; Sceptre, a four-year-old mare who had won every classic for her age except the Derby was entered; Oriole and another outsider completed the field. Ard Patrick won the race by a nose from Sceptre with Rock Sand running a spectacular third to the two flying older horses. Despite 142 pounds on Ard Patrick, 139 on Sceptre, and 130 on Rock Sand, they scorched the mile and a quarter in 2:08 for a record which still stands, being given more credence than an alleged 2:07 announced as the time for Diamond Jubilee, who won the event in 1900.

Rock Sand was beaten that day by older horses prepared and saved specifically for the race while he had been under severe training for several months. It was a gallant effort and added to rather than detracted from his stature. It should be noted that no three-year-old has ever been able to win the Eclipse carrying 130 pounds as did Rock Sand that day.

Soon after the Eclipse, Rock Sand completed his "triple" by winning the St. Leger, and then took another beating from a refreshed Sceptre in the Jockey Club Stakes for which she had been rested since the Eclipse. He was a tired young champion when the long season finally ended.

He had won all five starts in his own age group, and been second and third when he was entered with the best of the handicap thunderbolts.

When Rock Sand came out at four, Ard Patrick had departed for Germany where his bad legs sent him immediately to stud. Sceptre was still ready for a tussle as was Zinfandel, a son of Persimmon, who had been sidelined with injuries the year before. The three met in the Coronation Cup, Zinfandel winning, with Sceptre second and Rock Sand, "needing a race," a game but unsatisfactory third. Zinfandel, under smart handling was never again matched with Rock Sand, and received much doubtful acclaim from this one victory.

Rock Sand, on the other hand, finally whipped Sceptre in their next meeting, won four more Stakes consecutively, and retired with sixteen victories, one second, three thirds in twenty starts. He had won $236,820, a sum which could be multiplied by no less than four had he been available for the mammoth purses of the 1940's. He had carried tremendous weight at his different ages, had been under the hands of a trainer who believed in all-out workouts all through the season, had gone to the post with sorely inflamed suspensories in his final start—the Jockey Club Stakes—and won it on nerve and courage. He had been easy to handle, gentle, a kindly horse—his blood would be a soothing antidote to the fire of Hastings and Fair Play.

For a few months of 1905 Rock Sand was sent back to training, but when results were not quickly forthcoming he was retired to stud and bred to twenty mares in 1906, the same year his owner, Sir James Miller, died. Offers of $100,000, made by English horsemen, were refused by Miller's estate, and he was finally bought by Major Belmont for $125,000.

He came to America in July of 1908 and was sent to the Nursery Stud to join Henry of Navarre, Octagon, Hastings, and St. Blaise, the latter dying now in the Stallion Barn. Fair Play would join them soon.

Rock Sand served the seasons of 1909 to 1912 at the Nursery Stud. Later events would show it as a tragedy of American racing that he was not retained until his death.

In England, while Rock Sand was busy in Kentucky, his great son, Tracery, sent over by Belmont, rocketed to the top as a tremendous horse. The English, realizing that they had made a drastic error in letting Rock Sand go to the "colonies," now wanted him back, and were besieging Belmont with offers. Finally, along with Belmont's growing admiration for Fair Play, he decided to cut down his activities and concentrate on the cross of the Hastings-Fair Play blood on the Rock Sand mares produced at Nursery.

Not to England, however, did Rock Sand go when he recrossed the Atlantic. A French syndicate outbid the English with an offer of $125,000, his original price, and to France he went to stand but one season before his death, at fourteen, in July 1914.

His one crop of French foals disappeared into the shadows of World War I, and when it was over, the few which could be identified were four and five years of age, past their opportunity to prove their worth. He had left but sixteen living foals in England before going to America, and so it was through the produce of only four seasons at Nursery Stud that Rock Sand sent his glorious heritage down to those to follow. They have carried the banner well, proving beyond a question of doubt that his blood was of the true aristocracy.

The records show that he sired fifty-nine colts and sixty-one fillies in the United States, all but eleven at Nursery Stud. It was a small family which, because of the racing depression, could make no memorable financial record. Of the American crop, Friar Rock, born in 1913 to the mare, Friar Gold, who had previously produced Fair Play, by Hastings, was the most memorable. As a three-year-old in 1916, he won the Belmont, Brooklyn, Suburban, and Saratoga Cup. Friar Rock was sold for breeding to John E. Madden for $50,000 and produced Inchcape, the startling two-year-old which brought a price of $115,000 only to die before he could make his true score.

Many of Rock Sand's male descendants were marked for tragedy. Inchcape was one, and another was Tracery, who died at an early age after being exported to Argentina when his English career was done.

The sixty-one daughters of Rock Sand were his treasure. No other family of mares has ever carried on such a prepotent and splendid heritage as did they. Two of them, Hour Glass and Epine Blanche, went to France to produce Epinard and Hourless. The first, by Badojoz, became a sensational racer in France, England and the United

States; the second, by Negofol, was returned to this country to run brilliantly and to sire many fine handicap stars, including Mike Hall, one of the money-winning champions before the era of "crazy money" made financial records farcical.

Of Rock Sand's sixty-one fillies produced here, only forty became mothers, and this comparatively tiny family was augmented by seven more daughters from his English stud days. From these the American turf got such as Mad Hatter, Mad Play, Arc Light, Dunlin, Fairmont, Prince of Wales, Coventry, Missionary, Sporting Blood, Broomspun, Broomster, My Play, Chatterton, Osprey, and Hourless. They averaged sixteen triumphs and more than $70,000 each. In this list there is one great gap which is filled by the story of Man o' War.

(MAHUBAH) Mahubah was a dark bay with black points, shading to the seal-brown of Rock Sand, her sire. She stood just under sixteen hands in height and was of rangy, racy design. Her name was an Arabic word meaning "good greetings; good fortune."

She was born to Merry Token in the spring of 1910, while racing was still in the doldrums. She was strongly inbred, through Rock Sand, MacGregor, and Maniac to the Number 4 family of the Layton Barb Mare, many of whose daughters were richly endowed with speed, stamina, and the ability to reproduce in abundance. Mahubah, however, was destined to foal but five, and although those were the beginnings of one of the most magnificent thoroughbred families of history, it is tragic that Mahubah became barren when but ten years of age, and so remained until her death at twenty-one.

"Breeding mares," Major August Belmont often argued, "need not necessarily have experience or ability on the track. In fact, I am almost convinced that no racing at all is a better plan."

Thus Mahubah, already chosen for the Fair Play-Rock Sand experiment, was sent to the post for only one race as a two-year-old, placing second; twice at three years, winning and finishing fourth. That was all for Mahubah the racer. She had more important missions ahead.

Back she went to Nursery's pastures to wait for the spring when her "marriage" to Fair Play would take place. She would never be mated with any other horse, and was often called "Fair Play's wife."

Her first foal was the filly called Masda, a chestnut, a youngster of whistling speed but temperamental, difficult to manage, and apt to turn the fire of Fair Play into a tantrum rather than competitive drive.

Masda raced for four seasons. As a two-year-old, running under the training of S. C. Hildreth for Belmont, she ran seven times with two wins, two seconds, one third. She showed such startling speed at times that Hildreth was intensely interested in continuing the experiment. However, she was so difficult to handle that at his suggestion, Masda was sold after her first three-year-old start. For other owners she seemed to win only when she pleased, and she did not take kindly to routine. At four she joined the brood mares of Harry Payne Whitney at Brookdale Stud.

Mahubah failed to conceive after the birth of Masda, but was successful the next year, and that one was Man o' War. The following year she foaled the bay colt called Playfellow, and the next year another bay colt named My Play. The ensuing spring brought the second chestnut filly, Mirabelle.

And that was all.

Mahubah, although a healthy, strong, good-milking mother, had produced her last foal, and, although many expert veterinaries were called in, her barrenness was permanent.

When Playfellow was but a weanling he was sold by Major Belmont to J. F. Johnson, owner of the Quincy Stable. It must be remembered that at this time Man o' War was still a yearling, belonging now to Samuel Riddle, Masda was running in her erratic way, and there was no reason yet to know that the experiment was about to hit the golden jackpot. Even though the formula seemed sensational on paper, the individual products might still be nothing more than mediocre. This would happen later when Man o' War himself, bred to the great mare, Top Flight, in what was to be the mating of the ages, produced the nonentity, Sky Raider.

Then, too, World War was the order of the day for Major Belmont, and Playfellow was sold in the same cutting-down process which sent Man o' War to the auction at Saratoga where he became the property of Samuel D. Riddle in the summer of 1918.

Playfellow, then famous as a full-brother of Man o' War, the two-year-old, ran sensationally in two starts of his third year, smothering his opposition in two races at a mile at Belmont Park. Then his form took a sharp drop and he ran poorly for the next two years before going to stud. He changed hands many times, and it is possible that his value seemed less than it actually was because of the fabulous success of his older brother.

My Play, the younger bay brother, although trailed by a jinx through most of his career, was more than just "a brother to Man o' War." He was a terrific horse in his own right, and when death took him at eleven years of age it was a day of ill-luck for the future of racing.

He had matured slowly under the ownership of E. R. Simms and Henry Oliver who called themselves the Lexington Stable. He could not win in eleven tries at two, but at three he was better, and after that he became a star.

He spread a hoof during the running of the 1922 Kentucky Derby, where he finished fifth. This accident sidelined him for several weeks, but he managed to win three of six starts before the season ended. At four he captured the Aqueduct Handicap, the Waterfleet and Uncas Handicaps at Saratoga, and became the third of Mahubah's sons to run a mile in less than 1:37, a record held by no other mare.

He continued to run at five, and, although he was now a matured, game, and husky horse able to carry tremendous weight, bad luck still pursued him. He ran second four times, but finally won the Jockey Gold Cup at Belmont to end his racing career.

My Play went then to the Coldstream Stud to start his career as a sire in 1925, and to die suddenly on April 6, 1930. Within five years, despite only limited opportunity, My Play was the father of the winners of 323 races and $487,415.

Best known of his sons were Plucky Play and Head Play, the former a conqueror of Equipoise in the 1931 Arlington Handicap; the latter one of the figures in the famous stretch battle between jockeys Meade and Fischer which gave Burgoo King a nose victory over Head Play in the 1933 Kentucky Derby.

My Play joins in history with his more famous brother as the only brother team both of which have sired winners of more than $100,000. It is unfortunate that he could not have lived another decade to continue the brother act to a normal ending.

Mirabelle, Mahubah's second chestnut filly and her last foal, was born in 1920, small, rather frail, and was tabbed for breeding from the start. She trained at two, ran twice unplaced, and returned to the farm. She was an erratic breeder, often missing, and once having twins, but did foal the fine geldings Marabou and Mirage. She remained at Nursery until the dispersal sale in 1925 when she went to Elmendorf for $33,000 bid by Mr. Widener.

This, with the exception of Man o' War, ends the story of Mahubah's family. A pitifully small group, with neither of the daughters being exceptional breeders, it will still live forever in turf history because of the chestnut colt foaled in 1917. In him was the spark of greatness never seen before, and perhaps never to be seen again.

He was to be Mahubah's masterpiece, fashioned with the mixture, remixture, and countermixture of the blood of stalwart ancestors through nearly three hundred years.

He was to be the "mostest hoss."

COMPLETE RACING RECORD OF MAN O' WAR

1919	Track	Race	Dist.	Wt.	Fin.	Time Tr.	Odds	Valu
Jun 6	Belmont Park	Purse	5-8st	115	1^{6}	:59 ft	3-5	$50
Jun 9	Belmont Park	Keene Memorial	5½fst	115	1^{3}	1:05⅗sl	7-10	4,20
Jun 21	Jamaica	Youthful	5½f	120	$1^{2½}$	1:06⅗gd	1-2	3,85
Jun 23	Aqueduct	Hudson	5-8	130	$1^{1½}$	1:01⅗ft	1-10	2,82
Jly 5	Aqueduct	Tremont	3-4	130	1^{1}	1:13 ft	1-10	4,80
Aug 2	Saratoga	United States Hotel	3-4	130	1^{2}	1:12⅖ft	9-10	7,60
Aug 13	Saratoga	Sanford Memorial	3-4	130	$2^{½}$	1:11⅕ft	11-20	70
Aug 23	Saratoga	Grand Union Hotel Stakes	3-4	130	$1^{¼}$	1:12 ft	11-20	7,60
Aug 30	Saratoga	Hopeful Stakes	3-4	130	1^{4}	1:13 sl	9-20	24,60
Sep 23	Belmont Park	Belmont Futurity	3-4st	127	$1^{2½}$	1:11⅗ft	1-2	26,65
	Total (10)							$83,32

1920	Track	Race	Dist.	Wt.	Fin.	Time Tr.	Odds	Valu
May 18	Pimlico	Preakness	1 1-8	126	$1^{1½}$	1:51⅗ft	4-5	$23,00
May 29	Belmont Park	Withers	1	118	1^{2}	1:35⅘ft	1-7	4,82
Jun 12	Belmont Park	Belmont	1 3-8	126	1^{20}	2:14⅕ft	1-25	7,95
Jun 22	Jamaica	Stuyvesant	1	135	1^{8}	1:41⅗gd	1-100	3,85
Jly 10	Aqueduct	Dwyer	1 1-8	126	$1^{1½}$	1:49⅕ft	1-5	4,85
Aug 7	Saratoga	Miller	1 3-16	131	1^{6}	1:56⅗ft	1-30	4,70
Aug 21	Saratoga	Travers	1 1-4	129	$1^{2½}$	2:01⅘ft	2-9	9,27
Sep 4	Belmont Park	Lawrence Realization	1 5-8	126	1^{100}	2:40⅘ft	1-100	15,04
Sep 11	Belmont Park	Jockey Club	1 1-2	118	1^{15}	2:28⅘ft	1-100	5,85
Sep 18	Havre de Grace	Potomac Handicap	1 1-16	138	$1^{1½}$	1:44⅘ft	15-100	6,80
Oct 12	Kenilworth	Kenilworth Park Gold Cup	1 1-4	120	1^{7}	2:03 ft	1-20	80,00
	Total (11)							$166,14

RECAPITULATION

Year	Age	Sts.	1st	2d	3d	Unp.	Won
1919	2	10	9	1	0	0	$83,32
1920	3	11	11	0	0	0	166,14
Totals (2)		21	20	1	0	0	$249,46

MAN O' WAR'S TIME RECORDS MADE IN 1920

Date	Track	Stake	Dist.	Weight	Time
May 29	Belmont Park	Withers	1	118	1:35
Jly 10	Aqueduct	Dwyer	1 1-8	126	1:49
Jun 12	Belmont Park	Belmont	1 3-8	126	*2:14
Sep 11	Belmont Park	Jockey Club	1 1-2	118	2:28
Sep 4	Belmont Park	Lawrence Realization	1 5-8	126	2:40

* World's record still standing.

PAST PERFORMANCE RECORD

BELMONT PARK, N. Y., JUNE 6, 1919

SIXTH RACE—⅝ Mile Straight (Sept. 12, 1918—55⅗—2—110.) Purse **$700**. 2-year-olds. Maidens. Special Weights. Net Value to Winner, $500; second, $125; third, $75.

Horses	Wt.	PP	St.	¼	½	Str.	Fin.	Jockeys	Owners	W	P	S
Man o' War	115	7	1	2^1	2^4	1^3	1^6	J. Loftus	Gl. Riddle Fm.	3-5	1-5	out
Retrieve	112	6	4	1^{nk}	$1\frac{1}{2}$	2^4	$2\frac{1}{2}$	R. Troxler	W. Salmon	7	2½	4-5
Neddam	115	5	6	$4\frac{1}{2}$	4^1	3^1	3^4	M. Buxton	W. Booth*	20	5	8-5
Devildog	115	3	5	6^1	5^1	5^2	4^{nk}	G. Walls	Quincy Stable†	4	4-5	out
Gladiator	115	4	7	3^{nk}	$3\frac{1}{2}$	4^1	5^3	J. Butwell	W. Booth*	20	5	8-5
Lady Brighton	112	1	2	$5\frac{1}{2}$	6^2	$6\frac{1}{2}$	6^{nk}	J. Metcalf	Brighton Stable	10	3	1
American Boy	115	2	3	7	7	7	7	T. Rice	Quincy Stable†	4	4-5	out

* † Coupled in betting; no separate place or show betting.

Time: :59. Track—fast.

Winner—Ch. c. by Fair Play—Mahubah, by Rock Sand, trained by L. Feustel, bred by Mr. August Belmont. Went to post at 5:08. At post 2 minutes. Start good and slow. Won cantering; second and third driving. Man o' War broke fast, held sway throughout, and was under stout restraint at the end. Retrieve showed high early speed, but tired in the final eighth. Neddam closed gamely after racing greenly in the early stages. Devildog had no mishaps.

Scratched—Black Hackle 115.

BELMONT PARK, N. Y., JUNE 9, 1919

FOURTH RACE—5½ Furlongs Straight (July 17, 1915—1:03⅘—2—106). Seventh Running of the KEENE MEMORIAL STAKES. Value $5,000. 2-year-olds. Allowances. Net value to winner, $4,200; second, $700; third, $300.

Horses	Wt.	PP	St.	¼	½	Str.	Fin.	Jockeys	Owners	W	P	S
Man o' War	115	3	2	$2\frac{1}{2}$	3^2	3^2	1^3	J. Loftus	Gl. Riddle Fm.	7-10	1-3	out
On Watch	115	4	5	5^1	4^1	4^2	$2\frac{1}{2}$	W. Kelsay	G. Loft	5	7-5	3-5
Anniversary	115	6	6	6	5^2	5^5	3^4	T. Rice	Quincy Stable	12	3	6-5
Ralco	116½	5	1	$1\frac{1}{2}$	1^{nk}	$2\frac{1}{2}$	4^{nk}	J. Butwell	R. Parr	8	2½	6-5
My Laddie	112	2	4	3^1	$2\frac{1}{2}$	$1\frac{1}{2}$	5^8	R. Troxler	W. Salmon	50	15	5
Hoodwink	112	1	3	4^1	6	6	6	E. Ambrose	Mrs. W. Jeffords	4	7-5	1-2

Time: 1:05⅗.

Winner—Ch. c. by Fair Play—Mahubah by Rock Sand, trained by L. Feustel; bred by Mr. August Belmont. Went to post at 4:13. At post 1 minute. Start good and slow. Won easily; second and third driving. Man o' War, always well up, responded gamely to urging in the final eighth and drew away easily at the end. On Watch showed a game effort and finished fast. Anniversary closed gamely through the last quarter. Ralco tired. Laddie showed an improved effort. Hoodwink evidently disliked the going.

Scratched—Bonnie Mary, 125; Rouleau 112.

Overweight—Ralco 1½ pounds.

JAMAICA, N. Y., JUNE 21, 1919

THIRD RACE—5½ Furlongs (May 19, 1919—1:05—4—122). Seventh Running of the YOUTHFUL STAKES. Value $5,000. 2-year-olds. Allowances. Net value to winner, $3,850; second, $700; third, $300.

Horses	Wt.	PP	St.	¼	½	Str.	Fin.	Jockeys	Owners	W	P	S
Man o' War	120	4	3	1^1	1^2	1^4	1^{2½}	J. Loftus	Gl. Riddle Fm.	1-2	out	—
On Watch	108	2	1	3^2	2^{nk}	3^8	2^2	A. Schu'g'r	G. W. Loft	4½	4-5	out
Lady Brummel	105	3	4	4	3½	2½	3^{10}	L. Ensor	Brighton Stable	18-5	7-10	out
St. Allan	105	1	2	2^1	4	4	4	A. Collins	N. Sho. Stable	40	6	2

Time: :23⅕, :47⅗, 1:00⅕, 1:06⅗. Track—good.

Winner—Ch. c. by Fair Play—Mahubah, by Rock Sand, trained by L. Feustel; bred by Mr. August Belmont. Went to post at 3:47, at post 4 minutes. Start good and slow. Won easily; second and third driving. Man o' War, off in motion, drew away into a big early lead and was eased up in the last sixteenth. On Watch stood stretch gamely. Lady Brummel jumped in the air at the barrier's rise, but moved up with a rush and tired in the final eighth from her early effort. St. Allan apparently was outclassed.

Overweight—Lady Brummel, 3 pounds.

AQUEDUCT, N. Y., JUNE 23, 1919

THIRD RACE—⅝ Mile (July 8, 1918—58⅕—2—112). Twenty-ninth running of the HUDSON STAKES. Guaranteed value $3,500. 2-year-olds. Allowances. Net value to winner, $2,825; second, $400; third, $200.

Horses	Wt.	PP	St.	¼	½	Str.	Fin.	Jockeys	Owners	W	P	S
Man o' War	130	2	1	1½	1^1	1^1	1½	J. Loftus	Gl. Riddle Fm.*	1-10	out	—
Violet Tip	109	3	2	3^{nk}	4^1	2½	2^4	E. Ambrose	R. Parr	15	1	out
Shoal	115	1	5	5	5	3½	3^{12}	J. Collins	R. L. Gerry	15	1	out
Evergay	112	5	3	2½	2^1	4^2	4^6	L. Lyke	T. P. Thorne	40	4	out
Rockinghorse	115	4	4	4^3	3½	5	5	T. Nolan	Gl. Riddle Fm.*	1-10	out	—

* Coupled in betting; no separate place or show betting.

Time: 1:01⅗. Track—fast.

Winner—Ch. c. by Fair Play—Mahubah by Rock Sand, trained by L. Feustel; bred by Mr. August Belmont. Went to post at 3:36. At post 3 minutes. Start good and slow. Won easily; second and third driving. Man o' War, after breaking through the barrier to a false start, was away fast and assumed command at the elbow, then flew away to an easy victory and was easing up in the final forty yards. Violet Tip showed a good effort and was easily second best. Shoal ran sluggishly in the early running, but had little difficulty in disposing of Evergay. The latter showed a smart early effort. Rocking Horse tired badly in the final eighth and was not persevered with when thoroughly beaten.

Scratched—Dominique 115; Alias, 112; Rory O'Moore, 112; Sand Bed, 112.

AQUEDUCT, N. Y., JULY 5, 1919

THIRD RACE—¾ Mile (June 6, 1916—1:11—3—116). Thirtieth Running of the TREMONT STAKES. Guaranteed Value $6,000. 2-year-olds. Allowances. Net value to winner, $4,800; second, $700; third, $300.

Horses	Wt.	PP	St.	¼	½	Str.	Fin.	Jockeys	Owners	W	P	S
Man o' War	130	2	2	1^{1}	1^{1}	$1^{1\frac{1}{2}}$	1^{1}	J. Loftus	Gl. Riddle Fm.	1-10	out	—
Ralco	115	3	3	2^{2}	2^{3}	2^{5}	2^{20}	J. Butwell	R. Parr	10	1-6	out
Ace of Aces*	112	1	1	3	3	3	3	A. Collins	R. F. Carman	50	4	out

* Added starter.

Time: :23⅗, :47⅖, 1:13. Track—fast.

Winner—Ch. c. by Fair Play—Mahubah by Rock Island, trained by L. Feustel, bred by Mr. August Belmont. Went to post at 3:30. At post 2 minutes. Start good and slow. Won easily; second and third driving. Man o' War took the lead quickly, set a fast pace, and won all the way unextended. Ralco easily second best, was hard ridden through the final quarter. Ace of Aces began fast, but was immediately out-run, and was eased up when beaten, in the final eighth.

Scratched—Rocking Horse, 115.

SARATOGA, N. Y., AUGUST 2, 1919

THIRD RACE—¾ Mile (Aug. 22, 1918—1:10⅘—3—115). Thirty-sixth Running of the UNITED STATES HOTEL STAKES. Guaranteed Value $10,000. 2-year-olds. Allowances. Net value to winner, $7,600; second, $1,500; third, $750.

Horses	Wt.	PP	St.	¼	½	Str.	Fin.	Jockeys	Owners	W	P	S
Man o' War	130	8	1	1^{3}	1^{3}	1^{4}	1^{2}	J. Loftus	Gl. Riddle Fm.	9-10	2-5	1-5
Upset	115	1	3	$3^{\frac{1}{2}}$	2^{2}	2^{4}	2^{1}	E. Ambrose	H. P. Whitney	6	2	1
Homely	112	5	6	7^{1}	7^{1}	$3^{\frac{1}{2}}$	3^{1}	W. Kelsay	S. Lewis	25	10	5
Bonnie Mary	127	2	10	$5^{\frac{1}{2}}$	8^{8}	4^{2}	4^{8}	L. Ensor	P. Clark	4½	8-5	4-5
By Golly	115	6	4	6^{2}	6^{1}	$6^{\frac{1}{2}}$	5^{1}	H. Thurber	R. Bradley	10	3	8-5
Rouleau	112	10	8	8^{4}	5^{1}	8^{6}	6^{1}	C. Rob'son	M. Jones	20	8	4
Feodor	112	9	5	4^{3}	$4^{\frac{1}{2}}$	7^{2}	7^{1}	C. Kummer	R. Gerry	20	7	3
Carmandale	125	7	2	2^{1}	3^{1}	5^{1}	8^{1}	L. Fator	R. Carman	25	10-5	5
Sandy Beal	115	3	9	10	10	10	9^{1}	G. Corey	W. Murray	40	15	6
David Harum	112	4	7	9^{3}	9^{2}	9^{2}	10	L. McAtee	W. R. Coe	30	12	6

Time: :23, :47⅕, 1:12⅖. Track—fast.

Winner—Ch. c. by Fair Play—Mahubah, by Rock Sand, trained by L. Feustel; bred by Mr. August Belmont. Went to post at 3:46. At post 6 minutes. Start poor and slow. Won easily; second and third driving. Man o' War away fast, opened up a big lead at the back stretch turn, raced under restraint thereafter, and was eased up in the final sixteenth. Upset broke well and moved up stoutly in the early running but could never overtake the winner. Homely raced ending pressure all the way, saved ground throughout and held on gamely in the final drive. Bonnie Mary broke poorly and was taken to the outside, closed an immense gap in the first quarter and moved up steadily to the last eighth, where she began tiring. By Golly ran an even race. Rouleau was taken wide all the way. Feodor showed early speed, but failed to stay. Sandy Beal was away poorly.

Scratched—Sammy, 112; Royal Duck, 115; Marianne, 109.

SARATOGA, N. Y., AUGUST 13, 1919

FOURTH RACE—¾ Mile (Aug. 22, 1918—1:10⅗—3—115). Seventh Running of the SANFORD MEMORIAL. Guaranteed Value $5,000. 2-year-olds. Allowances. Net value to winner, $3,925; second, $700; third, $300.

Horses	Wt.	PP	St.	¼	½	Str.	Fin.	Jockeys	Owners	W	P	S
Upset	115	5	1	2^{h}	2^{1}	1^{h}	$1^{½}$	W. Knapp	H. P. Whitney	8	7-5	1-3
Man o' War	130	6	5	4^{4}	$3^{1½}$	3^{3}	2^{3}	J. Loftus	Gl. Riddle Fm.	11-20	out	—
Golden Broom	130	3	2	$1^{½}$	1^{1}	$2^{1½}$	3^{2}	E. Ambrose	Mrs. W. Jeffords	2½	1-2	—
Capt. Alcock*	112	4	7	7	7	6^{2}	$4^{1½}$	C. Rob'son	J. Madden	100	30	10
Armistice	112	2	3	5^{3}	5^{2}	$5^{½}$	5^{5}	L. McAtee	W. R. Coe	50	15	5
Donnacona	112	7	4	3^{1}	4^{5}	$4^{½}$	6^{1}	W. Kelsay	G. W. Loft	30	8	3
The Swimmer	115	1	6	6^{3}	$6^{1½}$	7	7	R. Simpson	T. F. Henry	50	15	5

* Added starter.

Time: :23⅕, :46⅘, 1:11⅕. Track—fast.

Winner—Ch. c. by Whisk Broom II—Pankhurst, by Voter, trained by James Rowe, bred by Mr. Harry Payne Whitney. Went to post at 4:10. At post 4 minutes. Start poor and slow. Won driving, second and third same. Upset followed the leader closely from the start, moved up with a rush in the last eighth, and, taking the lead, held on gamely when challenged and just lasted long enough to withstand Man o' War's challenge. The latter began slowly and moved up steadily to the stretch turn, where he got into close quarters, then came to the outside in the final eighth, and responding gamely to punishment was gaining in the closing strides. Golden Broom showed great speed in pacemaking, but tired when challenged. Captain Alcock began slowly and closed a big gap. Armistice ran well from a poor beginning. Donnacona ran forwardly in the early running, but was carried wide on the stretch turn and tired.

Scratched—Peace Pennant, 112; Ten Can, 112.

SARATOGA, N. Y., AUGUST 23, 1919

THIRD RACE—¾ Mile (Aug. 22, 1918—1:10⅗—3—115). Seventeenth Running of the GRAND UNION HOTEL STAKES. Guaranteed Value $10,000. 2-year-olds. Net value to winner, $7,600; second, $1,500; third, $750.

Horses	Wt.	PP	St.	¼	½	Str.	Fin.	Jockeys	Owners	W	P	S
Man o' War	130	2	3	1^h	1^3	1^3	1^1	J. Loftus	Gl. Riddle Fm.	11-20	out	—
Upset	125	6	1	4^h	4^1	2^3	2^4	W. Knapp	H. P. Whitney	7	2	1
Blazes	122	3	5	3^h	$3^{1/2}$	$3^{1/2}$	$3^{1/2}$	J. Butwell	R. Parr	8	2	4-5
King Thrush	115	10	6	$5^{1/2}$	5^1	4^1	$4^{1/2}$	E. Sande	J. K. Ross	8	2½	1
Peace Pennant	112	5	10	10	10	6^1	5^1	H. Thurber	W. F. Polson	50	15	8
Evergay	115	1	4	2^2	2^h	$5^{1/2}$	$6^{11/2}$	P. Musg've	T. P. Thorne	40	10	5
Hasten On	115	8	7	6^3	6^1	7^1	$7^{1/2}$	L. Ensor	J. McClell'nd*	20	7	3
Rouleau	112	9	8	9^3	$7^{1/2}$	$8^{1/2}$	8^1	H. Lunsf'd	M. Jones	50	15	8
The Trout	115	7	2	7^h	9^1	10	9^1	C. F'b'ther	J. McClell'nd*	20	7	3
Gladiator	115	4	9	$8^{11/2}$	8^1	9^1	10	W. Kelsay	W. Booth	10	4	8-5

* Coupled in betting; no separate place or show betting.

Time: :22⅗, :46⅗, 1:12. Track—fast.

Winner—Ch. c. by Fair Play—Mahubah, by Rock Sand, trained by L. Feustel; bred by Mr. August Belmont. Went to post at 3:55. At post 5 minutes. Start good and slow. Won eased up, second and third driving. Man o' War followed Upset in the early running under slight restraint, took the lead at his rider's leisure, and drew away in the stretch to win easing up through the last sixteenth. Upset began with a clear lead and raced on the outside of the leaders for the first half, then moved up gamely when called on, but could never overtake the winner. Blazes was hard ridden all the way, and, holding on gamely, outstayed King Thrush. The latter moved up rapidly while rounding the far turn into third place, but was forced wide on the stretch turn, and could never recover. Peace Pennant began slowly but saved ground on all the turns and closed a big gap. Evergay quit after going a good half mile. Hasten On raced wide all the way. Rouleau met with interference. The Trout was in close quarters throughout. Gladiator was eased up in the last sixteenth.

Scratched—Wildair, 115; Sandy Beal, 115; Neddam, 115.

THIRD RACE—¾ Mile (Aug. 22, 1918—1:10⅖—3—115). Fifteenth Running of the HOPEFUL STAKES. Value $30,000. 2-year-olds. Allowances. Net value to winner $24,600; second, $3,500; third, $1,500.

Horses	Wt.	PP	St.	¼	½	Str.	Fin.	Jockeys	Owners	W	P	S
Man o' War	130	3	4	2¹	2³	1⁵	1⁴	J. Loftus	Gl. Riddle Fm.	9-20	1-5	out
Cleopatra	112	1	8	5½	5⁸	3¹	2⁴	C. F'b'ther	W. R. Coe	8	2	4-5
Constancy	124	5	2	1²	1¹	2¹	3²	T. Nolan	J. K. Ross	10	3	6-5
Hasten On	115	8	5	4²	3½	4²	4¹	A. Schu'g'r	W. McClell'nd	40	15	5
Upset	125	6	6	6⁴	6³	6⁴	5³	W. Knapp	H. P. Whitney*	8	8-5	7-10
Dr. Clark†	115	4	1	3¹	4½	5²	6³	E. Ambrose	H. P. Whitney*	8	8-5	7-10
Ethel Gray	112	7	7	7³	7⁴	7⁴	7²	C. Kummer	M. Jones	15	5	2
Capt. Alcock	112	2	3	8	8	8	8	P. Musg've	J. E. Madden	15	5	2

* Coupled in betting; no separate place or show betting.

† Formerly ran as Sammy.

Time: :23, :47, 1:13. Track—slow.

Winner—Ch. c. by Fair Play—Mahubah, by Rock Sand, trained by L. Feustel; bred by Mr. August Belmont. Went to post at 4:03. At post 12 minutes. Start good and slow. Won, easily; second and third driving. Man o' War followed Constancy under slight restraint in the early running and assumed command at his leisure when entering the stretch, to win in a canter. Cleopatra broke slowly, but went around the leaders when rounding the stretch turn, then closed gamely in a stretch run and easily disposed of Constancy. The latter, a quick beginner, set a fast pace in the early running, but faltered in the final eighth. Hasten On, a forward contender, moved up strong on the inside then straightened out in the stretch, but was pinched off at the eighth pole by Constancy and could never recover. Upset, in a tangle at the start, was hard urged and did not appear to favor the going. Dr. Clark showed good speed for a half mile. Ethel Gray and Capt. Alcock could never improve their positions.

Scratched—Sandy Beal, 115.

BELMONT PARK, N. Y., SEPT. 13, 1919

THIRD RACE—¾ Mile Straight (May 19, 1908—1:08⅗—4—137). Thirtieth Running of the FUTURITY STAKES. $5,000 Added. 2-year-olds. Allowances. Net value to winner $26,650; second, $3,106.67; third, $1,503.33.

Horses	Wt.	PP	St.	¼	½	Str.	Fin.	Jockeys	Owners	W	P	S
Man o' War	127	8	2	$3\frac{1}{2}$	$1\frac{1}{2}$	1^2	$12\frac{1}{2}$	J. Loftus	Gl. Riddle Fm.	1-2	1-4	out
John P. Grier	117	9	7	2^1	$2\frac{1}{2}$	2^3	2^4	E. Ambrose	H. P. Whitney*	6	6-5	2-5
Dominique	122	2	1	$1\frac{1}{2}$	$3\frac{1}{2}$	$3\frac{1}{2}$	3^{nk}	C. Kummer	S. C. Hildreth	4	6-5	1-2
Cleopatra	117	3	6	$7\frac{1}{2}$	6^2	$4\frac{1}{2}$	$4\frac{1}{2}$	L. McAtee	W. R. Coe	20	7	3
Upset	120	6	4	$4\frac{1}{2}$	$4\frac{1}{2}$	5^1	5^1	T. Rice	H. P. Whitney*	6	6-5	2-5
Paul Jones	122	1	3	$5\frac{1}{2}$	$5\frac{1}{2}$	6^1	6^1	J. Butwell	R. Parr	40	10	5
On Watch	119	10	8	8^3	$7\frac{1}{2}^{1½}$	7^3	7^3	W. Kelsay	G. W. Loft	30	10	5
Dr. Clark†	122	4	5	9^5	9^3	8^4	8^6	A. Johnson	H. P. Whitney*	6	6-5	2-5
Capt. Alcock	119	5	10	10	10	10	9^2	L. Ensor	J. E. Madden	30	10	5
Miss Jemima	122	7	9	6^h	$8\frac{1}{2}$	9^2	10	C. Buxton	C. E. Rowe	25	8	4

* Coupled in betting; no separate place or show betting.

† Added starter.

Time: 1:11⅗. Track—fast.

Winner—Ch. c. by Fair Play—Mahubah by Rock Sand, trained by L. Feustel; bred by Mr. August Belmont. Went to post at 3:46. At post 8 minutes. Start good and slow. Won easily. Second and third driving. Man o' War was saved behind the leaders until in the last quarter, then took the lead at his rider's leisure and won easing up. John P. Grier was a forward contender for the entire race, and finished gamely through the last eighth. Dominique showed the most speed from the start and made the pace fast, but tired in the final drive. Cleopatra gained steadily and finished fast and gamely under punishment. Upset met with interference at the quarter post and came on gamely when clear in the last eighth. Paul Jones and On Watch tired in the stretch drive. The last three were pulled up at the finish.

Scratched—Arethusa, 116; Padraic, 117.

PIMLICO, MD., MAY 18, 1920

FOURTH RACE—1⅛ Miles (May 17, 1911—1:51—3—112). Purse $25,000 Added. Thirteenth Running of the PREAKNESS STAKES. 3-year-olds. Colts, Fillies, Geldings. Allowances. Net value to winner $23,000; second, $3,000; third, $2,000; fourth, $1,000.

Horses	Wt.	PP	St.	¼	½	¾	Str.	Fin.	Jockeys	Owners	Equiv. Odds
Man o' War	126	7	4	1^{2}	$1^{1½}$	1^{4}	1^{2}	$1^{1½}$	C. Kummer	Gl. R'dl Fm.	80-100
Upset	122	6	1	$3^{1½}$	3^{nk}	3^{h}	2^{2}	2^{5}	J. Rod'g'ez	H. P. Whitney	*285-100
Wildair	114	3	7	4^{nk}	4^{2}	4^{8}	3^{1}	3^{5}	E. Ambrose	H. P. Whitney	*
King Thrush	114	8	5	2^{2}	2^{1}	2^{h}	$4^{8½}$	4^{4}	E. Sande	J. K. L. Ross	850-100
Donnacona	114	4	9	$7^{1½}$	$6^{½}$	$5^{½}$	5^{4}	5^{8}	J. Pierce	G. W. Loft	†1615-100
Blazes	126	5	2	5^{2}	5^{4}	6^{4}	6^{3}	$6^{1½}$	C. F'b'ther	R. Parr	3190-100
On Watch	126	2	3	$8^{1½}$	7^{2}	7^{6}	7^{8}	7^{15}	N. Barrett	G. W. Loft	†
St. Allan	114	1	8	9	8^{6}	8^{8}	8^{9}	8^{3}	D. Sterling	No. Shore Stb.	4760-100
Fairway	114	9	6	6^{3}	9	9	9	9	J. Butwell	T. Clyde	3300-100

* Coupled in mutuels as H. P. Whitney entry.

† Coupled in mutuels as G. W. Loft entry.

Time: :23⅖, :47⅗, 1:12⅖, 1:38⅕, 1:51⅗. Track—fast.

$2 mutuels paid, Man o' War, $3.60 straight, $2.90 place, $2.90 show; H. P. Whitney entry, $2.50 place, $3.00 show.

Equivalent booking odds—Man o' War, 80 to 100 straight, 45 to 100 place, 45 to 100 show; H. P. Whitney entry, 25 to 100 place, 50 to 100 show.

Winner—Ch. c. by Fair Play—Mahubah by Rock Sand, trained by L. Feustel; bred by Mr. August Belmont. Went to post at 4:08. At post 6 minutes. Start good and slow. Won easily; second and third driving. Man o' War, rushed to the front in run to the first turn, set a terrific early pace, and, subduing King Thrush in the first three-quarters, had something in reserve when Upset challenged in the stretch. Upset hung on with determination, hard punished all the way. Wildair was stopping in the last eighth. Donnacona, away slowly, was cut off when the break came. King Thrush was speedy, but failed to stay the route. The others were always outpaced.

BELMONT PARK, N. Y., MAY 29, 1920

FOURTH RACE—1 Mile (Sept. 7, 1914—1:36⅗—3—117). Forty-fifth running of the WITHERS STAKES. $6,000. Guaranteed Value. 3-year-olds. Net value to winner $4,825; second, $700; third, $300.

Horses	Wt.	PP	St.	¼	½	¾	Str.	Fin.	Jockeys	Owners	W	P	S
Man o' War	118	2	1	1^{2}	$1^{1½}$	1^{2}	1^{2}	1^{2}	C. Kummer	Gl. Riddle Fm.	1-7	out	—
Wildair	118	1	3	$2^{½}$	2^{8}	2^{10}	2^{12}	2^{12}	E. Ambrose	H. P. Whitney	6	out	—
David Harum	118	3	2	3	3	3	3	3	C. F'b'ther	W. R. Coe	30	4	out

Time: :24, :47⅕, 1:11, 1:35⅘ (New American Record). Track—fast.

Winner—Ch. c. by Fair Play—Mahubah by Rock Sand, trained by L. Feustel; bred by Mr. August Belmont. Went to post at 4:12. At post 1 minute. Start good and slow. Won easily; second and third driving. Man o' War assumed command at the start, displayed wonderful speed under restraint, and won under a stout pull. Wildair made a game effort rounding the turn, but could never get up to the leader. David Harum was outpaced the entire race.

Scratched—Hasten On, 118.

BELMONT PARK, N. Y., JUNE 12, 1920

FOURTH RACE—1⅜ Miles (June 13, 1919—2:17⅖—3—126). Fifty-second Running of the BELMONT STAKES. Guaranteed Value $10,000 and Plate Valued at $250. 3-year-olds. Net value to winner, $7,700; second, $1,500.

Horses	Wt.	PP	St.	¼	½	¾	Str.	Fin.	Jockeys	Owners	W	P	S
Man o' War	126	1	1	1^{2}	1^{2}	1^{7}	1^{12}	1^{20}	C. Kummer	Gl. Riddle Fm.	1-25	out	—
Donnacona	126	2	2	2	2	2	2	2	N. Barrett	G. W. Loft	20	out	—

Time: 2:14⅕ (New Track Record). Track—fast.

Winner—Ch. c. by Fair Play—Mahubah by Rock Sand, trained by L. Feustel; bred by Mr. August Belmont. Went to post at 4:12. At post 1 minute. Start good and slow. Won easily. Man o' War, hard held in the early running, opened up a long lead entering the main track, but was taken under a pull in the final sixteenth. Donnacona was not persevered with when the leader drew away, and was eased up in the closing strides.

Scratched—David Harum, 126.

JAMAICA, N. Y., JUNE 22, 1920

FOURTH RACE—1 Mile (June 19, 1919—1:38⅘—3—129). Fifth Running of the STUYVESANT HANDICAP. Guaranteed Value $5,000. 3-year-olds. Net value to winner, $3,850; second $700.

Horses	Wt.	PP	St.	¼	½	¾	Str.	Fin.	Jockeys	Owners	W	P	S
Man o' War	135	1	1	1^{5}	1^{4}	1^{7}	1^{8}	1^{8}	C. Kummer	Gl. Riddle Fm.	1-100	out	—
Yellow Hand*	103	2	2	2	2	2	2	2	J. Callahan	R. Wilson	60	out	—

* Added starter.

Time: :25⅗, :49, 1:14⅕, 1:41⅗. Track good.

Winner—Ch. c. by Fair Play—Mahubah by Rock Sand, trained by L. Feustel; bred by Mr. August Belmont.

Went to post at 4:02. At post 4 minutes. Start good and slow. Won easily; second driving.

Man o' War, outbreaking his opponent, drew away into a long lead under stout restraint and was eased up in the last eighth. Yellow Hand, away slowly, was outrun for the entire journey.

Scratched—Dominique, 126; Irish Dream, 110; On Watch, 121; Krewer, 107.

AQUEDUCT, N. Y., JULY 10, 1920

FOURTH RACE—1⅛ Miles (June 25, 1917—1:49⅗—9—117). Thirty-second running of the DWYER STAKES. Purse $6,000 Guaranteed. 3-year-olds. Allowances. Net value to winner, $4,150; second, $700.

Horses	Wt.	PP	St.	¼	½	¾	Str.	Fin.	Jockeys	Owners	W	P	S
Man o' War	126	1	2	1½	1h	1h	1½	11½	C. Kummer	Gl. Riddle Fm.	1-5	out	—
John P. Grier	108	2	1	2	2	2	2	2	E. Ambrose	H. P. Whitney	18-5	out	—

Time: :23⅗, :46, 1:09⅗, 1:36, 1:49⅕. (New American Record.) Track—fast.

Winner—Ch. c. by Fair Play—Mahubah by Rock Sand, trained by L. Feustel, bred by Mr. August Belmont. Went to post at 4:05. At post 2 minutes. Start good and slow. Won ridden out; second driving. Man o' War rated in front under steady restraint for the first three quarters, responded courageously under intermittent punishment through the stretch, and drew clear under hard urging in the last sixteenth. John P. Grier ran in close pursuit of the leader the entire race, assumed a slight lead between calls in the stretch, but faltered the last seventy yards and Ambrose eased him up in the closing strides.

SARATOGA, N. Y., AUGUST 7, 1920

FOURTH RACE—1³⁄₁₆ Miles (August 16, 1918—1:56—4—131). Thirty-first Running of the MILLER STAKES. Purse, $2,500 Added. 3-year-olds. Net value to winner, $4,700; second, $700; third, $300.

Horses	Wt.	PP	St.	¼	½	¾	Str.	Fin.	Jockeys	Owners	W	P	S
Man o' War	131	2	1	11½	11½	13	14	16	E. Sande	Gl. Riddle Fm.	1-30	out	—
Donnacona	119	1	2	22	23	23	23	24	N. Barrett	G. W. Loft	15	out	—
King Albert	114	3	3	3	3	3	3	3	C. Borel	T. Monahan	150	10	out

Time: :24, :48⅕, 1:12⅘, 1:37⅘, 1:56⅗. Track—fast.

Winner—Ch. c. by Fair Play—Mahubah by Rock Sand, trained by L. Feustel, bred by August Belmont. Went to post at 4:32. At post 1 minute. Start good and slow. Won easily; second and third driving. Man o' War held his opponents safe all the way, was taken under stout restraint rounding the upper turn, and was never extended. Donnacona, in close pursuit of the leader for three-quarters, was not persevered with when the winner drew away. King Albert was outclassed, but raced gamely.

Scratched—Biff Bang, 114.

SARATOGA, N. Y., AUGUST 21, 1920

FOURTH RACE—1¼ Miles (August 2, 1920—2:01⅘—4—129). Fifty-first Running of the TRAVERS STAKES. Guaranteed Value $12,500. 3-year-olds. Allowances. Net value to winner, $9,275; second, $2,000; third, $1,000.

Horses	Wt.	PP	St.	¼	½	¾	Str.	Fin.	Jockeys	Owners	W	P	S
Man o' War	129	1	1	1^{1}	1^{2}	1^{4}	1^{4}	$1^{2½}$	A. Schu'g'r	Gl. Riddle Fm.	2-9	out	—
Upset	123	3	3	3	3	3	2^{11}	2^{7}	J. Rod'g'ez	H. P. Whitney	18-5	out	—*
John P. Grier	115	2	2	2^{6}	2^{5}	2^{1}	3	3	E. Ambrose	H. P. Whitney	18-5	out	—*

* Coupled in betting; no separate place or show betting.

Time: :23⅕, :46⅗, 1:10, 1:35⅗, 2:01⅘ (Equals track record). Track fast.

Winner Ch. c. by Fair Play—Mahubah by Rock Sand, trained by L. Feustel, bred by Mr. August Belmont. Went to post at 4:34. At post 1 minute. Start good and slow. Won easily; second and third driving. Man o' War took the lead at the start, and, setting a terrific pace in the early running, raced John P. Grier into defeat and was under restraint through the stretch. Upset, after being saved to the last turn, closed up resolutely in the last quarter and easily passed John P. Grier, but the leader easily held him safe. John P. Grier endeavored to keep pace with the leader for the first three-quarters, but tired badly in the stretch and finished eased up.

BELMONT PARK, N. Y., SEPT. 4, 1920

FOURTH RACE—1⅝ Miles (Sept, 6, 1919—2:47⅗—3—116). Purse $5,000 Added. Twenty-eighth Running of the LAWRENCE REALIZATION. 3-year-olds. Net value to winner, $15,040; second, $1,033.33.

Horses	Wt.	PP	St.	¼	½	¾	Str.	Fin.	Jockeys	Owners	W	P	S
Man o' War	126	2	2	1^{20}	1^{20}	1^{30}	1^{50}	1^{100}	C. Kummer	Gl. Riddle Fm.	1-100	1-100	out
Hoodwink*	116	1	1	2	2	2	2	2	E. Ambrose	Mrs. W. Jeffords	80	60	out

* Added starter.

Time: :23⅗, :47⅘, 1:13, 1:38⅘, 2:03⅗, 2:28⅘, 2:40⅘ (New American record). Track—fast.

Winner —Ch. c. by Fair Play—Mahubah, by Rock Sand, trained by L. Feustel; bred by Mr. August Belmont. Went to post at 3:42. At post 1 minute. Start good and slow. Won easily. Man o' War set a great pace under stout restraint the first three-quarters, displayed his flight of speed rounding the lower turn. In the stretch he was taken under restraint again. Hoodwink made no effort to keep pace with the leader.

Scratched—Sea Mint, 116.

BELMONT PARK, N. Y., SEPT. 11, 1920

FOURTH RACE—1½ Miles (Oct. 12, 1908—2:32⅕—3—106). Second Running of JOCKEY CLUB STAKES. Purse $5,000 Added. 3-year-olds and upward. Mares and Entire Horses. Weight for Age. Net value to winner $5,850; second $1,000.

Horses	Wt.	PP	St.	¼	½	¾	Str.	Fin.	Jockeys	Owners	W	P	S
Man o' War	118	2	1	1^4	1^5	1^8	1^{12}	1^{15}	C. Kummer	Gl. Riddle Fm.	1-100	out	—
Damask	118	1	2	2	2	2	2	2	E. Ambrose	H. P. Whitney	80	out	—

Time: :25, :49⅗, 1:14⅕, 1:38⅘, 2:03⅗, 2:28⅘ (New American record). Track—fast.

Winner—Ch. c. by Fair Play—Mahubah, by Rock Sand, trained by L. Feustel; bred by Mr. August Belmont. Went to post at 3:44. At post 1 minute. Start good and slow. Won easily; second driving. Man o' War under steady restraint the first mile, opened up a long lead in the stretch, and won under a pull. Damask ran a creditable race.

Scratched—Sea Mint, 118.

HAVRE DE GRACE, SEPT. 18, 1920

FIFTH RACE—1$\frac{1}{16}$ Miles (Sept. 22, 1917—1:45—5—105). Purse $10,000 Added. Sixth Running of the POTOMAC HANDICAP. 3-year-olds. Net value to winner, $6,800; second, $2,000; third, $1,000; fourth, $500.

Horses	Wt.	PP	St.	¼	½	¾	Str.	Fin.	Jockeys	Owners	Equiv. Odds
Man o' War	138	4	1	$1^{1½}$	$1^{1½}$	1^1	$1^{1½}$	$1^{1½}$	C. Kummer	Gl. Riddle Fm.	15-100
Wildair	108	3	2	3^2	3^4	2^5	2^{10}	2^{15}	F. C'ltletti	H. P. Whitney	1010-100
Blazes	104½	1	4	$2^{1½}$	2^{nk}	3^5	3^3	3^2	A. Schu'g'r	R. Parr	*955-100
Paul Jones	114	2	3	4	4	4	4	4	J. Rod'g'ez	R. Parr	*

* Coupled in betting as R. Parr entry.

Time: :23, :47⅗, 1:11⅗, 1:38⅕, 1:44⅘ (New track record). Track—fast.

$2 mutuels paid, Man o' War, $2.30 straight; no place or show mutuels sold.

Equivalent booking odds—Man o' War, 15 to 100 straight.

Winner—Ch. c. by Fair Play—Mahubah, by Rock Sand, trained by L. Feustel; bred by Mr. August Belmont. Went to post at 4:49. At post 1 minute. Start good and slow. Won easily; second and third driving. Man o' War was a bit fractious at the post, but broke well and assumed command under a strong pull rounding the first turn, then Kummer rated him along easily and he drew away without effort when Wildair challenged about the middle of the stretch, and was easing up at the finish. Wildair ran a splendid race, but at no time appeared dangerous, but was easily best of the others. Blazes ran well for the first three-quarters, then tired. Paul Jones showed no speed at any stage.

Scratched—King Thrush, 103; Siren Maid, 87; Shoal, 92.

Overweight—Blazes, 2½ pounds.

KENILWORTH PARK, OCT. 12, 1920

FOURTH RACE—1¼ Miles (Oct. 18, 1916—2:09⅗—5—102). Purse $75,000 and $5,000 Gold Cup. 3-year-olds and upward. Weight-for-Age. Net value to winner, $75,000 and $5,000 Gold Cup.

Horses	Wt.	PP	St.	¼	½	¾	Str.	Fin.	Jockeys	Owners	Equiv. Odds
Man o' War	120	2	1	1^2	1^2	1^5	1^6	1^7	C. Kummer	Gl. Riddle Fm.	5-100
Sir Barton	126	1	2	2	2	2	2	2	F. Keogh	J. K. L. Ross	555-100

Time: :23, :46⅖; :59½; 1:11⅘, 1:37⅗, 2:03 (New Track record). Track—fast.

$2 mutuels paid, Man o' War, $2.10 straight; no place or show mutuels sold.

Equivalent booking odds—Man o' War, 5 to 100 straight.

Winner—Ch. c. by Fair Play—Mahubah, by Rock Sand, trained by L. Feustel; bred by Mr. August Belmont. Went to post at 3:37. At post 1 minute. Start good and slow. Won easily; second driving. Man o' War bounded to the front when the barrier was released, and, setting a great pace for this track, won all the way never fully extended. Keogh went to the whip before they had gone a quarter but was unable to improve his position.

Scratched—Wickford, 126.

WINNING HORSES DEFEATED BY MAN O' WAR

Horse	Races Won	Stakes Won	Money Won
Sir Barton, ch. c., by Star Shoot	13	13	$116,857
Dr. Clark, ch. g., by Broomstick	44	5	101,659
Captain Alcock, ch. c., by Ogden	17	7	69,550
Damask, br. c., by All Gold	18	7	68,000
On Watch, br. c., by Colin	21	9	64,245
Paul Jones, br. g., by Sea King	14	5	64,171
Blazes, br. c., by Wrack	19	7	63,740
*Yellow Hand, b. g., by Rossendale	20	11	61,450
*Cleopatra, ch. f., by Corcyra	8	6	55,937
Dominique, ch. c., by Peter Quince	25	4	45,304
Miss Jemima, br. f., by Black Toney	21	5	42,057
Upset, ch. c., by Whisk Broom II	5	2	37,504
John P. Grier, ch. c., by Whisk Broom II	10	4	37,003
Carmandale, b. c., by Meridian	22	3	34,221
Wildair, b. c., by Broomstick	9	3	32,126
Gladiator, b. c., by Superman	10	4	28,548
Neddam, b. c., by Ormondale	22	2	26,715
Ralco, bl. c., by Rock View	14	4	24,523
Sandy Beal, ch. c., by Superman	9	2	22,856
*Constancy, b. f., by Ambassador II	6	2	21,729
*St. Allan, b. c., by Bridge of Allan	15	—	21,439
American Boy, b. c., by Superman	15	—	19,397
Shoal, b. c., by Danger Rock	11	2	17,959
*Donnacona, b. c., by Prince Palatine	6	1	16,677
Fairway, br. c., by Bryn Mawr	10	1	16,123
Bonnie Mary, b. f., by Ultimus	3	3	15,600
David Harum, b. g., by Star Shoot	15	—	15,415
Anniversary, br. g., by Celt	7	1	15,204
*Rouleau, br. c., by Tracery	7	—	14,583
*King Thrush, ch. c., by Thrush	9	—	13,221
Peace Pennant, b. c., by McGee	5	1	13,020
The Trout, b. c., by Rapid Water	7	—	12,657
Feodor, ch. c., by Ivan the Terrible	16	—	12,497
*Golden Broom, ch. c., by Sweeper II	1	1	10,150
By Golly, b. c., by Helmet	6	—	8,959
Ethel Gray, br. f., by Hessian	3	—	8,447
The Swimmer, ch. g., by Ivan the Terrible	7	—	8,050
Hasten On, b. c., by Great Britain	7	—	7,792
Ace of Aces, br. c., by Meridian	8	—	7,467
Rocking Horse, ch. g., by Trap Rock	4	—	6,658
*Devil Dog, br. c., by Darley Dale	5	—	5,868
Homely, ch. f., by Sea King	2	1	4,801
Lady Brummel, ch. f., by Brummel	4	—	4,458
My Laddie, bl. c., by Celt	3	1	4,317
Evergay, b. c., by Magellan	2	—	2,164
Violet Tip, b. f., by Fair Play	1	1	2,160
Hoodwink, ch. c., by Disguise	1	—	2,753
Retrieve, ch. f., by Celt	1	—	875
Totals (forty-eight horses)	508	117	$1,306,906

* Imported

In the following checklist are included all the 386 foals sired by Man o' War in his 22 years at stud. After the name of each horse is given the name of his dam. In each year the stakes winners are given first, in capitals, then other winners. The number of wins through 1946 is shown. Horses which raced without winning are indicated by a zero in the win column, non-starters by a dash. In each classification colts are named first, then fillies.

1922: 13 Foals

	Wins
AMERICAN FLAG, ch. c.: *Lady Comfey, by Roi Herode	8
BY HISSELF, br. c.: *Colette, by Collar....	8
GUN BOAT, ch. c.: Star Fancy, by *Star Shoot	8
FLORENCE NIGHTINGALE, b. f.: The Nurse, by Yankee	5
MAID AT ARMS, ch. f.: Thrasher, by Trap Rock	7
First Mate, ch. c.: Shady, by Broomstick	7
Flagship, ch. c.: Understudy, by *Star Ruby	10
Lightship, ch. f.: Smoky Lamp, by Broomstick	3
Flotilla, ch. f.: *Santissima, by St. Angelo	—
Friendship Two, ch. c.: Sea Name, by *Seahorse 2nd	—
Homeric, ch. c.: *Batanoea, by Roi Herode	—
Seaplane, b. f.: *Bathing Girl, by Spearmint	—
Br. f.: Masquerade, by Disguise...........Died	

1923: 18 Foals

CRUSADER, ch. c.: Star Fancy, by *Star Shoot	18
MARS, ch. c.: Christmas Star, by *Star Shoot	13
CORVETTE, ch. f.: *Batanoea, by Roi Herode	6
EDITH CAVELL, b. f.: The Nurse, by Yankee	10
TAPS, ch. f.: Shady, by Broomstick.........	5
Dress Parade, ch. c.: Thrasher, by Trap Rock	6
Old Guard, ch. g.: Understudy, by *Star Ruby	9
Volunteer, ch. c.: Flirtatious, by *Golden Garter	5
War Lord, ch. c.: Ursula Emma, by Broomstick	7
Warship, ch. g.: Mistress Ballot, by Ballot	1
Medal, ch. f.: *Meddlesome 2nd, by *Meddler	3
Siren, br. f.: Star Puss, by Jim Gaffney	3
Swanee, ch. f.: Honey Girl, by Friar Rock	1
Artillery, ch. c.: Miss Starlight, by *Watercress	0
Assembly, br. f.: Highest Appeal, by Ultimus	0
Fortress, br. f.: Masquerade, by Disguise	—
Marina, ch. f.: Gold Tassel, by *Star Shoot	—
Ch. c.: Fairy Wand, by *Star Shoot....Died	

1924: 23 Foals

SCAPA FLOW, b. c.: Florence Webber, by *Peep o' Day.....................	5
BROADSIDE, br. c.: *Blue Glass, by *Prince Palatine	11
SON O' BATTLE, b. c.: *Batanoea, by Roi Herode	10
WAR EAGLE, ch. c.: *Earine, by Sea Sick	11
FRILETTE, b. f.: *Frillery, by Broomstick	6
YEDDO, ch. f.: *Yokohama, by Santoi......	5
Point Breeze, ch. c.: Summer Breeze, by *McGee	5
Purple Pirate, ch. c.: Billet, by *Star Shoot	4
Revolver, ch. c.: Helen Blaze, by *Wrack	6
Sea Lion, ch. c.: Sea Puss, by *Star Shoot	2
Mix-Up, ch. f.: *Meddlesome 2nd, by *Meddler	17
Port-Hole, ch. f.: Shady, by Broomstick	1
War Feathers, ch. f.: *Tuscan Red, by William Rufus	1
Armada, dk. ch. f.: *Crepuscule, by *Meddler	0
Bivouac, ch. c.: Topaz, by Uncle............	0
Hail Columbia, br. or blk. f.: *Colette, by Collar........	0
Harp o' th' Winds, ch. f.: Starina, by *Star Shoot	0
Bivouac, ch. c.: Topaz, by Uncle...........	—
Jibber Jib, ch. f.: *Santissima, by St. Angelo	—
Machine Gun, b. f.: *Moneta 3rd, by Spearmint	—
Red White and Blue, ch. f.: *Lady Comfey, by Roi Herode.............	—
Ship of War, blk. f.: Waterblossom, by Waterboy	—
Stewardess, ch. f.: Scribble, by Ultimus	—

1925: 20 Foals

GENIE, ch. c.: Fairy Wand, by *Star Shoot	10
CAESARION, ch. c.: Cleopatra, by Corcyra	1
IRONSIDES, b. c.: Bee's Wax, by Celt.........	14
BATEAU, b. f.: *Escuina, by Ecouen....	11
Crow's Nest, ch. c.: Jeanne Bowdre, by Luke McLuke	10
Field Marshal, ch. c.: Little Flower, by *Star Ruby	13
War Flier, ch. c.: True Flier, by Pennant	4
War Whoop, ch. c.: Highest Appeal, by Ultimus	3
Binnacle, ch. f.: Smoky Lamp, by Plaudit	1
Canteen, ch. f.: Offensive, by Yankee....	1
Marine Blue, ch. f.: Topaz, by Uncle....	1
Sister Ship, ch. f.: Star Fancy, by *Star Shoot	8
Stream Line, ch. f.: Waterblossom, by Waterboy	5
Valkyr, ch. f.: *Princess Palatine, by *Prince Palatine	9
Cassandra, ch. f.: Discretion, by The Manager	0

Miss Shrapnel, ch. f.: Problem, by Superman 0
Admiral's Lassie, ch. f.: *Sun Disc, by Sundridge .... —
Periscope, ch. f.: Scrutiny, by Ballot.... —
War Darling, ch. f.: Early Bird, by Whisk Broom 2nd .... —
Windlass, ch. f.: Milky Way, by *Star Shoot .... —

1926: 18 Foals

CLYDE VAN DUSEN, ch. g.: Uncle's Lassie, by Uncle 12
ANNAPOLIS, br. c.: Panoply, by Peter Pan 21
BATTLESHIP GREY, gr. c.: Alice Blue Gown, by Luke McLuke 8
HARD TACK, ch. c.: Tea Biscuit, by *Rock Sand 3
MARINE, b. c.: *Damaris 2nd, by Sunstar 19
DREADNAUGHT, b. or br. f.: Crack o' Doom, by Ultimus 2
Constitution, b. c.: Florence Webber, by *Peep o' Day 1
Marine Compass, ch. c.: Milky Way, by *Star Shoot 1
Shipmaster, ch. c.: Scribble, by Ultimus 2
War Time, b. c.: Pen Rose, by Sweep.... 4
Serenity, b. f.: *Nature's Smile, by Rabelais 1
Warrior Lass, ch. f.: Sweetheart, by Ultimus 1

Red Gown (ran as Naomi), ch. f.: Ursula Emma, by Broomstick............. 0
Torpedo, ch. f.: *Pasta, by Thrush 0
Gobs, ch. c.: *Santissima, by St. Angelo —
War Horse, ch. c.: Early Bird, by Whisk Broom 2nd .... —
Betsy Ross, b. f.: *Escuina, by Ecouen.. —
War Woman, ch. f.: Topaz, by Uncle.... —

1927: 20 Foals

BATTLESHIP, ch. c.: *Quarantaine, by Sea Sick 17
ALDERSHOT, ch. c.: Coronis, by *Voter.... 10
QUARTER DECK, br. c.: *Trace, by Tracery 8
Armageddon, ch. c.: *L'Avenir, by Rabelais 5
Dock Light, ch. c.: Milky Way, by *Star Shoot 5
Full Dress, blk. c.: Shady, by Broomstick 7
Gun Man, ch. c.: Thrasher, by Trap Rock 5
Red Cross Sister, ch. f.: Scribble, by Ultimus 2
Vagrant, b. f.: *Sanberia, by Santry.... 3

Broadway Limited, ch. c.: *Starflight, by Sunstar 0
Joshua, ch. c.: Summit, by Ultimus........ 0
War Flag, b. c.: Whetstone, by Sweep.. 0
Baton Rouge, br. f.: Baton, by Hainault 0
Shipshape, b. f.: Beatitude, by *Hourless 0
Sweet Gun, ch. f.: Eventide, by Uncle.... 0
Powerful, br. c.: *Queen of Jest, by Black Jester .... —
Sergt. Mike Donaldson, ch. c.: Off Color, by Jim Gaffney............. —
Boadicea, b. f.: *Scoot 2nd, by Vamose —
Uniform, ch. f.: *King's Feather, by Roi Herode .... —
Br. c.: Tripping, by Delhi..................Died

1928: 18 Foals

Wins

ANCHORS AWEIGH, br. c.: Good Bye, by Ultimus 7
FLEET FLAG, ch. c.: *Lady Comfey, by Roi Herode 18
IRON CLAD, ch. c.: Violet Mahoney, by Colin 3
SEA FOX, ch. g.: Trasher, by Trap Rock 24
Frigate Bird, br. c.: *Pameta, by William the Third 16
Roan Antelope, gr. c.: *Garristown, by Roi Herode 9
War, ch. c.: Milky Way, by *Star Shoot 8
Allez Vite, ch. f.: May Alley, by *Star Shoot 3
Problematical, ch. f.: Problem, by Superman 1

David, ch. c.: Christmas Star, by *Star Shoot 0
King's Navy, ch. c.: *King's Feather, by Roi Herode 0
Firetop, ch. f.: Summit, by Ultimus 0
Gun Play, b. f.: *Scoot 2nd, by Vamose 0
War Widow, b. f.: Veuve Clicquot, by *McGee 0
Ship Ahoy, ch. g.: Early Bird, by Whisk Broom 2nd .... —
Float, b. or br. f.: *Queen of Jest, by Black Jester .... —
Galleon Gold, ch. f.: Golden Haze, by *Golden Broom .... —
Sarah Constant, ch. f.: Etoile d'Or, by *Golden Broom .... —

1929: 20 Foals

BOATSWAIN, b. or br. c.: Baton, by Hainault 3
WAR HERO, b. c.: Whetstone, by Sweep 6
Blockade, ch. c.: Rock Emerald, by Trap Rock .... †
Happy Warrior, ch. c.: Eventide, by Uncle 9
Sebastapool, ch. c.: *Maimouna, by Sardanapale 4
Temple Bells, ch. c.: Golden Haze, by *Golden Broom 1
Tug o' War, br. c.: All Aboard, by Sweep 12
Afloat, ch. f.: Problem, by Superman.... 2
Argosie, br. f.: *Lady Comfey, by Roi Herode 1
Horatia, ch. f.: Etoile d'Or, by *Golden Broom 2

Arms, ch. c.: May Alley, by *Star Shoot 0
Crows Feet, ch. f.: Scribble, by Ultimus 0
Victress, ch. f.: *Princess Polly, by *Prince Palatine 0
Drystone, dk. b. f.: *Keystone, by Marajax 0
Cabin Boy, ch. g.: Guesswork, by *Star Shoot (twin) .... —
Fighting Chance, ch. f.: Guesswork, by *Star Shoot (twin) .... —
Escadrille, b. f.: *Escuina, by Ecouen.... —
Thirty Knots, ch. f.: Brush Along, by Sweep .... —
Tokio Belle, b. f.: *Yokohama, by Santoi .... —
Who Won, b. or br. f.: Boosting, by *North Star 3rd .... —

218

B. C.: Insignia, by Star Hampton ....Died
† Blockade, not raced under Jockey Club rules, won the Maryland Hunt Cup three times.

1930: 16 Foals

WAR GLORY, ch. c.: Annette K., by Harry of Hereford 11
NEMI, b. f.: *Messaline, by Caligula.... †3
SPEED BOAT, ch. f.: Friar's Carse, by Friar Rock 3
Flashing Colors, ch, c.: Alzada, by Sir Martin 20
Octaroro, ch. c.: *Maimouna, by Sardanapale 10
Pre War, ch. c.: *Sherbert, by Sunstar 25
War Stripes, ch. c.: Insignia, by Star Hampton 8
Ship Ablaze, ch. f.: Golden Haze, by *Golden Broom 2
War Banner, ch. f.: Golden Masque, by *Golden Broom 4

Fast Colors, ch. c.: Off Color, by Jim Gaffney 0
Emergency Aid, b. f.: *Keystone, by Marajax 0
Strong, b. f.: *Lady Comfey, by Roi Herode 0
Changing Colors, ch. c.: Green Fruit, by The Finn .... —
Decked Up, ch. f.: Guesswork, by *Star Shoot .... —
Soldiers Dance, ch. f.: Starlight, by *Star Shoot 1
War Wedding, ch. f.: May Alley, by *Star Shoot .... —
† Nemi raced only in England.

1931: 17 Foals

IDENTIFY, ch. c.: Footprint, by Grand Parade 12
Holystone, ch. c.: Brush Along, by Sweep .... †1
Shot and Shell, ch. c.: *Maimouna, by Sardanapale 14
War Letters, ch. c.: Scribble, by Ultimus 7
Chauvism, br. f.: Boosting, by *North Star 3rd 5
Dead Reckoning, ch. f.: Guesswork, by *Star Shoot 1
Fortification, ch. f.: Off Color, by Jim Gaffney 12
Neverfail, br. f.: *Keystone, by Marajax 1
Proud Girl, b. or br. f.: Exalted, by High Time 4
Time Off, ch. f.: Daylight Saving, by *Star Shoot 1

Fighting Mike, ch. c.: Golden Haze, by *Golden Broom 0
Turret, ch. c.: *Zohra, by Sardanapale 0
Marching Along, ch. f.: Annette K., by Harry of Hereford¯ 0
Shell Hole, ch. f.: Golden Masque, by *Golden Broom 0
Strong Drink, b. c.: Veuve Clicquot, by *McGee .... —
War Gain, ch. c.: Mary A., by Fair Gain —
Redoubt, ch. f.: May Alley, by *Star Shoot .... —
† Holystone became an outstanding show horse for Crispin Oglebay.

1932: 18 Foals

STAR SHADOW, b. or br. c.: Shady, by Broomstick 17
ANN O'RULEY, ch. f.: Priscilla Ruley, by *Ambassador 4th 17
Cannons Roar, ch. c.: Fine Gold, by *Golden Broom 4
Deserter, ch. c.: Off Color, by Jim Gaffney 21
Right Rank, ch. c.: Exalted, by High Time 10
Soldiers Dream, ch. c.: Golden Haze, by *Golden Broom 3
Unknown Soldier, ch. c.: Black Carse, by Black Toney 4
Ship Executive, ch. c.: *Lady Comfey, by Roi Herode .... †8
Gas Bag, b. f.: Golden Masque, by *Golden Broom 1
Judy O'Grady, b. or br. f.: Bel Agnes, by *Ambassador 4th 2
War Band, ch. f.: Bandymo, by Uncle 1
War Dancer, br. f.: On Her Toes, by High Time 1

Martial Law, ch. f.: Painted Lady, by *Golden Broom 0
Pellet, br. f.: *Nature's Smile, by Rabelais '.............. 0
Mister Atkins, b. or br. c.: *Albus, by Phalaris .... —
Anchors Ahead, ch. f.: Friar's Carse, by Friar Rock .... —
War Grey, b. f.: Quaker Lady, by Isard 2nd .... —
Ch. c.: *Liseuse, by Rabelais ....Died
† Ship Executive was a steeplechase stakes winner.

1933: 17 Foals

INDOMITABLE, b. or br. c.: Violet Mahoney, by Colin 18
JEAN BART, b. c.: *Escuina, by Ecouen 6
KEARSARGE, b. or br. c.: Baton, by Hainault 4
Booming Guns, b. or br. c.: Annette K., by Harry of Hereford 3
St. Elmo, ch. c.: Smoky Lamp, by Plaudit 1
War Vessel, ch. c.: On Her Toes, by High Time .... †3
Sweet as Sugar, ch. f.: Good as Gold, by *Golden Broom 1
Under the Guns, ch. f.: *Maimouna, by Sardanapale 1
War Haste, ch. f.: Hasten, by *Carlaris 2
War Lassie, b. f.: Golden Masque, by *Golden Broom 2

Drafted, b. or br. c.: Brush Along, by Sweep 0
Battle Station, ch. f.: Confusion, by Friar Rock 0
Flaming Swords, b. or br. f.: Exalted, by High Time 0
Red Grape, ch. f.: Ripe Grape, by Friar Rock 0
Smooth Sailing, ch. f.: Suppress, by Superman 0
Star o' War, br. or blk. f.: Three Stars, by Star Master 0
Brave Maid, ch. f.: Fine Gold, by *Golden Broom .... —
† War Vessel was a steeplechase winner in England.

219

1934: 17 Foals

Wins

WAR ADMIRAL, br. c.: Brushup, by Sweep 21
WAND, b. f.: Baton, by Hainault 3
MATEY, ch. c.: Tavy, by *St. Germans 4
SAMMIE, br. c.: *Thread, by Gains-
  borough 5
REGAL LILY, ch. f.: Regal Lady, by
  Supremus 7
Bomber, br. or blk. c.: Black Carse,
  by Black Toney 10
Bugle Call, ch. c.: Boosting, by *North
  Star 3rd 3
Coxswain, ch. g.: Calypso, by Friar
  Rock 2
Matelot, ch. c.: Polly Pledge, by *Ar-
  chaic 3
Over the Top, ch. c.: Cresta, by Whisk
  Broom 2nd 5

War Tumult, ch. c.: Confusion, by Friar
  Rock 0
De Grasse, b. c.: *Escuina, by Ecouen —
Enameled, ch. f.: Painted Lady, by
  *Golden Broom .... —
Fairy Day, ch. f.: Ides, by *Archaic .... —
Fleet Parade, b. or br. f.: Brush Along,
  by Sweep .... —
Pomp and Glory, br. f.: Exalted, by
  High Time .... —
Sloop, ch. f.: Fine Gold, by *Golden
  Broom .... —

1935: 22 Foals

U-BOAT, blk. f.: Artifice, by *Light Bri-
  gade 13
John One, ch. c.: On Her Toes, by High
  Time 4
Jolly Tar, ch. c.: Tavy, by *St.
  Germans 3
Sailmaker, ch. c.: Center Stone, by
  Tryster .... †1
Warbridge, ch. c.: Bridgeen, by Domi-
  nant 5
Warlaine, ch. c.: *Madelaine, by Aber-
  glaube 14
Gulf Breeze, ch. f.: Sordavala, by The
  Finn 1
Hostile, ch. f.: Traumerette, by *Traum-
  er 1
Rambler Rose, br. f.: *Lady Rosemary,
  by Blandford 1
Warring Lady, blk. f.: Shady, by
  Broomstick 1

Manalong, ch. c.: Brush Along, by
  Sweep 0
Mayorcito, ch. c.: Calypso, by Friar
  Rock 0
War Peril, blk. c.: *Helsingfors 2nd,
  by Ramrod 0
Fine as Silk, ch. f.: Good as Gold, by
  *Golden Broom 0
Martial Air, br. f.: Baton, by Hainault 0
My Lady Fair, ch. f.: Regal Lady, by
  Supremus 0
Tropic Isle, br. f.: Exalted, by High
  Time 0
War Infant, ch. f.: Oh Baby, by
  Campfire 0
Harranette, br. f.: Annette K., by Harry
  of Hereford .... —
Miss Dodo, ch. f.: Cresta, by Whisk
  Broom 2nd .... —
War Brush, ch. f.: Brushup, by Sweep —

Warring Nymph, ch. f.: Carola, by Friar
  Rock .... —
† Sailmaker won in England.

1936: 18 Foals

HOSTILITY, b. f.: *Marguerite de Valois,
  by *Teddy 1
WAR REGALIA, ch. f.: Regal Lady, by
  Supremus 3
Catapult, b. c.: Center Stone, by Trys-
  ter 14
Deck, b. c.: Neshaminy, by St. James 3
Fleet Admiral, ch. g.: Annette K., by
  Harry of Hereford 11
Red War, ch. g.: Exalted, by High Time 9
Batalet, b. f.: *Escuina, by Ecouen 1
Betty War, ch. f.: Gilded Easel, by
  Leonardo 2nd 1
Fourragere, b. f.: Brocado, by The
  Porter 1
Marching, ch. f.: Bridgeen, by Domi-
  nant 1

Brandywine Fox, b. c.: Parmachenee
  Belle, by *Troutbeck 0
War Sack, b. c.: *Albus, by Phalaris 0
Racing Colors, br. f.: Gold and Black,
  by Big Blaze 0
Gunpowder, b. c.: Fluffy, by Pennant .... —
Warcraft, b. c.: Foxcraft, by Foxlaw .... —
Mandalay, ch. f.: *Madelaine, by Aber-
  glaube .... —
Twilight Gun, ch. f.: Golden Haze, by
  *Golden Broom .... —
War Swept, br. f.: Brush Along, by
  Sweep .... —

1937: 22 Foals

DORIMAR, b. f.: Neshaminy, by St.
  James 10
SALAMINIA, ch. f.: Alcibiades, by Su-
  premus 5
WAR BEAUTY, ch. f.: Silver Beauty, by
  *Stefan the Great 5
Army Song, b. c.: Song, by *Royal
  Minstrel 17
Blue Uniform, gr. c.: Alice Blue Gown,
  by Luke McLuke 6
Muffled Drums, ch. g.: Cresta, by Whisk
  Broom 2nd 9
Phoebus, ch. c.: Guiding Star, by *Hol-
  lister 6
Rollo, ch. c.: *Lady Rosemary, by
  Blandford 9
Scotch Tar, b. g.: Caledonia, by *Craig-
  angower 5
Big Beauty, ch. f.: Golden Haze, by
  *Golden Broom 1
Coquelicot, ch. f.: Fleur, by Pennant 1
Furlough, ch. f.: Flying Hour, by Ga-
  letian 1
Jeanne d'Arc, ch. f.: Jeanne Bowdre,
  by Luke McLuke 3
Rose-Ouzel, b. f.: Gilded Easel, by Leo-
  nardo 2nd 1

Boat, blk. f.: Crotala, by Black Toney 0
Golden Manda, br. f.: Golden Fair, by
  *Wrack 0
Ma Minnie, b. f.: Baton, by Hainault 0
Manspell, ch. f.: Idle Spell, by *Sir
  Gallahad 3rd 0
Perfect Love, ch. f.: Shady, by Broom-
  stick 0
Amphibian, ch. f.: Sordavala, by The
  Finn .... —

220

Army Colors, ch. f.: Bridgeen, by Dominant .... —
War Flurry, br. f.: Last Boat, by *Sir Gallahad 3rd .... —

1938: 19 Foals

war relic, c.: Friar's Carse, by Friar Rock 9
battle colors, ch. g.: Beaugingham, by *Sun Briar 8
war hazard, ch. f.: Artifice, by *Light Brigade 6
Fairymant, ch. c.: Star Fairy, by The Satrap 1
Field of Gold, ch. g.: Sun Tweed, by *Sun Briar 3
Sky Raider, c.: Top Flight, by *Dis Donc 2
War Bonnet, ch. g.: Golden Haze, by *Golden Broom 12
War Bugle, b. g.: Song, by *Royal Minstrel 11
War Skipper, ch. g.: Traumerette, by *Traumer 1
War Stone, ch. g.: Center Stone, by Tryster 5
Admiralette, b. f.: Brushup, by Sweep ... 1

Great War, gr. c.: Great Belle, by *Stefan the Great 0
War Flower, ch. f.: Crotala, by Black Toney 0
Hamalca, ch. c.: Sable Muff, by *Light Brigade .... —
Warrior Son, ch. c.: Bridgeen, by Dominant .... —
Racquette Lake, b. f.: Forest Nymph, by Luke McLuke .... —
Stark War, b. f.: Betty Stark, by *Sobieski .... —
War Gem, ch. f.: Sun Emerald, by *Sun Briar .... —
War Jitters, ch. f.: On Her Toes, by High Time .... —

1939: 21 Foals

Wins

soldier song, b. c.: Song, by *Royal Minstrel 12
War Vessel, ch. c.: On Her Toes, by High Time .... †3
Air Raider, b. g.: Apogee, by *Pharamond 2nd 7
Fairy Manah, ch. c.: Star Fairy, by The Satrap 2
Gun Site, ch. g.: Friar's Carse, by Friar Rock 1
Middlestone, br. g.: Center Stone, by Tryster 5
War Reward, ch. c.: On Her Toes, by High Time 5
Navy Cruiser, br. f.: Artifice, by *Light Brigade 2
Seaway, b. f.: Silway, by Silvern 4

Enchantress, ch. f.: Beaugingham, by Sun Beau or *Sun Briar 0
Military Brush, br. f.: Brushup, by Sweep 0
H. M. War, ch. c.: Bridgeen, by Dominant .... —
Army Flirt, ch. f.: Great Belle, by *Stefan the Great .... —
Fighting Polly, b. f.: Polymera, by *Polymelian .... —
Maidoduntreath, br. f.: Mid Victorian,

by Victorian .... —
Red Haze, ch. f.: Golden Haze, by *Golden Broom .... —
War Cloth, ch. f.: Sun Tweed, by *Sun Briar .... —
War Party, gr. f.: (twin): Crotala, by Black Toney .... —
War Sky, gr. f.: Mock Modesty, by *Royal Minstrel .... —
War Victory, ch. f.: Sun Emerald, by *Sun Briar .... —
Ch. c.: Cresta, by Whisk Broom 2nd...Died
† Admiralty was a steeplechase stakes winner.

1940: 15 Foals

fairy manhurst, ch. c.: Star Fairy, by *The Satrap 4
Crest o' War, ch. c.: Cresta, by Whisk Broom 2nd 1
Signal Corps, b. g.: *Albus, by Phalaris 6
War Commander, ch. g.: Alpi, by Pilate 4
War Gleam, ch. c.: Sun Emerald, by *Sun Briar 13
War Joy, b. g.: Jubilesta, by Insco 3
Blois, b. f.: *Mademoiselle de Valois, by Sardanapale 2
Opera Singer, b. f.: Song, by *Royal Minstrel 2
Yellow Poppy, ch. f.: *Forsythia 2nd, by *Stefan the Great 1

Bashful, gr. f.: Mock Modesty, by *Royal Minstrel 0
Navy Contracts, b. c.: Betty Stark, by *Sobieski .... —
War Course, b. c.: Harmonessa, by *Bull Dog .... —
Bombstick, b. f.: Slapstick, by Broomstick .... —
Mere Polly, ch. f.: Polymera, by *Polymelian .... —
Miss Smug, ch. f.: Snobling, by *Snob 2nd .... —

1941: 13 Foals

Army Power, b. g.: Harmonessa, by *Bull Dog .... †
Free France, ch. c.: La France, by *Sir Gallahad 3rd 2
General War, ch. c.: Snobling, by *Snob 2nd 1
Mightiest, blk. g.: Third Party, by *Teddy 5
War Delegate, ch. g.: Leonissa, by *Sickle 3
War Dressing, b. c.: Gauze, by *Teddy 7
War Peak, ch. c.: Smatterings, by John P. Grier .... †
Velvet Glove, br. f.: On Hand, by On Watch 1
War Waac, ch. f.: Alpi, by Pilate 1

Ammunition, ch. f.: Artifice, by *Light Brigade 0
Post War, ch. c.: *Source, by Ali Bey —
Spotted Beauty, str. ro. f.: Silver Beauty, by *Stefan the Great .... —
†Winner in 1947.

1942: 10 Foals

War Archive, ch. g.: Beaugingham, by Sun Beau or *Sun Briar 1
War Atlas, ch. g.: Leonissa, by *Sickle 1

221

Miss War, b. f.: Harmonica, by *Bull Dog 3
War Damsel, ch. f.: Jubilesta, by Insco 2

Yoemanry, ch. c.: *Source, by Ali Bey 0
War Hysteria, ch. f.: Brushup, by Sweep 0
Yacht, br. f.: Polymera, by *Polymelian 0
War Liberator, b. c.: Snobling, by *Snob 2nd .... —
War Memorial, ch. f.: Northern Belle, by John P. Grier .... —
Ch. c.: Singing Witch, by *Royal Minstrel .... Died

1943: 10 Foals
WAR KILT, ch. f.: Friar's Carse, by Friar Rock 3

Drum Major, ch. c.: Artifice, by *Light Brigade 2
Monitor, ch. c.: Alwiser, by Wise Counsellor 2
Northern Trust, ch. g.: Northern Belle, by John P. Grier .... †
War Sword, ch. g.: Harmonessa, by *Bull Dog 1

Our Colors, b. f.: Brushup, by Sweep 0
War Blast, ch. f.: Alpi, by Pilate 0
Wild Geranium, ch. f.: Leonissa, by *Sickle 0
Patrol, ch. c.: Jubilesta, by Insco .... —
Aye Aye, blk. f.: Waterford, by *Sickle —
†Winner in 1947.

BOX SCORE BY YEARS
OF HIS FOALS

	Foals	2-Y-O Wnrs.	Wnrs.	Stakes Wnrs.	Non-Wnrs.	Unr.
1922	13	8	7	5	0	5
1923	18	13	11	5	2	3
1924	23	13	8	6	4	6
1925	20	14	7	4	2	4
1926	18	12	10	6	2	4
1927	20	9	2	3	6	5
1928	18	9	6	4	5	4
1929	21	10	3	2	4	7
1930	16	9	7	3	3	4
1931	17	10	10	1	4	3
1932	18	12	7	3	2	4
1933	17	10	8	3	6	1
1934	17	10	6	5	1	6
1935	22	10	5	1	8	4
1936	18	10	4	2	3	5
1937	22	14	3	3	5	3
1938	19	11	5	3	2	6
1939	21	9	3	2	2	10
1940	15	9	4	1	1	5
1941	13	9	3	0	1	3
1942	10	4	1	0	3	3
1943	10	5	1	1	3	2
	386	220	121	61	69	97

Note. Seven unnamed foals included, one each in 1922, 1923, 1927, 1929, 1932, 1939, and 1942. In stakes winners, steeplechasers omitted.

SIRE RECORD BY YEARS

Yr.	Rank	Wnrs.	1st	2nd	3rd	Amt. Won
1924		7	14	6	8	$ 29,865
1925	4	19	51	30	25	213,933
1926	1	18	49	37	31	408,137
1927	7	24	62	49	65	210,872
1928	2	33	87	85	79	303,533
1929	2	27	73	64	59	267,583
1930	16	24	61	39	37	124,750
1931		19	43	48	36	81,070
1932	11	23	56	52	50	121,261
1933	12	26	75	61	45	87,480
1934		22	55	59	44	61,235
1935	14	33	75	77	66	104,675
1936	9	26	71	55	35	129,837
1937	2	29	74	70	65	262,705
1938	7	27	70	63	61	166,182
1939		21	40	48	41	101,595
1940		23	47	40	42	85,990
1941	5	24	66	52	35	202,500
1942		21	36	41	37	44,764
1943		22	50	36	40	86,335
1944		20	45	55	50	83,963
1945		14	26	36	38	63,097
1946		16	32	43	55	72,590
1947		17	28	34	44	68,700
1948		13	29	44	32	54,470
1949		8	25	21	19	39,220
		1,340	1,245	1,139		$3,476,342

BROODMARE SIRE RECORD

Yr.	Rank	Mares	Wnrs.	*Wins	1st Monies
1929		2	2	4	$ 5,875
1930		7	8	18	16,150
1931		8	9	19	14,850
1932		14	18	54	30,730
1933	2	27	30	79	142,584
1934		28	33	84	78,575
1935	7	32	44	125	151,740
1936	8	35	47	139	141,005
1937	3	42	56	144	216,215
1938	5	48	67	159-1	203,907
1939	3	48	65	166-1	219,977
1940	6	43	61	139	150,770
1941	3	61	86	222-2	211,622
1942	2	69	100	252-2	362,126
1943	2	66	88	229-6	384,080
1944	2	81	128	314-3	607,781
1945	2	73	102	229-2	591,436
1946	2	88	145	379-2	948,204
1947	2	93	145	369-6	858,575
1948	2	85	135	337-4	866,941
1949	1	96	159	385-1	1,018,857
				3,873-30	$7,222,000

* Dead heats for first place are added after a hyphen. Thus, in addition to 3,873 wins there were 30 dead heats for first place.

COMPLETE DATA ON THE 172 STAKES WON BY HIS GET

The following is a complete list of the stakes won by Man o' War's children. There are 172 triumphs for a total winning of $1,776,520. No other sire has ever approached this showing.

ACORN STAKES, Belmont Park.
1939—Hostility (3) $12,100
ADIRONDACK HANDICAP, Saratoga.
1932—Speed Boat (2) 3,075
ALABAMA STAKES, Saratoga.
1925—Maid at Arms (3) 10,625
1937—Regal Lily (3) 7,425
1940—Salaminia (3) 9,450
1941—War Hazard (3) 8,975
AMSTERDAM CLAIMING STAKES, Saratoga.
1932—Fleet Flag (4) 2,325
1936—Ann O'Ruley (4) 3,325
ARDSLEY HANDICAP, Empire City.
1924—By Hisself (2) 4,935
1930—Anchors Aweigh (2) 3,735
ARLINGTON FALL HANDICAP, Arlington Downs.
1936—Star Shadow (4) 3,200
ASTORIA STAKES, Aqueduct.
1925—Edith Cavell (2) 4,875
AU REVOIR HANDICAP, Arlington Downs.
1936—Star Shadow (4) 2,140
AUTUMN DAYS STAKES, Empire City.
1924—By Hisself (2) 4,075
1930—Anchors Aweigh (2) 3,325
BALDWIN HANDICAP, Jamaica.
1930—Anchors Aweigh (2) 4,475
BALLSTON HANDICAP, Saratoga.
1928—Son o' Battle (4) 2,875
BELDAME HANDICAP, Aqueduct.
1926—Frilette (2) 4,125
BELMONT STAKES, Belmont Park.
1925—American Flag (3) 38,500
1926—Crusader (3) 48,550
1937—War Admiral (3) 38,020
BEN ALI HANDICAP, Lexington.
1929—Broadside (5) 3,200
BILLY BARTON STEEPLECHASE, Pimlico.
1931—Annapolis (5) 2,000
BOWIE HANDICAP, Pimlico.
1927—Edith Cavell (4) 8,825
1928—Genie (3) 9,500
BROADWAY HANDICAP, Aqueduct.
1928—Ironsides (3) 4,175
BRYAN AND O'HARA MEMORIAL HANDICAP, Bowie.
1929—Bateau (4) 39,600
CHAMPLAIN HANDICAP, Saratoga.
1930—Caesarion (5) 3,400
CHESAPEAKE STAKES, Havre de Grace.
1931—Anchors Aweigh (3) 9,950
1937—War Admiral (3) 8,250
CINCINNATI DERBY, River Downs.
1926—Crusader (3) 20,150
COACHING CLUB AMERICAN OAKS, Belmont Park.
1925—Florence Nightingale (3) 13,400
1926—Edith Cavell (3) 12,100
1928—Bateau (3) 14,825

CONFEDERATION HANDICAP, Blue Bonnets.
1929—Marine (3) 2,750
CONNAUGHT CUP HANDICAP, Woodbine Park.
1931—Marine (5) 980
DEBUT STAKES, Belmont Park.
1930—Aldershot (3) 3,925
DEMOISELLE STAKES, Jamaica.
1945—War Kilt (2) 8,230
DIANA HANDICAP, Saratoga.
1939—War Regalia (3) 2,550
DIXIE HANDICAP, Pimlico.
1927—Mars (4) 26,375
DWYER STAKES, Aqueduct.
1925—American Flag (3) 8,900
1926—Crusader (3) 15,000
1928—Genie (3) 19,600
1933—War Glory (3) 4,250
EASTERN SHORE HANDICAP, Havre de Grace.
1936—War Admiral (2) 11,250
EDGEMERE HANDICAP, Aqueduct.
1928—Ironsides (3) 6,300
EMPIRE CITY DERBY, Empire City.
1928—Genie (3) 7,550
EVENING HANDICAP, Hialeah.
1941—Dorimar (4) 4,810
FASHION STAKES, Belmont Park.
1927—Bateau (2) 5,800
FORDHAM CLAIMING STAKES, Empire City.
1930—Aldershot (3) 2,170
FUTURITY STAKES, Belmont Park.
1926—Scapa Flow (2) 65,980
GALLANT FOX HANDICAP, Jamaica.
1940—Salaminia (3) 11,150
GARDEN CITY CLAIMING STAKES, Jamaica.
1931—Quarter Deck (4) 2,250
GAZELLE STAKES, Aqueduct.
1926—Corvette (3) 2,875
1928—Bateau (3) 3,200
1937—Regal Lily (3) 5,125
GLENDALE STEEPLECHASE, Aqueduct.
1926—Gun Boat (4) 6,200
GOVERNOR'S HANDICAP, Narragansett Park.
1935—Identify (4) 5,210
1941—War Relic (3) 8,660
GRAND NATIONAL STEEPLECHASE HANDICAP, Belmont Park.
1934—Battleship (7) 5,900
GRAND NATIONAL HANDICAP STEEPLECHASE, Liverpool, England.
1938—Battleship (11) 37,545
GRANITE STATE HANDICAP, Rockingham Park.
1935—Identify (4) 3,950

225

GREAT LAKES HANDICAP, Lincoln
Fields.
1931—Battleship (4) 5,025
HAMPTON CUP HANDICAP, Rockingham
Park.
1934—Sea Fox (6) 3,810
HAVRE DE GRACE CUP, Havre de Grace.
1926—Crusader (3) 14,250
HENDRIE STEEPLECHASE HANDICAP,
Woodbine Park.
1943—Admiralty (4) 1,045
HURON HANDICAP, Saratoga.
1926—Crusader (3) 4,050
1932—War Hero (3) 2,850
1936—Jean Bart (3) 2,410
1937—Sammie (3) 2,410
IDLE HOUR STAKES, Lexington, Ky.
1928—Clyde Van Dusen (2) 2,890
INDEPENDENCE HANDICAP, Latonia, Ky.
1929—Broadside (5) 10,525
ILLINOIS OAKS, Washington Park.
1927—Yeddo (3) 5,120
JAMES ROWE MEMORIAL HANDICAP,
Bowie.
1930—Battleship (3) 3,880
JEROME HANDICAP, Belmont Park.
1931—Ironclad (3) 3,050
JOCKEY CLUB GOLD CUP, Belmont Park.
1926—Crusader (3) 13,300
1938—War Admiral (4) 5,500
JUNIOR CHAMPION STAKES, Aqueduct.
1925—Mars (2) 7,550
KENNER STAKES, Saratoga.
1929—Marine (3) 5,100
1933—War Glory (3) 1,820
1941—War Relic (3) 3,225
KENTUCKY DERBY, Churchill Downs.
1929—Clyde Van Dusen (3) 53,950
1937—War Admiral (3) 52,050
KENTUCKY JOCKEY CLUB STAKES,
Churchill Downs.
1928—Clyde Van Dusen (2) 32,800
KING EDWARD GOLD CUP, Woodbine
Park.
1930—Marine (4) 5,220
KNICKERBOCKER HANDICAP, Empire
City.
1929—Hard Tack (3) 4,050
LADIES' HANDICAP, Belmont Park.
1940—Salaminia (3) 12,250
LATONIA OAKS, Latonia, Ky.
1926—Edith Cavell (3) 10,920
LAUREL STAKES, Laurel.
1944—Soldier Song (5) 7,875
LAWRENCE REALIZATION, Belmont Park.
1933—War Glory (3) 21,400
1943—Fairy Manhurst (3) 7,475
LONG BEACH CLAIMING HANDICAP,
Jamaica.
1931—Quarter Deck (4) 2,725
MANHATTAN HANDICAP, Belmont Park.
1929—Ironsides (4) 6,675
MANOR HANDICAP, Laurel Park.
1924—American Flag (2) 9,225
1925—Crusader (2) 11,100
MARYLAND HANDICAP, Laurel Park.
1925—Maid at Arms (3) 8,900
1926—Crusader (3) 8,850
1933—War Glory (3) 4,930

MATRON STAKES, Belmont Park.
1925—Taps (2) 15,075
1928—Dreadnaught (2) 21,725
1936—Wand (2) 12,075
MATRON HANDICAP, Rockingham Park.
1941—War Beauty (4) 1,905
MIAMI CUP, Hialeah.
1928—War Eagle (4) 24,100
MOMUS HANDICAP, Fair Grounds.
1928—War Eagle (4) 2,040
MYLES STANDISH STAKES, Suffolk
Downs.
1936—Kearsarge (2) 2,310
MONTAUK CLAIMING STAKES, Belmont
Park.
1937—Star Shadow (5) 2,205
NARRAGANSETT SPECIAL, Narragansett
Park.
1941—War Relic (3) 22,400
OCTOBER CLAIMING HANDICAP, Jamaica.
1929—Annapolis (3) 3,600
ORPHANAGE STAKES, Idle Hour Farm.
1928—Clyde Van Dusen (2) 3,925
PIMLICO FUTURITY, Pimlico.
1936—Matey (2) 25,000
PIMLICO CUP, Pimlico.
1926—Edith Cavell (3) 8,825
1928—Edith Cavell (5) 10,025
PIMLICO FALL SERIAL W.-F.-A. RACE
NO. 2, Pimlico.
1926—Mars (3) 3,425
PIMLICO FALL SERIAL W.-F.-A. RACE
NO. 3, Pimlico.
1926—Mars (3) 4,625
PIMLICO OAKS, Pimlico.
1925—Maid at Arms (3) 4,430
PIMLICO SPECIAL, Pimlico.
1937—War Admiral (3) 5,680
PINGREE HANDICAP, Detroit.
1934—Sea Fox (6) 2,300
PREAKNESS STAKES, Pimlico.
1937—War Admiral (3) 45,600
PRINCE GEORGES AUTUMN HANDICAP,
Bowie.
1934—Identify (3) 2,555
R. J. MACKENZIE MEMORIAL HANDICAP,
Thorncliffe Park.
1930—Marine (4) 3,340
1931—Marine (5) 3,420
RHODE ISLAND HANDICAP, Narragansett
Park.
1937—War Admiral (4) 8,340
RIGGS HANDICAP, Pimlico.
1926—Crusader (3) 22,450
1928—Genie (3) 23,775
ROCKINGHAM PARK HANDICAP, Rockingham Park.
1935—Identify (4) 7,370
SARANAC HANDICAP, Saratoga.
1926—Mars (3) 9,300
1929—Hard Tack (3) 10,100
1933—War Glory (3) 3,900
SARATOGA CUP, Saratoga.
1932—War Hero (3) 7,825
1938—War Admiral (4) 6,600
1941—Dorimar (4) 9,850
SARATOGA HANDICAP, Saratoga.
1927—Mars (4) 8,000
1930—Marine (4) 7,400
1938—War Admiral (4) 7,500

226

SCARSDALE HANDICAP, Empire City.
1928—Genie (3) 4,040
SCHUYLERVILLE STAKES, Saratoga.
1925—Taps (2) 3,925
SELIMA STAKES, Laurel Park.
1927—Bateau (2) 23,925
1939—War Beauty (2) 26,560
SOUTHERN MARYLAND HANDICAP, Bowie.
1929—Bateau (4) 39,600
STATLER HOTEL HANDICAP, Fort Erie.
1930—Marine (4) 2,100
STONY BROOK CLAIMING STAKES, Aqueduct.
1935—Ann O'Ruley (3) 2,195
1936—Ann O'Ruley (4) 2,295
SUBURBAN HANDICAP, Belmont Park.
1926—Crusader (3) 13,150
1927—Crusader (4) 11,875
1929—Bateau (4) 14,100
TEST STAKES, Saratoga.
1933—Speed Boat (3) 1,820
TOBOGGAN HANDICAP, Belmont Park.
1935—Identify (4) 4,225
TORONTO CUP, Woodbine Park.
1930—Son o' Battle (6) 12,500

TRAVERS   Saratoga.
1926—Mars (3) 15,050
1932—War Hero (3) 23,150
U. S. HOTEL STAKES, Saratoga.
1926—Scapa Flow (2) 11,525
VALLEY STAKES, Fairmount Park.
1928—Clyde Van Dusen (2) 6,430
WALDEN HANDICAP, Pimlico.
1925—Mars (2) 9,725
1932—War Glory (2) 5,370
WASHINGTON HANDICAP, Laurel Park.
1926—Mars (3) 24,150
1937—War Admiral (3) 15,350
WHITNEY STAKES, Saratoga.
1929—Bateau (4) 5,850
1938—War Admiral (4) 2,725
WHITE MOUNTAIN HANDICAP, Rockingham Park.
1935—Identify (4) 1,965
1939—U-Boat (4) 4,730
WIDENER HANDICAP, Hialeah.
1938—War Admiral (4) 49,550
WILL ROGERS MEMORIAL HANDICAP, Hollywood Park.
1941—Battle Colors (3) 7,925

227

MAN O' WAR AS A BROODMARE SIRE

In the following checklist are the daughters of Man o' War which have produced stakes winners on the flat. Foaling dates of the mares and their stakes winners are given. When not otherwise indicated, mares were unraced. After each stakes winner is given the name of its sire.

Amphibian, 1937
War Allies, 1942   *Alibhai

Anchors Ahead, 1932
Ocean Blue, 1938   Blue Larkspur
Price Level, 1942   *Sickle
Air Hero, 1943   *Blenheim 2nd

Armada, 1924 (placed)
Don Guzman, 1930   St. James
High Fleet, 1933   Jack High
Grass Cutter, 1935   *Sickle
Sir Francis, 1942   *Sickle

Assembly, 1923 (unplaced)
Gold Foam, 1932   *Golden Broom

Ann O'Ruley, 1932 (stakes winner)
Bonnet Ann, 1939   Blue Larkspur

Army Colors, 1937
Istan, 1945   *Heliopolis

Baton Rouge, 1927 (placed)
Firethorn, 1932   *Sun Briar
Creole Maid, 1935   *Pharamond 2nd

Blois, 1940 (winner)
Roman Zephyr, 1947   Roman

Boadicea, 1927
Manatella, 1934   *The Satrap
Manie O'Hara, 1935   *The Satrap

Boat, 1937 (unplaced)
Rampart, 1942   Trace Call
Noble Hero, 1945   *Heliopolis
Greek Ship, 1947   *Heliopolis

Coquelicot, 1937 (winner)
Pavot, 1942   Case Ace
Lovat, 1943   Jamestown

Crows Feet, 1929 (unplaced)
No Wrinkles, 1940   Wise Counsellor

Dead Reckoning, 1931 (winner)
Director J. E., 1941   *Sickle

Dorimar, 1937 (stakes winner)
Lady Dorimar, 1946   Our Boots

Drystone, 1929 (unplaced)
Buttermilk, 1934   Milkman

Emergency Aid, 1930 (unplaced)
Grey Nurse, 1936   *Sir Greysteel

Escadrille, 1929
Giant Killer, 1933   *St. Germans

Fairy Day, 1934
Larky Day, 1941   Blue Larkspur

Firetop, 1928 (placed)
Columbiana, 1933   Petee-Wrack
Red Vulcan, 1938   Pompey

Flaming Swords, 1933 (placed)
Blue Swords, 1940   Blue Larkspur

Fleet Parade, 1934
Trojan Fleet, 1942   Case Ace

Float, 1928
Float Me, 1941   Menow

Frilette, 1924 (stakes winner)
Jabot, 1931   *Sickle
Cravat, 1935   *Sickle
Hindu Kush, 1942   *Mahmoud

Furlough, 1937 (winner)
Ace Card, 1942   Case Ace
Adile, 1946   *Mahmoud

Gas Bag, 1932 (winner)
Thumbs Up, 1939   *Blenheim 2nd

Golden Manda, 1937
Manyunk, 1945   Unbreakable

Gun Play, 1928 (unplaced)
Dawn Play, 1934   Clock Tower

Jibber Jib, 1924
Be Jabbers, 1935   Bud Lerner

Judy O'Grady, 1932 (winner)
Westminster, 1941   *Bull Dog
Snow Goose, 1944   *Mahmoud

Maid at Arms, 1922 (stakes winner)
Army Game, 1932   *Bright Knight

Ma Minnie, 1937 (placed)
Mahout, 1943   *Mahmoud

Pellet, 1932 (unplaced)
Layout, 1941   *Sickle

Port-Hole, 1924 (winner)
Harmonica, 1944   Snark

Rambler Rose, 1935 (winner)
Trymenow, 1942   Menow

Red Gown, 1926 (unplaced)
Dressy, 1934   *Sickle

Red Haze, 1939
Eternal War, 1944   Eternal Bull

Salaminia, 1937 (stakes winner)
Athenia, 1943   *Pharamond 2nd

Sarah Constant, 1928
Gerald, 1934   *Pharamond 2nd

Sea Plane, 1922
Aquaplane, 1926   High Time

Seaway, 1939 (winner)
Ol' Skipper, 1946   Occupation

Shell Hole, 1931 (placed)
Phidias, 1943   Rosemont

Ship Ablaze, 1930
(winner, placed in stakes)
Mystery Lady, 1945   *Bull Dog

Ship of War, 1924
Billy M., 1931   Peter Pan
Dauber, 1935   Pennant

Siren, 1923 (winner)
Black Buddy, 1931   Bud Lerner

Sister Ship, 1925 (stakes winner)
Signalman, 1931   High Cloud

Speed Boat, 1930 (stakes winner)
Level Best, 1938   Equipoise

Spotted Beauty, 1941
Royal Blood, 1945   Coldstream

Vagrant, 1927 (winner)
They Say, 1943   Roman

Valkyr, 1925 (winner)
Vicar, 1931   Flying Ebony
Vicaress, 1932   Flying Ebony
Vagrancy, 1939   *Sir Galahad 3rd
Hypnotic, 1943   *Hypnotist 2nd

Wand, 1934 (stakes winner)
Halberd, 1940   *Blenheim 2nd

War Feathers, 1924 (winner)
War Minstrel, 1934   *Royal Minstrel
War Magic, 1935   *Pharamond 2nd
War Plumage, 1936   On Watch

War Flower, 1938 (unplaced)
Ace Admiral, 1945   *Heliopolis

War Grey, 1932
Grey Wing, 1939   Halcyon
Loyal Legion, 1944   Halcyon

War Jitters, 1938
The Shaker, 1943   Roman

War Lassie, 1933 (winner)
Rodney Stone, 1941   *Bull Dog

Warrior Lass, 1926 (winner)
Knickerbocker, 1936   *Teddy

War Swept, 1936
Roman Bath, 1947   Roman

War Wedding, 1930
Marriage, 1936   *Strolling Player

War Woman, 1926
Mata Hari, 1931   Peter Hastings

Windlass, 1925
Anhelation, 1933   *Grandace
Weigh Anchor, 1937   *Grandace

Dams of Steeplechase Stakes Winners

Admiral's Lassie, 1925
Our Sailor, 1931   Transmute

Drystone, 1929 (unplaced)
Leche Hombre, 1944   Milkman

Escadrille, 1929
Knight's Quest, 1938   *Sir Gallahad 3rd

Float, 1928
Mandingham, 1934   *The Satrap

Marching Along, 1931 (unplaced)
Pebalong, 1944   Big Pebble

Racing Colors, 1936 (placed)
War Trophy, 1942   Trace Call

Soldiers Dance, 1930
Arms of War, 1938   *Quatre Bras 2nd

War Path, 1924 (unplaced)
Bushranger, 1930   *Stefan the Great

RECORD OF HIS YEARLINGS SOLD BY AUCTION

In the following list are the horses by Man o' War which were sold at auction as yearlings, with their prices and their earnings on the race course. Of the 45 sold, 33 raced, 23 won, and three (Son o' Battle, U-Boat, War Beauty) were stakes winners.

The high prices ran through 1929, by which time eight head had sold for $85,500; the entire crop that year earned only a little over $54,000. In 1936, 17 of the crop of 22 registered foals were sold for $252,500; collectively they won $54,383. In 1936,

In the earnings column below a zero indicates that the horse raced without earning anything, a dash (—) indicates that the horse did not race. Fillies are marked f.

Year Sold	Horse, Dam	Price	Earnings
1924	Siren, f., Star Puss	$ 8,000	$ 2,100
1925	War Feathers, f., Tuscan Red	50,500	1,350
	SON O' BATTLE, Scrutiny	16,000	27,225
1926	Periscope, f., *Batanoea	13,000	
	Crows Nest, Jeanne Bowdre	25,000	10,200
1927	War Time, Pen Rose	30,000	5,228
1928	Broadway Limited, *Starflight	65,000	0
1929	War, Milky Way	45,000	8,280
1932	Turret, *Zohra	5,000	50
1933	Cannons Roar, Fine Gold	2,000	2,850
	Deserter, Off Color	4,000	19,165
1934	Smooth Sailing, f., Suppress	1,000	(£1,059)
	War Vessel, On Her Toes	650	
1935	War Haste, f., Hasten	325	1,420
	Enameled, f., Painted Lady	1,300	
1936	Harranette, f., Annette K	4,600	
	U-BOAT, f., Artifice	1,800	17,460
	Warbridge, Bridgeen	18,000	3,740
	Manalong, Brush Along	4,000	0
	War Brush, f., Brushup	1,700	
	Mayorito, Calypso	4,700	0
	Warring Nymph, f., Carola	800	
	Sailmaker, Center Stone	7,000	(£117)
	Miss Dodo, f., Cresta	3,400	
	Tropic Isle, f., Exalted	3,600	300
1936	War Peril, *Helsingfors 2nd	$ 8,300	$ 1,155
	Warlaine, *Madelaine	2,700	12,995
	War Infant, f., Oh Baby	4,500	0
	John One, On Her Toes	9,000	4,715
	Warring Lady, f., Shady	6,500	560
	Gulf Breeze, f., Sordavala	2,700	2,150
	Hostile, f., Traumerette	2,200	860
1938	Manspell, f., Idle Spell	4,900	0
	Perfect Love, f., Shady	12,100	125
	WAR BEAUTY, f., Silver Beauty	4,200	42,840
	Amphibian, f., Sordavala	3,900	
1939	Rocquette Lake, f., Forest Nymph	2,200	
1940	Maidoduntreath, f., Mid Victorian	7,500	
1941	Crest o' War, Cresta	2,200	2,250
	Mere Polly, f., Polymera	3,200	
	War Gleam, Sun Emerald	4,500	16,330
1942	General War, Snobling	1,450	3,1&
	Post War, *Source	900	
	Mightiest, Third Party	2,000	9,735
1943	War Liberator, Snobling	4,050	—
	45 head (22 colts, 23 fillies)	$405,375	$196,188 plus £1,176

INDEX